Houghton
Mifflin
Harcourt

W9-AZD-940

GO MATH!

Volume 2

Made in the United States
Text printed on 100%
recycled paper

**Houghton
Mifflin
Harcourt**

2017 Edition

Printed in the U.S.A.

ISBN 978-0-544-71059-7

12 0877 20

4500789750   D E F G

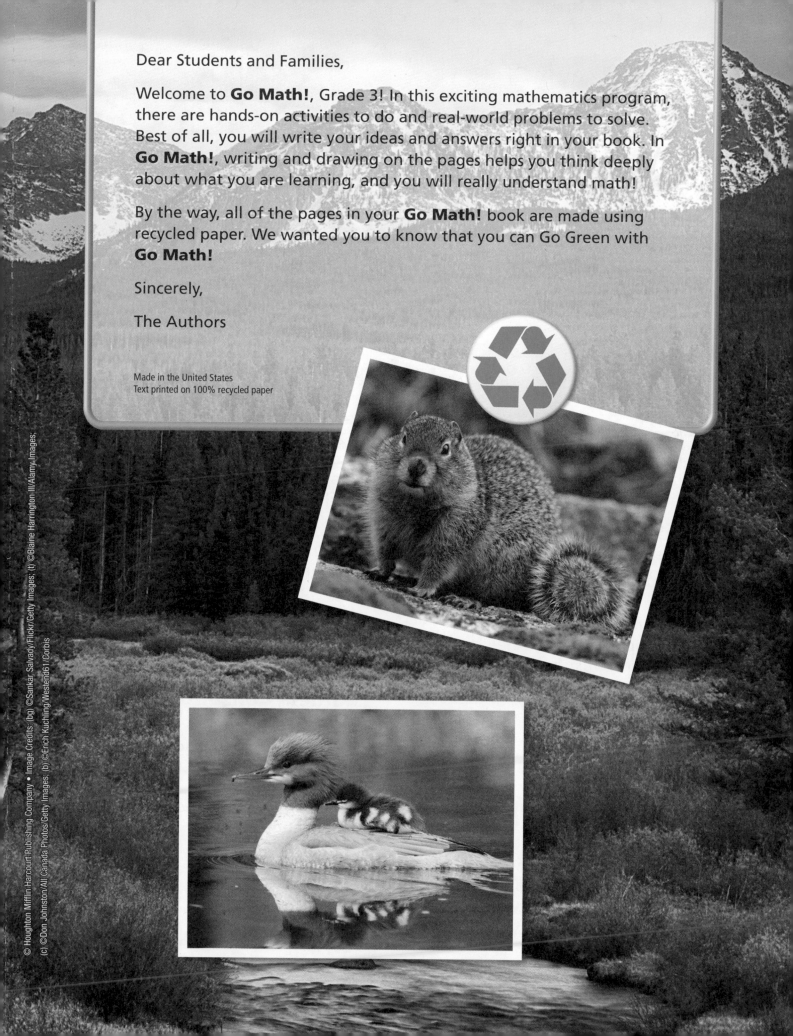

Dear Students and Families,

Welcome to **Go Math!**, Grade 3! In this exciting mathematics program, there are hands-on activities to do and real-world problems to solve. Best of all, you will write your ideas and answers right in your book. In **Go Math!**, writing and drawing on the pages helps you think deeply about what you are learning, and you will really understand math!

By the way, all of the pages in your **Go Math!** book are made using recycled paper. We wanted you to know that you can Go Green with **Go Math!**

Sincerely,

The Authors

Made in the United States
Text printed on 100% recycled paper

Authors

Juli K. Dixon, Ph.D.
Professor, Mathematics Education
University of Central Florida
Orlando, Florida

Edward B. Burger, Ph.D.
President, Southwestern University
Georgetown, Texas

Steven J. Leinwand
Principal Research Analyst
American Institutes for
  Research (AIR)
Washington, D.C.

Contributor

Rena Petrello
Professor, Mathematics
Moorpark College
Moorpark, CA

Matthew R. Larson, Ph.D.
K-12 Curriculum Specialist for
  Mathematics
Lincoln Public Schools
Lincoln, Nebraska

Martha E. Sandoval-Martinez
Math Instructor
El Camino College
Torrance, California

English Language Learners Consultant

Elizabeth Jiménez
CEO, GEMAS Consulting
Professional Expert on English
  Learner Education
Bilingual Education and
  Dual Language
Pomona, California

VOLUME 1
Whole Number Operations

Big Idea Develop a conceptual understanding of whole number operations and data. Use strategies for addition and subtraction within 1,000 and multiplication and division within 100.

Big Idea

GO DIGITAL

Go online! Your math lessons are interactive. Use *i*Tools, Animated Math Models, the Multimedia *e*Glossary, and more.

Chapter 1 Overview

In this chapter, you will explore and discover answers to the following **Essential Questions**:

- How can you add and subtract whole numbers and decide if an answer is reasonable?
- How do you know when an estimate will be close to an exact answer?
- When do you regroup to add or subtract whole numbers?
- How might you decide which strategy to use to add or subtract?

Chapter 2 Overview

In this chapter, you will explore and discover answers to the following **Essential Questions**:

- How can you represent and interpret data?
- What are some ways to organize data so it is easy to use?
- How can analyzing data in graphs help you solve problems?

Chapter 3 Overview

In this chapter, you will explore and discover answers to the following **Essential Questions**:

• How can you use multiplication to find how many in all?
• What models can help you multiply?
• How can you use skip counting to help you multiply?
• How can multiplication properties help you find products?
• What types of problems can be solved by using multiplication?

Practice and Homework

Lesson Check and Spiral Review in every lesson

Chapter 4 Overview

In this chapter, you will explore and discover answers to the following **Essential Questions**:

• What strategies can you use to multiply?
• How are patterns and multiplication related?
• How can multiplication properties help you find products?
• What types of problems can be solved by using multiplication?

Chapter 5 Overview

In this chapter, you will explore and discover answers to the following **Essential Questions**:

• How can you use multiplication facts, place value, and properties to solve multiplication problems?

• How are patterns and multiplication related?

• How can multiplication properties help you find products?

• What types of problems can be solved by using multiplication?

Chapter 6 Overview

In this chapter, you will explore and discover answers to the following **Essential Questions**:

• How can you use division to find how many in each group or how many equal groups?

• How are multiplication and division related?

• What models can help you divide?

• How can subtraction help you divide?

Chapter 7 Overview

In this chapter, you will explore and discover answers to the following **Essential Questions**:

- What strategies can you use to divide?
- How can you use a related multiplication fact to divide?
- How can you use factors to divide?
- What types of problems can be solved by using division?

© Houghton Mifflin Harcourt Publishing Company

viii

Big Idea

GO DIGITAL

Go online! Your math lessons are interactive. Use *i*Tools, Animated Math Models, the Multimedia eGlossary, and more.

Essential Question
What are equal parts of a whole?

Chapter 8 Overview

In this chapter, you will explore and discover answers to the following **Essential Questions**:

• How can you use fractions to describe how much or how many?

• Why do you need to have equal parts for fractions?

• How can you solve problems that involve fractions?

Chapter 9 Overview

In this chapter, you will explore and discover answers to the following **Essential Questions**:

• How can you compare fractions?

• What models can help you compare and order fractions?

• How can you use the size of the pieces to help you compare and order fractions?

• How can you find equivalent fractions?

Chapter 10 Overview

In this chapter, you will explore and discover answers to the following **Essential Questions**:

- How can you tell time and use measurement to describe the size of something?
- How can you tell time and find the elapsed time, starting time, or ending time of an event?
- How can you measure the length of an object to the nearest half or fourth inch?

Chapter 11 Overview

In this chapter, you will explore and discover answers to the following **Essential Questions**:

- How can you solve problems involving perimeter and area?
- How can you find perimeter?
- How can you find area?
- What might you need to estimate or measure perimeter and area?

Measurement

Big Idea Develop a conceptual understanding of measurement, including time, linear, and liquid measures. Develop concepts of area and perimeter.

Geometry

Big Idea Describe, analyze, and compare two-dimensional shapes. Develop a conceptual understanding of dividing shapes into equal areas and writing the area as a fraction.

Science, Technology, Engineering, and Math (STEM) Activities   STEM 1

GO DIGITAL

Go online! Your math lessons are interactive. Use *i*Tools, Animated Math Models, the Multimedia eGlossary, and more.

Chapter 12 Overview

In this chapter, you will explore and discover answers to the following **Essential Questions**:

• What are some ways to describe and classify two-dimensional shapes?

• How can you describe the angles and sides in polygons?

• How can you use sides and angles to describe quadrilaterals and triangles?

• How can you use properties of shapes to classify them?

• How can you divide shapes into equal parts and use unit fractions to describe the parts?

Personal Math Trainer
Online Assessment and Intervention

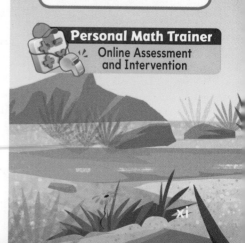

Big Idea Fractions

The Missouri quarter shows explorers Lewis and Clark traveling down the Missouri River. The Gateway Arch is in the background.

Real World Project

Coins in the U.S.

Many years ago, a coin called a *piece of eight* was sometimes cut into 8 equal parts. Each part was equal to one eighth ($\frac{1}{8}$) of the whole. Now, U.S. coin values are based on the dollar. Four quarters are equal in value to 1 dollar. So, 1 quarter is equal to one fourth ($\frac{1}{4}$) of a dollar.

Get Started

WRITE ▸ *Math*

Work with a partner. In which year were the Missouri state quarters minted? Use the Important Facts to help you. Then write fractions to answer these questions:

1. 2 quarters are equal to what part of a dollar?
2. 1 nickel is equal to what part of a dime?
3. 2 nickels are equal to what part of a dime?

Important Facts

- The U.S. government minted state quarters every year from 1999 to 2008 in the order that the states became part of the United States.
- 1999—Delaware, Pennsylvania, New Jersey, Georgia, Connecticut
- 2000—Massachusetts, Maryland, South Carolina, New Hampshire, Virginia
- 2001—New York, North Carolina, Rhode Island, Vermont, Kentucky
- 2002—Tennessee, Ohio, Louisiana, Indiana, Mississippi
- 2003—Illinois, Alabama, Maine, Missouri, Arkansas
- 2004—Michigan, Florida, Texas, Iowa, Wisconsin
- 2005—California, Minnesota, Oregon, Kansas, West Virginia
- 2006—Nevada, Nebraska, Colorado, North Dakota, South Dakota
- 2007—Montana, Washington, Idaho, Wyoming, Utah
- 2008—Oklahoma, New Mexico, Arizona, Alaska, Hawaii

_____

_____

_____

_____

Completed by _____

Understand Fractions

© Houghton Mifflin Harcourt Publishing Company • Image Credits: ©PhotoDisc / Getty Images

 Show What You Know

 Personal Math Trainer
Online Assessment
and Intervention

Check your understanding of important skills.

Name _____

▶ **Equal Parts** Circle the shape that has equal parts.

1.

2.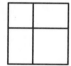

▶ **Combine Plane Shapes** Write the number of needed to cover the shape.

3.

_____ triangles

4.

_____ triangles

5.

_____ triangles

▶ **Count Equal Groups** Complete.

6.

_____ groups
_____ in each group

7.

_____ groups
_____ in each group

 Math in the Real World

Casey shared a pizza with some friends. They each ate $\frac{1}{3}$ of the pizza. How many people shared the pizza?

Chapter 8   441

Vocabulary Builder

▶ **Visualize It** ....

Complete the bubble map by using the words with a ✓.

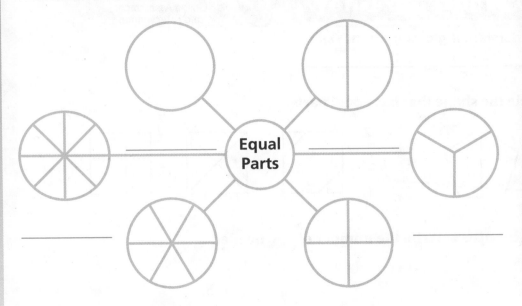

Preview Words

denominator
✓ eighths
equal parts
✓ fourths
fraction
fraction greater than 1
✓ halves
numerator
✓ sixths
✓ thirds
unit fraction
✓ whole

▶ **Understand Vocabulary** ....

Read the description. Write the preview word.

1. It is a number that names part of a whole or part

   of a group. _____

2. It is the part of a fraction above the line, which tells
   how many parts are being counted.

   _____

3. It is the part of a fraction below the line, which tells
   how many equal parts there are in the whole or in the

   group. _____

4. It is a number that names 1 equal part of a whole and

   has 1 as its numerator. _____

• **Interactive Student Edition**
• **Multimedia eGlossary**

denominator

denominador

11

Eighths

octavos

17

Equal Parts

partes iguales

21

Fourths

cuartos

26

fraction

fracción

27

Fraction Greater than 1

fraccíon mayor que 1

28

Halves

mitades

32

numerator

numerador

53

These are eighths

The part of a fraction below the line, which tells how many equal parts there are in the whole or in the group

Example: $\frac{1}{5}$ ← denominator

These are fourths

Parts that are exactly the same size

6 equal parts

A number which has a numerator that is greater than its denominator

Examples:

   $\frac{6}{3}$ $\frac{2}{1}$

A number that names part of a whole or part of a group

Examples:

   $\frac{1}{3}$

The part of a fraction above the line, which tells how many parts are being counted

Example: $\frac{1}{5}$ ← numerator

These are halves

Sixths

sextos

74

Thirds

tercios

77

unit fraction

fraccíon unitaria

79

Whole

entero

84

These are thirds

These are sixths

All of the parts of a shape or group

Example:

$$\frac{2}{2} = 1$$

This is one whole.

A fraction that has 1 as its top number, or numerator

Example: $\frac{1}{3}$ is a unit fraction

Going to the Mint

For 2 to 4 players

Word Box
denominator
eighths
equal parts
fourths
fraction
fraction greater
   than 1
halves
numerator
sixths
thirds
unit fraction
whole

Materials

- 3 red playing pieces
- 3 blue playing pieces
- 3 green playing pieces
- 3 yellow playing pieces
- 1 number cube

How to Play

1. Put your 3 playing pieces in the START circle of the same color.

2. To get a playing piece out of START, you must toss a 6 on the number cube.
   - If you toss a 6, move 1 of your playing pieces to the same colored circle on the path.
   - If you do not toss a 6, wait until your next turn.

3. Once you have a playing piece on the path, toss the number cube to take a turn. Move the playing pieces that many tan spaces. You must get all 3 of your playing pieces on the path.

4. If you land on a space with a question, answer it. If you are correct, move ahead 1 space.

5. To reach FINISH, move your playing pieces up the path that is the same color as your playing pieces. The first player to get all three playing pieces on FINISH wins.

Game

START

FINISH

Why is $\frac{1}{4}$ a unit fraction?

What is the name of the part of a fraction above the line?

How many fourths are in a whole?

What is a fraction?

What is the meaning of a whole?

How many sixths does three thirds equal?

Why is $\frac{4}{3}$ a fraction greater than 1?

Which is a whole: $\frac{3}{8}$ or $\frac{8}{8}$?

START

442B

START

FINISH

START

What are sixths?

What kind of number has a numerator greater than its denominator?

What kind of fraction is $\frac{1}{3}$?

If a whole has two equal parts, what are the equal parts called?

How many equal parts called thirds are in a whole?

What are equal parts?

If there are 8 equal parts in a whole, what are the equal parts called?

What is the meaning of *denominator*?

The Write Way

Reflect

Choose one idea. Write about it.

- Draw and explain the ideas of *equal* and *unequal parts*. Use a separate piece of paper for your drawing.
- Tell the most important idea to understand about fractions.
- Define *numerator and denominator* so that a younger child would understand.

Name _____

Equal Parts of a Whole

Essential Question What are equal parts of a whole?

Learning Objective You will describe equal parts of a whole.

🔑 Unlock the Problem

Lauren shares a sandwich with her brother. They each get an equal part. How many equal parts are there?

🔒 Each whole shape below is divided into equal parts. A **whole** is all of the parts of one shape or group. **Equal parts** are exactly the same size.

- What do you need to find?

_____

_____

- How many people share the sandwich? _____

2 halves

3 thirds

4 fourths

_____ **sixths**

_____ **eighths**

Lauren's sandwich is divided into halves.

So, there are _____ equal parts.

- Draw a picture to show a different way Lauren's sandwich could have been divided into halves.

 Math Talk

Math Processes and Practices ③

Verify the Reasoning of Others Are your halves the same shape as your classmates' halves? Explain why both halves represent the same size.

Try This! Write whether the shape is divided into *equal* parts or *unequal* parts.

A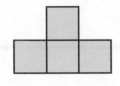

4 _____ parts
fourths

B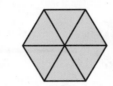

6 _____ parts
sixths

C

2 _____ parts
These are not halves.

Share and Show MATH BOARD

1. This shape is divided into 3 equal parts. What is the name for the parts?

_____

Math Talk   Math Processes and Practices ③

Apply How do you determine if the shapes are divided into equal parts?

Write the number of equal parts. Then write the name for the parts.

2.

_____ equal parts

_____

3.

_____ equal parts

_____

✓4.

_____ equal parts

_____

Write whether the shape is divided into *equal* parts or *unequal* parts.

5.

_____ parts

6.

_____ parts

✓7.

_____ parts

Name _____

Write the number of equal parts. Then write the name for the parts.

8.

_____ equal parts

_____

9.

_____ equal parts

_____

10.

_____ equal parts

_____

11.

_____ equal parts

_____

12.

_____ equal parts

_____

13.

_____ equal parts

_____

Write whether the shape is divided into *equal* parts or *unequal* parts.

14.

_____ parts

15.

_____ parts

16.

_____ parts

17. Draw lines to divide the circle into 8 eighths.

18. **GO DEEPER** Thomas wants to divide a square piece of paper into 4 equal parts. Draw two different quick pictures to show what his paper could look like.

Problem Solving • Applications

Use the pictures for 19–20.

19. Mrs. Rivera made 2 pans of corn casserole for a large family dinner. She cut each pan into parts. What is the name of the parts in A?

   _____

20. **THINK SMARTER** Alex said his mom divided Pan B into eighths. Does his statement make sense? Explain.

   _____

Pan A   **Pan B**

   _____

21. **Math Processes and Practices ⑥** **Explain** why the rectangle is divided into 4 equal parts.

   _____

   _____

22. **GO DEEPER** Shakira cut a triangle out of paper. She wants to divide the triangle into 2 equal parts. Draw a quick picture to show what her triangle could look like.

23. **THINK SMARTER** Parker divides a fruit bar into 3 equal parts. Circle the word that makes the sentence true.

   The fruit bar is divided into | thirds / halves / fourths |.

Name _____

Equal Parts of a Whole

Learning Objective You will describe equal parts of a whole.

Write the number of equal parts.
Then write the name for the parts.

1.

   ___4___ equal parts

   ___fourths___

2.

   _____ equal parts

   _____

Write whether the shape is divided into *equal* parts or *unequal* parts.

3.

   _____ parts

4.

   _____ parts

Problem Solving (Real World)

5. Diego cuts a round pizza into eight equal slices. What is the name for the parts?

   _____

6. Madison is making a place mat. She divides it into 6 equal parts to color. What is the name for the parts?

   _____

7. **WRITE** ▸*Math* Describe how 4 friends could share a sandwich equally.

   _____

   _____

Lesson Check

1. How many equal parts are in this shape?

2. What is the name for the equal parts of the whole?

Spiral Review

3. Use a related multiplication fact to find the quotient.

$$49 \div 7 =$$

4. Find the unknown factor and quotient.

$$9 \times \boxed{} = 45$$

$$45 \div 9 = \boxed{}$$

5. There are 5 pairs of socks in one package. Matt buys 3 packages of socks. How many pairs of socks does Matt buy?

6. Mrs. McCarr buys 9 packages of markers for an art project. Each package has 10 markers. How many markers does Mrs. McCarr buy?

FOR MORE PRACTICE
GO TO THE
Personal Math Trainer

Name _____

Equal Shares

Essential Question Why do you need to know how to make equal shares?

Learning Objective You will draw models to make equal shares.

🔑 Unlock the Problem

Four friends share 2 small pizzas equally. What are two ways the pizza could be divided equally? How much pizza will each friend get?

🔲 **Draw to model the problem.**

Draw 2 circles to show the pizzas.

• How might the two ways be different?

_____

_____

🔲 One Way

There are _____ friends.

So, divide each pizza into 4 slices.

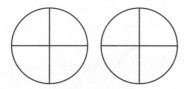

There are _____ equal parts.

Each friend can have 2 equal parts. Each friend will get 2 eighths of all the pizza.

🔲 Another Way

There are _____ friends.

So, divide all the pizza into 4 slices.

There are _____ equal parts.

Each friend can have 1 equal part. Each friend will get 1 half of a pizza.

Math Talk

Math Processes and Practices ②

Use Reasoning Why does dividing the pizza into different size slices still allow the friends to have an equal share?

Try This! Four girls share 3 oranges equally. Draw a quick picture to find out how much each girl gets.

• Draw 3 circles to show the oranges.

• Draw lines to divide the circles equally.

• Shade the part 1 girl gets.

• Describe what part of an orange each girl gets.

_____

🔑 Example

Melissa and Kyle are planning to share one pan of lasagna with 6 friends. They do not agree on the way to cut the pan into equal parts. Will each friend get an equal share using Melissa's way? Using Kyle's way?

Melissa's Way   **Kyle's Way**

- Will Melissa's shares and Kyle's shares have the same shape? _____

- Will their shares using either way be the same size? _____

So, each friend will get an _____ share using either way.

- Explain why both ways let the friends have the same amount.

_____

_____

Share and Show 📋 MATH BOARD

Math Talk   Math Processes and Practices ⑥

Explain another way the oranges could have been divided. Tell how much each friend will get.

1. Two friends share 4 oranges equally. Use the picture to find how much each friend gets.

Think: There are more oranges than friends.

_____

Draw lines to show how much each person gets. Write the answer.

✓ 2. 8 sisters share 3 eggrolls equally.

_____

✓ 3. 6 students share 4 bagels equally.

_____

Name _____

On Your Own

Draw lines to show how much each person gets. Write the answer.

4. 3 classmates share 2 granola bars equally.

_____

5. 4 brothers share 2 sandwiches equally.

_____

Draw to show how much each person gets. Shade the amount that one person gets. Write the answer.

6. 8 friends share 4 sheets of construction paper equally.

_____

7. **Math Processes and Practices 4** **Model Mathematics** 4 sisters share 3 muffins equally.

_____

8. **GO DEEPER** Maria prepared 5 quesadillas. She wants to share them equally among 8 of her neighbors. How much of a quesadilla will each neighbor get?

_____

© Houghton Mifflin Harcourt Publishing Company

🔑 Unlock the Problem

9. **THINK SMARTER** Julia holds a bread-baking class. She has 4 adults and 3 children in the class. The class will make 2 round loaves of bread. If Julia plans to give each person, including herself, an equal part of the baked breads, how much bread will each person get?

a. What do you need to find? _____

_____

b. How will you use what you know about drawing equal

shares to solve the problem? _____

_____

c. Draw a quick picture to find the share
   of bread each person will get.

d. So, each person will get

_____ of a loaf of bread.

10. **THINK SMARTER** Lara and three girl friends share three sandwiches equally.

How much does each girl get? Mark all that apply.

Ⓐ 3 fifths of a sandwich   Ⓒ 1 whole sandwich

Ⓑ 3 fourths of a sandwich   Ⓓ one half and 1 fourth of a sandwich

Equal Shares

Learning Objective You will draw models to make equal shares.

Draw lines to show how much each person gets. Write the answer.

1. 6 friends share 3 sandwiches equally.

3 sixths of a sandwich _____

_____

2. 4 teammates share 5 granola bars equally.
   Draw to show how much each person gets.
   Shade the amount that one person gets.
   Write the answer.

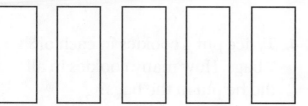

_____

Problem Solving Real World

3. Three brothers share 2 sandwiches equally. How much of a sandwich does each brother get?

_____

_____

4. Six neighbors share 4 pies equally. How much of a pie does each neighbor get?

_____

_____

5. **WRITE** ▸Math Draw a diagram to show 3 pizzas shared equally among 6 friends.

_____

_____

Lesson Check

1. Two friends share 3 fruit bars equally. How much does each friend get?

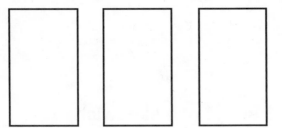

_____

2. Four brothers share 3 pizzas equally. How much of a pizza does each brother get?

_____

Spiral Review

3. Find the quotient.

$$3\overline{)27}$$

_____

4. Tyrice put 4 cookies in each of 7 bags. How many cookies in all did he put in the bags?

_____

5. Ryan earned $5 per hour raking leaves. He earned $35. How many hours did he rake leaves?

_____

6. Hannah has 229 horse stickers and 164 kitten stickers. How many more horse stickers than kitten stickers does Hannah have?

_____

FOR MORE PRACTICE GO TO THE Personal Math Trainer

Lesson 8.3

Name _____

Unit Fractions of a Whole

Essential Question What do the top and bottom numbers of a fraction tell?

Learning Objective You will use fraction models to recognize and name the quantity formed by one part when a whole is divided into equal parts.

A **fraction** is a number that names part of a whole or part of a group.

In a fraction, the top number tells how many equal parts are being counted.

The bottom number tells how many equal parts are in the whole or in the group.

$$\longrightarrow \quad \frac{1}{6}$$

A **unit fraction** names 1 equal part of a whole. It has 1 as its top number. $\frac{1}{6}$ is a unit fraction.

Unlock the Problem

Luke's family picked strawberries. They put the washed strawberries in one part of a fruit platter. The platter had 6 equal parts. What fraction of the fruit platter had strawberries?

Find part of a whole.

Shade 1 of the 6 equal parts.

Read: one sixth   **Write:** $\frac{1}{6}$

So, _____ of the platter had strawberries.

Math Talk   Math Processes and Practices ②

Reason Abstractly How can you make a whole if you know what one equal part looks like?

Use a fraction to find a whole.

This shape ⬜ is $\frac{1}{4}$ of the whole. Here are examples of what the whole could look like.

Ⓐ   Ⓑ   Ⓒ

© Houghton Mifflin Harcourt Publishing Company

Chapter 8   455

Try This! Look again at the examples at the bottom of page 455. Draw two other pictures of how the whole might look.

Share and Show MATH BOARD

1. What fraction names the shaded part? _____

   Think: 1 out of 3 equal parts is shaded.

Math Talk Math Processes and Practices ④

Use Models When using a fraction model, how do you know what the denominator of the fraction will be?

Write the number of equal parts in the whole. Then write the fraction that names the shaded part.

2.

_____ equal parts

_____

3.

_____ equal parts

_____

4.

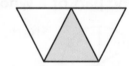

_____ equal parts

_____

5.

_____ equal parts

_____

6.

_____ equal parts

_____

7.

_____ equal parts

_____

Name _____

On Your Own

Write the number of equal parts in the whole.
Then write the fraction that names the shaded part.

8.

_____ equal parts

_____

9.
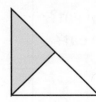

_____ equal parts

_____

10.

_____ equal parts

_____

11.

_____ equal parts

_____

12.

_____ equal parts

_____

13. **GO DEEPER**

_____ equal parts

_____

Math Processes and Practices ④ Use Diagrams   Draw a picture of the whole.

14. $\frac{1}{2}$ is

15. $\frac{1}{3}$ is ▨

16. $\frac{1}{6}$ is ▬

17. $\frac{1}{4}$ is

Problem Solving • Applications (Real World)

Use the pictures for 18–19.

Kylie's Lunch	Dylan's Lunch
sandwich	pizza
apple	fruit bar

18. The missing parts of the pictures show what Kylie and Dylan ate for lunch. What fraction of the pizza did Dylan eat? What fraction of the fruit bar did he eat?

_____

19. What fraction of the apple did Kylie eat? Write the fraction in numbers and in words.

_____ _____

20. (Math Processes and Practices 3) **Make Arguments** Diego drew lines to divide the square into 6 pieces as shown. Then he shaded part of the square. Diego says he shaded $\frac{1}{6}$ of the square. Is he correct? Explain how you know.

_____

_____

21. (THINK SMARTER) Riley and Chad each have a granola bar broken into equal pieces. They each eat one piece, or $\frac{1}{4}$, of their granola bar. How many more pieces do Riley and Chad need to eat to finish both granola bars? Draw a picture to justify your answer.

_____

22. (THINK SMARTER) What fraction names the shaded part? Explain how you know how to write the fraction.

_____

Unit Fractions of a Whole

Learning Objective You will use fraction models to recognize and name the quantity formed by one part when a whole is divided into equal parts.

Write the number of equal parts in the whole. Then write the fraction that names the shaded part.

1.

_____6_____ equal parts

$$\frac{1}{6}$$
_____

2.

_____ equal parts

_____

Draw a picture of the whole.

3. $\frac{1}{3}$ is

4. $\frac{1}{8}$ is

Problem Solving Real World

5. Tyler made a pan of cornbread. He cut it into 8 equal pieces and ate 1 piece. What fraction of the cornbread did Tyler eat?

_____

6. Anna cut an apple into 4 equal pieces. She gave 1 piece to her sister. What fraction of the apple did Anna give to her sister?

_____

7. **WRITE** ▸Math Draw a picture to show what 1 out of 3 equal parts looks like. Then write the fraction.

_____

_____

Lesson Check

1. What fraction names the shaded part?

_____

2. Tasha cut a fruit bar into 3 equal parts. She ate 1 part. What fraction of the fruit bar did Tasha eat?

_____

Spiral Review

3. Alex has 5 lizards. He divides them equally among 5 cages. How many lizards does Alex put in each cage?

_____

4. Find the product.

$$8 \times 1 = \boxed{}$$

_____

5. Leo bought 6 chew toys for his new puppy. Each chew toy cost $4. How much did Leo spend for the chew toys?

_____

6. Lilly is making a picture graph. Each picture of a star is equal to two books she has read. The row for the month of December has 3 stars. How many books did Lilly read during the month of December?

_____

FOR MORE PRACTICE
GO TO THE
Personal Math Trainer

Name _____

Fractions of a Whole

Essential Question How does a fraction name part of a whole?

  Unlock the Problem Real World

The first pizzeria in America opened in New York in 1905. The pizza recipe came from Italy. Look at Italy's flag. What fraction of the flag is not red?

🔓 **Name equal parts of a whole.**

A fraction can name more than 1 equal part of a whole.

The flag is divided into 3 equal parts, and 2 parts are not red.

2 parts not red → **2** ← numerator
3 equal parts in all → **3** ← denominator

Read: two thirds or two parts out of three equal parts

Write: $\frac{2}{3}$

So, _____ of the flag is not red.

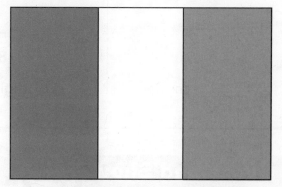

▲ Italy's flag has three equal parts.

Math Idea
When all the parts are shaded, one whole shape is equal to all of its parts. It represents the whole number 1.
$$\frac{3}{3} = 1$$

The **numerator** tells how many parts are being counted.

The **denominator** tells how many equal parts are in the whole or in the group.

You can count equal parts, such as sixths, to make a whole.

| One $\frac{1}{6}$ part | Two $\frac{1}{6}$ parts | Three $\frac{1}{6}$ parts | Four $\frac{1}{6}$ parts | Five $\frac{1}{6}$ parts | Six $\frac{1}{6}$ parts |

$\frac{1}{6}$ $\frac{2}{6}$ $\frac{3}{6}$ $\frac{}{6}$ $\frac{}{6}$ $\frac{}{6}$

For example, $\frac{6}{6}$ = one whole, or 1.

Try This! Write the missing word or number to name the shaded part.

A

$\frac{2}{6}$

_____ sixths

B

$\frac{5}{8}$

_____ eighths

C

$\frac{}{3}$

two thirds

D

$\frac{}{6}$, or 1

six sixths, or one whole

Share and Show MATH BOARD

Math Talk Math Processes and Practices ⑧

Generalize What do the numerator and denominator of a fraction tell you?

1. Shade two parts out of eight equal parts. Write a fraction in words and in numbers to name the shaded part.

Think: Each part is $\frac{1}{8}$.

Read: _____ eighths   **Write:** _____

Write the fraction that names each part. Write a fraction in words and in numbers to name the shaded part.

2.

Each part is ____.

_____ fourths

_____

✔ 3.

Each part is ____.

_____ sixths

_____

✔ 4.

Each part is ____.

_____ fourths

_____

© Houghton Mifflin Harcourt Publishing Company

462

Name _____

On Your Own

Write the fraction that names each part. Write a fraction in words and in numbers to name the shaded part.

5.

Each part is ____.

_____ eighths

_____

6.

Each part is ____.

_____ thirds

_____

7.

Each part is ____.

_____ sixths

_____

Shade the fraction circle to model the fraction. Then write the fraction in numbers.

8. six out of eight

_____

9. three fourths
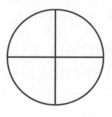

_____

10. three out of three
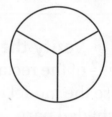

_____

11. A flag is divided into four equal sections. One section is white. What fraction of the flag is not white?

_____

12. A garden has six sections. Two sections are planted with tomatoes. Which fraction represents the part of the garden without tomatoes?

_____

13. Jane is making a memory quilt from some of her old favorite clothes that are too small. She will use T-shirts for the shaded squares in the pattern. What names the part of the quilt that will be made of T-shirts?

_____

© Houghton Mifflin Harcourt Publishing Company

Problem Solving • Applications

Use the diagrams for 14–15.

Pepperoni   Cheese   Veggie

14. **GO DEEPER** Mrs. Ormond ordered pizza. Each pizza had 8 equal slices. What fraction of the pepperoni pizza was eaten? What fraction of the cheese pizza is left?

_____

15. **THINK SMARTER** **Pose a Problem** Use the picture of the veggie pizza to write a problem that includes a fraction. Solve your problem.

_____

_____

16. **Math Processes and Practices ③** **Verify the Reasoning of Others** Kate says that $\frac{2}{4}$ of the rectangle is shaded. Describe her error. Use the model to write the correct fraction for the shaded part.

_____

_____

_____

17. **THINK SMARTER** Select a numerator and a denominator for the fraction that names the shaded part of the shape.

Numerator	Denominator
○ 2	○ 3
○ 3	○ 5
○ 5	○ 6
○ 6	○ 8

Fractions of a Whole

Learning Objective You will use fraction models to name equal parts of a whole.

Write the fraction that names each part. Write a fraction in words and in numbers to name the shaded part.

1.

   Each part is ____$\frac{1}{6}$____.

   ____three____ sixths

   ____$\frac{3}{6}$____

2.

   Each part is _____.

   _____ eighths

   _____

Shade the fraction circle to model the fraction. Then write the fraction in numbers.

3. four out of six

   _____

4. eight out of eight

   _____

5. Emma makes a poster for the school's spring concert. She divides the poster into 8 equal parts. She uses two of the parts for the title. What fraction of the poster does Emma use for the title?

   _____

6. Lucas makes a flag. It has 6 equal parts. Five of the parts are red. What fraction of the flag is red?

   _____

7. **WRITE** ▸Math Draw a rectangle and divide it into 4 equal parts. Shade 3 parts. Then write the fraction that names the shaded part.

   _____

   _____

Lesson Check

1. What fraction names the shaded part?

2. What fraction names the shaded part?

Spiral Review

3. Sarah biked for 115 minutes last week. Jennie biked for 89 minutes last week. How many minutes did the girls bike?

4. Harrison made a building using 124 blocks. Greyson made a building using 78 blocks. How many more blocks did Harrison use than Greyson?

5. Von buys a bag of 24 dog treats. He gives his puppy 3 treats a day. How many days will the bag of dog treats last?

6. How many students chose swimming?

Favorite Activity	
Skating	☺ ☺
Swimming	☺ ☺ ☺ ☺ ☺
Biking	☺ ☺ ☺ ☺
Key: Each ☺ = 5 votes.	

FOR MORE PRACTICE
GO TO THE
Personal Math Trainer

Name _____

Fractions on a Number Line

Essential Question How can you represent and locate fractions on a number line?

Learning Objective You will use fraction strips to represent fractions and recognize fractions as points on a number line.

🔑 Unlock the Problem

Billy's family is traveling from his house to his grandma's house. They stop at gas stations when they are $\frac{1}{4}$ and $\frac{3}{4}$ of the way there. How can you represent those distances on a number line?

You can use a number line to show fractions. The length from one whole number to the next whole number represents one whole. The line can be divided into any number of equal parts, or lengths.

> ### Math Idea
> A point on a number line shows the endpoint of a length, or distance, from zero. A number or fraction can name the distance.

🔓 Activity Locate fractions on a number line.

Materials ■ fraction strips

Billy's House   Grandma's House
0   1

$\frac{0}{4}$ $\frac{4}{4}$

STEP 1 Divide the line into four equal lengths, or fourths.
Place four $\frac{1}{4}$-fraction strips end-to-end above the line to help.

STEP 2 At the end of each strip, draw a mark on the line.

STEP 3 Count the fourths from zero to 1 to label the distances from zero.

STEP 4 Think: $\frac{1}{4}$ is 1 out of 4 equal lengths.
Draw a point at $\frac{1}{4}$ to represent the distance from 0 to $\frac{1}{4}$.
Label the point *G1*.

STEP 5 Think: $\frac{3}{4}$ is 3 out of 4 equal lengths.
Draw a point at $\frac{3}{4}$ to represent the distance from 0 to $\frac{3}{4}$.
Label the point *G2*.

① Example Complete the number line to name the point.

Materials ■ color pencils

Write the fraction that names the point on the number line.

Think: This number line is divided into six equal lengths, or sixths.

The length of one equal part is _____.

Shade the fraction strips to show the location of the point.

There are _____ out of _____ equal lengths shaded.
The shaded length shows $\frac{5}{6}$.

So, _____ names the point.

Share and Show **MATH BOARD**

1. Complete the number line. Draw a point to show $\frac{2}{3}$.

Math Talk Math Processes and Practices ④

Use Models What does the length between each mark on this number line represent?

Write the fraction that names the point.

2. point A _____   ✓ 3. point B _____   ✓ 4. point C _____

468

© Houghton Mifflin Harcourt Publishing Company

Name _____

On Your Own

Use fraction strips to help you complete the number line. Then locate and draw a point for the fraction.

5. $\frac{2}{6}$

6. $\frac{2}{3}$

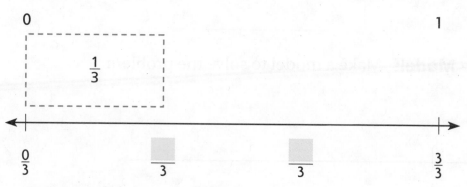

Write the fraction that names the point.

7. point C _____   8. point D _____   9. point E _____

---

10. There is a walking trail at the park. Four laps around the trail is a distance of 1 mile. How many laps does it take to walk $\frac{3}{4}$ mile?

11. **GO DEEPER** A recipe for pasta makes enough for eight servings. How many servings can be made using $\frac{4}{8}$ of each ingredient in the recipe?

Unlock the Problem

12. **THINK SMARTER** Javia ran 8 laps around a track to run a total of 1 mile on Monday. How many laps will she need to run on Tuesday to run $\frac{3}{8}$ of a mile?

a. What do you need to find?

_____

_____

_____

b. How will you use what you know about number lines to help you solve the problem?

_____

_____

_____

_____

c. **Math Processes and Practices 4** **Use Models** Make a model to solve the problem.

←_____→

d. Complete the sentences.

There are _____ laps in 1 mile.

Each lap represents _____ of a mile.

_____ laps represent the distance of three eighths of a mile.

So, Javia will need to run _____ laps to run $\frac{3}{8}$ of a mile.

Personal Math Trainer

13. **THINK SMARTER +** Locate and draw point *F* on the number line to represent the fraction $\frac{2}{4}$.

470

Fractions on a Number Line

Learning Objective You will use fraction strips to represent fractions and recognize fractions as points on a number line.

**Use fraction strips to help you complete the number line.
Then locate and draw a point for the fraction.**

1. $\frac{1}{3}$

Write the fraction that names the point.

2. point A _____

3. point B _____

4. point C _____

Problem Solving · Real World

5. Jade ran 6 times around her neighborhood to complete a total of 1 mile. How many times will she need to run to complete $\frac{5}{6}$ of a mile?

_____

6. A missing fraction on a number line is located exactly halfway between $\frac{3}{6}$ and $\frac{5}{6}$. What is the missing fraction?

_____

7. **WRITE** ▸*Math* Explain how showing fractions with models and a number line are alike and different.

_____

_____

Lesson Check

1. What fraction names point *G* on the number line?

0   1

$\frac{0}{4}$ G $\frac{2}{4}$ $\frac{3}{4}$ $\frac{4}{4}$

_____

2. What fraction names point *R* on the number line?

0   1

$\frac{0}{3}$ $\frac{1}{3}$ R $\frac{3}{3}$

_____

Spiral Review

3. Each table in the cafeteria can seat 10 students. How many tables are needed to seat 40 students?

_____

4. Use the Commutative Property of Multiplication to write a related number sentence.

$$4 \times 9 = 36$$

_____

5. Pedro shaded part of a circle. What fraction names the shaded part?

6. Find the quotient.

$$8 \div 1 = \boxed{}$$

_____

FOR MORE PRACTICE
GO TO THE
Personal Math Trainer

Name _____

Personal Math Trainer
Online Assessment
and Intervention

Vocabulary

Choose the best term from the box to complete
the sentence.

Vocabulary
denominator
fraction
numerator

1. A _____ is a number that names part
   of a whole or part of a group. (p. 455)

2. The _____ tells how many equal parts are in
   the whole or in the group. (p. 461)

Concepts and Skills

Write the number of equal parts. Then write the name
for the parts.

3.

____ equal parts

_____

4.

____ equal parts

_____

5.

____ equal parts

_____

Write the number of equal parts in the whole. Then write the
fraction that names the shaded part.

6.

____ equal parts

_____

7.

____ equal parts

_____

8.

____ equal parts

_____

© Houghton Mifflin Harcourt Publishing Company

Write the fraction that names the point.

0   1

$\frac{0}{6}$ A B $\frac{3}{6}$ $\frac{4}{6}$ C $\frac{6}{6}$

9. point A _____

10. point B _____

11. point C _____

12. **GO DEEPER**   Jessica ordered a pizza. What fraction of the pizza has mushrooms? What fraction of the pizza does not have mushrooms?

_____

13. Which fraction names the shaded part?

_____

14. Six friends share 3 oatmeal squares equally. How much of an oatmeal square does each friend get?

_____

474

Relate Fractions and Whole Numbers

Essential Question When might you use a fraction greater than 1 or a whole number?

Learning Objective You will locate and draw points as fractions and whole numbers on a number line and then use models to write fractions greater than 1.

Unlock the Problem

Steve ran 1 mile and Jenna ran $\frac{4}{4}$ of a mile. Did Steve and Jenna run the same distance?

🔑 **Locate 1 and $\frac{4}{4}$ on a number line.**

- Shade 4 lengths of $\frac{1}{4}$ and label the number line.

- Draw a point at 1 and $\frac{4}{4}$.

> **Math Idea**
> If two numbers are located at the same point on a number line, then they are equal and represent the same distance.

Since the distance _____ and _____ end at the same point, they are equal.

So, Steve and Jenna ran the _____ distance.

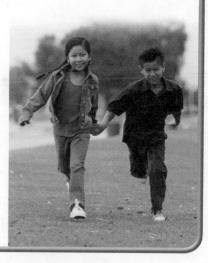

Try This! Complete the number line. Locate and draw points at $\frac{3}{6}$, $\frac{6}{6}$, and 1.

A Are $\frac{3}{6}$ and 1 equal? Explain.

Think: Do the distances end at the same point?

_____

_____

So, $\frac{3}{6}$ and 1 are _____.

B Are $\frac{6}{6}$ and 1 equal? Explain.

Think: Do the distances end at the same point?

_____

_____

So, $\frac{6}{6}$ and 1 are _____.

CONNECT The number of equal parts the whole is divided into is the denominator of a fraction. The number of parts being counted is the numerator. A **fraction greater than 1** has a numerator greater than its denominator.

Examples

Each shape is 1 whole. Write a whole number and a fraction greater than 1 for the parts that are shaded.

> **Remember**
>
> $\frac{4}{1}$ ← numerator
> ← denominator

A

There are 2 wholes.

Each whole is divided into $2 = \frac{8}{4}$
4 equal parts, or fourths.

There are _____ equal parts shaded.

B

There are 3 wholes.

Each whole is divided into $3 = \frac{3}{1}$
1 equal part.

There are _____ equal parts shaded.

1. Explain what *each whole is divided into 1 equal part* means in Example B.

   _____

   _____

> **Read Math**
>
> Read $\frac{3}{1}$ as *three ones*.

2. How do you divide a whole into 1 equal part?

   _____

   _____

Try This!

Each shape is 1 whole. Write a whole number and a fraction greater than 1 for the parts that are shaded.

Name _____

Share and Show

1. Each shape is 1 whole. Write a whole number and a fraction greater than 1 for the parts that are shaded.

There are _____ wholes.

Each whole is divided into _____ equal parts.

There are _____ equal parts shaded.

 $=\dfrac{}{}$

Use the number line to find whether the two numbers are equal. Write *equal* or *not equal*.

2. $\dfrac{1}{8}$ and $\dfrac{8}{8}$ _____

3. $\dfrac{8}{8}$ and 1 _____

4. 1 and $\dfrac{4}{8}$ _____

On Your Own

Use the number line to find whether the two numbers are equal. Write *equal* or *not equal*.

Math Talk — Math Processes and Practices ①

Evaluate How do you know whether the two fractions are equal or not equal when using a number line?

5. $\dfrac{0}{3}$ and 1 _____

6. 1 and $\dfrac{2}{3}$ _____

7. $\dfrac{3}{3}$ and 1 _____

Each shape is 1 whole. Write a fraction for the parts that are shaded.

8.

2 = _____

9.

1 = _____

10.

3 = _____

11.

2 = _____

© Houghton Mifflin Harcourt Publishing Company

Math Processes and Practices ⑥ Make Connections Draw a model of the fraction or fraction greater than 1. Then write it as a whole number.

12. $\frac{8}{4}$ = _____

13. $\frac{6}{6}$ = _____

14. $\frac{5}{1}$ = _____

Problem Solving • Applications Real World

15. **GO DEEPER** Jeff rode his bike around a bike trail that was $\frac{1}{3}$ of a mile long. He rode around the trail 9 times. Write a fraction greater than 1 for the distance. How many miles did Jeff ride?

_____

16. **THINK SMARTER** **What's the Error?** Andrea drew the number line below. She said that $\frac{9}{8}$ and 1 are equal. Explain her error.

_____

17. **THINK SMARTER** Each shape is 1 whole. Which numbers name the parts that are shaded? Mark all that apply.

Ⓐ 4   Ⓒ $\frac{26}{6}$ Ⓔ $\frac{6}{4}$

Ⓑ 6   Ⓓ $\frac{24}{6}$

Name _____

Relate Fractions and Whole Numbers

Learning Objective You will locate and draw points as fractions and whole numbers on a number line and then use models to write fractions greater than 1.

Use the number line to find whether the two numbers are equal. Write *equal* or *not equal*.

1. $\frac{0}{6}$ and 1

2. 1 and $\frac{6}{6}$

3. $\frac{1}{6}$ and $\frac{6}{6}$

_____not equal_____

_____

_____

Each shape is 1 whole. Write a fraction for the parts that are shaded.

4. 1 = _____

5. 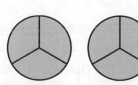 4 = _____

Problem Solving

6. Rachel jogged along a trail that was $\frac{1}{4}$ of a mile long. She jogged along the trail 8 times. How many miles did Rachel jog?

_____

7. Jon ran around a track that was $\frac{1}{8}$ of a mile long. He ran around the track 24 times. How many miles did Jon run?

_____

8. **WRITE** ▶*Math* Write a problem that uses a fraction greater than 1.

_____

_____

Lesson Check

1. Each shape is 1 whole. What fraction greater than 1 names the parts that are shaded?

_____

2. Each shape is 1 whole. What fraction greater than 1 names the parts that are shaded?

_____

Spiral Review

3. Tara has 598 pennies and 231 nickels. How many pennies and nickels does she have?

$$598$$
$$+\ 231$$

_____

4. Dylan read 6 books. Kylie read double the number of books that Dylan read. How many books did Kylie read?

_____

5. Alyssa divides a granola bar into halves. How many equal parts are there?

_____

6. There are 4 students in each small reading group. If there are 24 students in all, how many reading groups are there?

_____

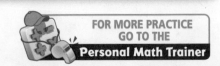

Name _____

Fractions of a Group

Essential Question How can a fraction name part of a group?

Learning Objective You will use fractions to name parts of a group.

 Unlock the Problem *Real World*

Jake and Emma each have a collection of marbles. What fraction of each collection is blue?

You can use a fraction to name part of a group.

Jake's Marbles

number of
blue marbles → [ ] ← numerator
total number → 8 ← denominator
of marbles

Read: three eighths, or three out of eight

Write: $\frac{3}{8}$

So, _____ of Jake's marbles are blue.

Emma's Marbles

bags of
blue marbles → [ ] ← numerator
total number → 4 ← denominator
of bags

Read: one fourth, or one out of four

Write: $\frac{1}{4}$

So, _____ of Emma's marbles are blue.

Try This! **Name part of a group.**

Draw 2 red counters and 6 yellow counters.

Write the fraction of counters that are red.

_____ ← number of red counters
_____ ← total number of counters

Write the fraction of counters that are not red.

_____ ← number of yellow counters
_____ ← total number of counters

So, _____ of the counters are red and _____ are not red.

Fractions Greater Than 1

Sometimes a fraction can name more than a whole group.

Daniel collects baseballs. He has collected 8 so far. He puts them in cases that hold 4 baseballs each. What part of the baseball cases has Daniel filled?

Think: 1 case = 1
Daniel has two full cases of 4 baseballs each.

So, 2, or $\frac{8}{4}$, baseball cases are filled.

Try This! Complete the whole number and the fraction greater than 1 to name the part filled.

Ⓐ

Think: 1 pan = 1

_____, or $\frac{}{6}$

Ⓑ

Think: 1 box = 1

_____, or $\frac{}{8}$

Share and Show MATH BOARD

1. What fraction of the counters are red? _____

Think: How many red counters are there? How many counters are there in all?

Write a fraction to name the red part of each group.

2.   _____

3.   _____

Math Talk — Math Processes and Practices 6

Explain another way to name the fraction for Exercise 3.

Name _____

Write a whole number and a fraction greater than 1 to name the part filled.

4.

Think: 1 carton = 1

_____

 5.

Think: 1 container = 1

_____

Write a fraction to name the blue part of each group.

6.

_____

7.

_____

8.

_____

9.

_____

Write a whole number and a fraction greater than 1 to name the part filled.

10.

Think: 1 container = 1

_____

11. THINK SMARTER

Think: 1 carton = 1

_____

Draw a quick picture on your MathBoard. Then write a fraction to name the shaded part of the group.

12. Draw 8 circles.
Shade 8 circles.

_____

13. Draw 8 triangles.
Make 4 groups.
Shade 1 group.

_____

14. Draw 4 rectangles.
Shade 2 rectangles.

_____

Problem Solving • Applications

Use the graph for 15–16.

School Marble Tournament

15. **GO DEEPER** The bar graph shows the winners of the Smith Elementary School Marble Tournament. How many games were played? What fraction of the games did Scott win?

_____   _____

16. **Math Processes and Practices 1** **Analyze** What fraction of the games did Robyn NOT win?

 WRITE ▸ *Math*
Show Your Work

_____

17. **THINK SMARTER** Li has 6 marbles. Of them, $\frac{1}{3}$ are blue. The rest are red. Draw a picture to show Li's marbles.

18. **WRITE** ▸ *Math* **What's the Question?** A bag has 2 yellow cubes, 3 blue cubes, and 1 white cube. The answer is $\frac{1}{6}$.

_____

19. **THINK SMARTER** Makayla picked some flowers. What fraction of flowers are yellow or red? What fraction of the flowers are NOT yellow or red? Show your work.

_____

© Houghton Mifflin Harcourt Publishing Company

Fractions of a Group

Learning Objective You will use fractions to name parts of a group.

Write a fraction to name the shaded part of each group.

1. $\frac{6}{8}$ or $\frac{3}{4}$

2.   _____

Write a whole number and a fraction greater than 1 to name the part filled. Think: 1 container = 1

3.

4.

_____   _____   _____   _____

Draw a quick picture. Then, write a fraction to name the shaded part of the group.

5. Draw 4 circles.
   Shade 2 circles.

6. Draw 6 circles.
   Make 3 groups.
   Shade 1 group.

_____

Problem Solving · Real World

7. Brian has 3 basketball cards and 5 baseball cards. What fraction of Brian's cards are baseball cards?

8. **WRITE** ▸*Math* Draw a set of objects where you can find a fractional part of the group using the total number of objects and by using subgroups.

_____

_____

Lesson Check

1. What fraction of the group is shaded?

_____

2. What fraction of the group is shaded?

_____

Spiral Review

3. What multiplication number sentence does the array represent?

☐☐☐☐☐☐
☐☐☐☐☐☐
☐☐☐☐☐☐

_____

_____

4. Juan has 436 baseball cards and 189 football cards. How many more baseball cards than football cards does Juan have?

_____

_____

5. Sydney bought 3 bottles of glitter. Each bottle of glitter cost $6. How much did Sydney spend on the bottles of glitter?

_____

6. Add.

262
+ 119

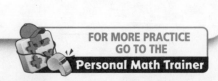

FOR MORE PRACTICE
GO TO THE
Personal Math Trainer

Find Part of a Group Using Unit Fractions

Essential Question How can a fraction tell how many are in part of a group?

Learning Objective You will use two-color counters to model and find parts of a group.

? Unlock the Problem

Audrey buys a bouquet of 12 flowers. One third of them are red. How many of the flowers are red?

- How many flowers does Audrey buy in all? _____
- What fraction of the flowers are red? _____

Activity

Materials ■ two-color counters ■ MathBoard

- Put 12 counters on your MathBoard.
- Since you want to find $\frac{1}{3}$ of the group, there should be _____ equal groups. Draw the counters below.

- Circle one of the groups to show _____.

  Then count the number of counters in that group.

There are _____ counters in 1 group. $\frac{1}{3}$ of 12 = _____

So, _____ of the flowers are red.

- What if Audrey buys a bouquet of 9 flowers and one third of them are yellow? Use your MathBoard and counters to find how many of the flowers are yellow.

_____

 Math Talk

Math Processes and Practices ❸

Apply How can you use the numerator and denominator in a fraction to find part of a group?

Try This! **Find part of a group.**

Raul picks 20 flowers from his mother's garden.
One fourth of them are purple. How many of the
flowers are purple?

STEP 1 Draw a row of 4 counters.

Think: To find $\frac{1}{4}$, make 4 equal groups.

STEP 2 Continue to draw as many rows of
4 counters as you can until you have 20 counters.

STEP 3 Then circle _____ equal groups.

Think: Each group represents $\frac{1}{4}$ of the flowers.

$$\frac{1}{4} \qquad \frac{1}{4} \qquad \frac{1}{4} \qquad \frac{1}{4}$$

There are _____ counters in 1 group.

$\frac{1}{4}$ of 20 = _____

So, _____ of the flowers are purple.

Math Talk Math Processes and Practices ⑥

Describe why you count the number of counters in just one of the groups when finding $\frac{1}{2}$ of any number.

1. Use the model to find $\frac{1}{2}$ of 8. _____

   Think: How many counters are in 1 of the 2 equal groups?

Circle equal groups to solve. Count the number of flowers in 1 group.

2. $\frac{1}{4}$ of 8 = _____

3. $\frac{1}{3}$ of 6 = _____

4. $\frac{1}{6}$ of 12 = _____

Name _____

On Your Own

Circle equal groups to solve. Count the number of flowers in 1 group.

5. $\frac{1}{4}$ of 12 = ____

6. $\frac{1}{3}$ of 15 = ____

7. $\frac{1}{4}$ of 16 = ____

8. $\frac{1}{6}$ of 30 = ____

9. $\frac{1}{3}$ of 12 = ____

10. THINK SMARTER

$\frac{1}{2}$ of 6 = ____

THINK SMARTER **Draw counters. Then circle equal groups to solve.**

11. $\frac{1}{8}$ of 16 = ____

12. $\frac{1}{6}$ of 24 = ____

13. GO DEEPER Gerry has 50 sports trading cards. Of those cards, $\frac{1}{5}$ of them are baseball cards, $\frac{1}{10}$ of them are football cards, and the rest are basketball cards. How many more basketball cards than baseball cards does Gerry have?

_____

14. GO DEEPER Barbara has a mixed garden that has 16 rows of different flowers and vegetables. One-fourth of the rows are lettuce, $\frac{1}{8}$ of the rows are pumpkins, and $\frac{1}{2}$ of the rows are red tulips. The other rows are carrots. How many rows of carrots are in Barbara's garden?

_____

Problem Solving • Applications

Use the table for 15–16.

Flower Seeds Bought	
Name	Number of Packs
Ryan	8
Brooke	12
Cole	20

15. **Math Processes and Practices ④ Use Diagrams** One fourth of the seed packs Ryan bought are violet seeds. How many packs of violet seeds did Ryan buy? Draw counters to solve.

_____

16. **GO DEEPER** One third of Brooke's seed packs and one fourth of Cole's seed packs are daisy seeds. How many packs of daisy seeds did they buy altogether? Explain how you know.

WRITE *Math*
Show Your Work

_____

_____

_____

17. **THINK SMARTER Sense or Nonsense?** Sophia bought 12 pots. One sixth of them are green. Sophia said she bought 2 green pots. Does her answer make sense? Explain how you know.

_____

_____

_____

Personal Math Trainer

18. **THINK SMARTER +** A florist has 24 sunflowers in a container. Mrs. Mason buys $\frac{1}{4}$ of the flowers. Mr. Kim buys $\frac{1}{3}$ of the flowers. How many sunflowers are left? Explain how you solved the problem.

_____

_____

_____

Find Part of a Group Using Unit Fractions

Learning Objective You will use two-color counters to model and find parts of a group.

Circle equal groups to solve. Count the number of items in 1 group.

1. $\frac{1}{4}$ of 12 = ___3___

2. $\frac{1}{8}$ of 16 = _____

○ ○ ○ ○ ○ ○ ○ ○
○ ○ ○ ○ ○ ○ ○ ○

3. $\frac{1}{3}$ of 12 = _____

○ ○ ○
○ ○ ○
○ ○ ○
○ ○ ○

4. $\frac{1}{3}$ of 9 = _____

○ ○ ○
○ ○ ○
○ ○ ○

Problem Solving Real World

5. Marco drew 24 pictures. He drew $\frac{1}{6}$ of them in art class. How many pictures did Marco draw in art class?

_____

6. Caroline has 16 marbles. One eighth of them are blue. How many of Caroline's marbles are blue?

_____

7. **WRITE** ▸ *Math* Explain how to find which is greater: $\frac{1}{4}$ of 12 or $\frac{1}{3}$ of 12.

_____

_____

Lesson Check

1. Ms. Davis made 12 blankets for her grandchildren. One third of the blankets are blue. How many blue blankets did she make?

_____

2. Jackson mowed 16 lawns. One fourth of the lawns are on Main Street. How many lawns on Main Street did Jackson mow?

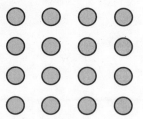

_____

Spiral Review

3. Find the difference.

$$509 - 175$$

4. Find the quotient.

$$6\overline{)54}$$

_____

5. There are 226 pets entered in the pet show. What is 226 rounded to the nearest hundred?

_____

6. Ladonne made 36 muffins. She put the same number of muffins on each of 4 plates. How many muffins did she put on each plate?

_____

FOR MORE PRACTICE GO TO THE Personal Math Trainer

Name _____

Problem Solving • Find the Whole Group Using Unit Fractions

Essential Question How can you use the strategy *draw a diagram* to solve fraction problems?

Learning Objective You will use the strategy *draw a diagram* to find parts of a group by drawing counters.

Unlock the Problem

Cameron has 4 clown fish in his fish tank. One third of the fish in the tank are clown fish. How many fish does Cameron have in his tank?

Use the graphic organizer to help you solve the problem.

Read the Problem	Solve the Problem
What do I need to find? I need to find _____ are in Cameron's fish tank.	**Describe how to draw a diagram to solve.** The denominator in $\frac{1}{3}$ tells you that there are _____ equal parts in the whole group. Draw 3 circles to show _____ equal parts. Since 4 fish are $\frac{1}{3}$ of the whole group, draw _____ counters in the first circle.
What information do I need to use? Cameron has _____ clown fish. _____ of the fish in the tank are clown fish.	Since there are _____ counters in the first circle, draw _____ counters in each of the remaining circles. Then find the total number of counters.
How will I use the information? I will use the information in the problem to draw a _____.	So, Cameron has _____ fish in his tank.

🔓 Try Another Problem

A pet store has 2 gray rabbits. One eighth of the rabbits at the pet store are gray. How many rabbits does the pet store have?

Read the Problem	Solve the Problem
What do I need to find?	
What information do I need to use?	
How will I use the information?	

1. **Math Processes and Practices 8** **Draw Conclusions** How do you know that your answer is reasonable?

_____

_____

2. How did your diagram help you solve the problem? _____

_____

Math Talk

© Houghton Mifflin Harcourt Publishing Company • Image Credits: (tr) ©Getty Images

Math Processes and Practices ①

Make Sense of Problems Suppose $\frac{1}{2}$ of the rabbits are gray. How can you find the number of rabbits at the pet store?

x

494

Name _____

Share and Show

Unlock the Problem

✓ Circle the question.
✓ Underline important facts.
✓ Put the problem in your own words.
✓ Choose a strategy you know.

1. Lily has 3 dog toys that are red. One fourth of all her dog toys are red. How many dog toys does Lily have?

   First, draw _____ circles to show _____ equal parts.

   Next, draw _____ toys in _____ circle since

   _____ circle represents the number of red toys.

   Last, draw _____ toys in each of the remaining circles. Find the total number of toys.

   So, Lily has _____ dog toys.

2. **THINK SMARTER** What if Lily has 4 toys that are red? How many dog toys would she have?

   _____

3. The pet store sells bags of pet food. There are 4 bags of cat food. One sixth of the bags of food are cat food. How many bags of pet food does the pet store have?

   _____

4. Rachel owns 2 parakeets. One fourth of all her birds are parakeets. How many birds does Rachel own?

   _____

On Your Own

5. **THINK SMARTER** Before lunchtime, Abigail and Teresa each read some pages from different books. Abigail read 5, or one fifth, of the pages in her book. Teresa read 6, or one sixth, of the pages in her book. Whose book had more pages? How many more pages?

_____

6. **Math Processes and Practices 2** **Represent a Problem** Six friends share 5 meat pies. Each friend first eats half of a meat pie. How much more meat pie does each friend need to eat to finish all the meat pies and share them equally? Draw a quick picture to solve.

_____

7. **GO DEEPER** Braden bought 4 packs of dog treats. He gave 4 treats to his neighbor's dog. Now Braden has 24 treats left for his dog. How many dog treats were in each pack? Explain how you know.

_____

_____

_____

_____

_____

WRITE _Math_ • **Show Your Work**

8. **THINK SMARTER** Two hats are $\frac{1}{3}$ of the group. How many hats are in the whole group?

_____ hats

Problem Solving • Find the Whole Group Using Unit Fractions

Learning Objective You will use the strategy *draw a diagram* to find parts of a group by drawing counters.

Draw a quick picture to solve.

1. Katrina has 2 blue ribbons for her hair. One fourth of all her ribbons are blue. How many ribbons does Katrina have in all?

   _____8 ribbons_____

2. One eighth of Tony's books are mystery books. He has 3 mystery books. How many books does Tony have in all?

   _____

3. Brianna has 4 pink bracelets. One third of all her bracelets are pink. How many bracelets does Brianna have?

   _____

4. Ramal filled 3 pages in a stamp album. This is one sixth of the pages in the album. How many pages are there in Ramal's stamp album?

   _____

5. Jeff helped repair one half of the bicycles in a bike shop last week. If Jeff worked on 5 bicycles, how many bicycles did the shop repair last week?

   _____

6. **WRITE** ▸*Math* Write a problem about a group of objects in your classroom. Tell how many are in one equal part of the group. Solve your problem. Draw a diagram to help you.

_____

_____

Lesson Check

1. A zoo has 2 male lions. One sixth of the lions are male lions. How many lions are there at the zoo?

_____

2. Max has 5 red model cars. One third of his model cars are red. How many model cars does Max have?

_____

Spiral Review

3. There are 382 trees in the local park. What is the number of trees rounded to the nearest hundred?

_____

4. The Jones family is driving 458 miles on their vacation. So far, they have driven 267 miles. How many miles do they have left to drive?

$$\begin{array}{r} 458 \\ -\ 267 \\ \hline \end{array}$$

_____

5. Ken has 6 different colors of marbles. He has 9 marbles of each color. How many marbles does Ken have in all?

_____

6. Eight friends share two pizzas equally. How much of a pizza does each friend get?

_____

FOR MORE PRACTICE GO TO THE Personal Math Trainer

Name _____

Personal Math Trainer
Online Assessment
and Intervention

1. Each shape is divided into equal parts. Select the shapes that show thirds. Mark all that apply.

  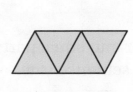

Ⓐ   Ⓑ   Ⓒ   Ⓓ

2. What fraction names the shaded part of the shape?

Ⓐ   8 sixths

Ⓑ   8 eighths

Ⓒ   6 eighths

Ⓓ   2 sixths

3. Omar shaded a model to show the part of the lawn that he finished mowing. What fraction names the shaded part? Explain how you know how to write the fraction.

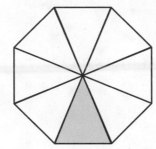

_____

_____

4. What fraction names point *A* on the number line?

_____

5. Jamal folded this piece of paper into equal parts.
Circle the word that makes the sentence true.

The paper is folded into

sixths
eighths
fourths

.

6. Caleb took 18 photos at the zoo. One sixth of his
photos are of giraffes. How many of Caleb's photos are
of giraffes?

_____ photos

7. Three teachers share 2 packs of paper equally.

How much paper does each teacher get? Mark all
that apply.

Ⓐ 3 halves of a pack

Ⓑ 2 thirds of a pack

Ⓒ 3 sixths of a pack

Ⓓ 1 half of a pack

Ⓔ 1 third of a pack

Name _____

8. Lilly shaded this design.

Select one number from each column to show
the part of the design that Lilly shaded.

Numerator	Denominator
○ 1	○ 3
○ 3	○ 4
○ 5	○ 5
○ 6	○ 6

9. Marcus baked a loaf of banana bread for a party.
He cut the loaf into equal size pieces. At the end of the
party, there were 6 pieces left. Explain how you can find
the number of pieces in the whole loaf if Marcus told you
that $\frac{1}{3}$ of the loaf was left. Use a drawing to show your
work.

_____

_____

_____

_____

10. The model shows one whole. What fraction of the model is NOT shaded?

_____

11. Together, Amy and Thea make up $\frac{1}{4}$ of the midfielders on the soccer team. How many midfielders are on the team? Show your work.

_____ midfielders

12. Six friends share 4 apples equally. How much apple does each friend get?

   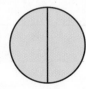

_____

13. Each shape is 1 whole.

For numbers 13a–13e, choose Yes or No to show whether the number names the parts that are shaded.

13a. 4   ○ Yes   ○ No

13b. 8   ○ Yes   ○ No

13c. $\frac{8}{2}$ ○ Yes   ○ No

13d. $\frac{8}{4}$ ○ Yes   ○ No

13e. $\frac{2}{8}$ ○ Yes   ○ No

Name _____

14. Alex has 3 baseballs. He brings 2 baseballs to school. What fraction of his baseballs does Alex bring to school?

_____

15. GO DEEPER Janeen and Nicole each made fruit salad for a school event.

Part A

Janeen used 16 pieces of fruit to make her salad. If $\frac{1}{4}$ of the fruits were peaches, how many peaches did she use? Make a drawing to show your work.

_____ peaches

Part B

Nicole used 24 pieces of fruit. If $\frac{1}{6}$ of them were peaches, how many peaches in all did Janeen and Nicole use to make their fruit salads? Explain how you found your answer.

_____

_____

16. There are 8 rows of chairs in the auditorium. Three of the rows are empty. What fraction of the rows are empty?

_____

© Houghton Mifflin Harcourt Publishing Company

17. Tara ran 3 laps around her neighborhood for a total of 1 mile yesterday. Today she wants to run $\frac{2}{3}$ of a mile. How many laps will she need to run around her neighborhood?

_____ laps

18. Gary painted some shapes.

Select one number from each column to show a fraction greater than 1 that names the parts Gary painted.

Numerator	Denominator
○ 3	○ 3
○ 4	○ 4
○ 8	○ 8
○ 24	○ 24

Personal Math Trainer

19. (THINK SMARTER +) Angelo rode his bike around a bike trail that was $\frac{1}{4}$ of a mile long. He rode his bike around the trail 8 times. Angelo says he rode a total of $\frac{8}{4}$ miles. Teresa says he is wrong and that he actually rode 2 miles. Who is correct? Use words and drawings to explain how you know.

_____

_____

_____

_____

_____

Chapter 9
Compare Fractions

✓ Show What You Know

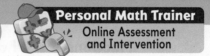
Personal Math Trainer
Online Assessment and Intervention

Check your understanding of important skills.

Name _____

▶ Halves and Fourths

1. Find the shape that is divided into 2 equal parts. Color $\frac{1}{2}$.

2. Find the shape that is divided into 4 equal parts. Color $\frac{1}{4}$.

▶ Parts of a Whole   Write the number of shaded parts and the number of equal parts.

3.   ____ shaded parts

____ equal parts

4.   ____ shaded parts

____ equal parts

▶ Fractions of a Whole

Write the fraction that names the shaded part of each shape.

5. _____

6. _____

7. _____

Hannah keeps her marbles in bags with 4 marbles in each bag. She writes $\frac{3}{4}$ to show the number of red marbles in each bag. Find another fraction to name the number of red marbles in 2 bags.

Vocabulary Builder

▶ **Visualize It** •••••••••••••••••••••••••••••••••••

Complete the flow map by using the words with a ✓.

Fractions and Whole Numbers

What is it?		What are some examples?
_____	→	$\frac{2}{3} > \frac{1}{3}$
_____	→	$\frac{1}{4} < \frac{2}{4}$
_____	→	$\frac{1}{2} = \frac{2}{4}$
_____	→	$\frac{1}{3}, \frac{1}{4}$
_____	→	$\frac{2}{2}, \frac{4}{2}$

Review Words

compare
denominator
eighths
equal parts
equal to (=)
fourths
fraction
✓ greater than (>)
halves
✓ less than (<)
numerator
order
sixths
thirds
✓ unit fractions
✓ whole numbers

Preview Word

✓ equivalent
fractions

▶ **Understand Vocabulary** ••••••••••••••••••••••••

Write the review word or preview word that answers the riddle.

1. We are two fractions that name the same amount.

   _____

2. I am the part of a fraction above the line. I tell how many parts are being counted.

   _____

3. I am the part of a fraction below the line. I tell how many equal parts are in the whole or in the group.

   _____

GO DIGITAL
• Interactive Student Edition
• Multimedia eGlossary

denominator

denominador

11

Eighths

octavos

17

Equal Parts

partes iguales

21

equivalent fractions

fracciones equivalentes

23

greater than (>)

mayor que

31

less than (<)

menor que

41

numerator

numerador

53

unit fraction

fracción unitaria

79

These are eighths

The part of a fraction below the line, which tells how many equal parts there are in the whole or in the group

Example: $\frac{1}{5}$ ← denominator

Two or more fractions that name the same amount

Example: $\frac{1}{2}$ and $\frac{3}{6}$ are equivalent fractions

Parts that are exactly the same size

6 equal parts

A symbol used to compare two numbers when the lesser number is given first

Example:
Read 3 < 7 as "three is less than seven."

A symbol used to compare two numbers when the greater number is given first

Example:
Read 6 > 4 as "six is greater than four."

A fraction that has 1 as its top number, or numerator

Example: $\frac{1}{3}$ is a unit fraction

The part of a fraction above the line, which tells how many parts are being counted

Example: $\frac{1}{5}$ ← numerator

Pick It

For 3 players

Materials
- 4 sets of word cards

How to Play

1. Each player is dealt 5 cards. The remaining cards are a draw pile.

2. To take a turn, ask any player if he or she has a word that matches one of your word cards.

3. If the player has the word, he or she gives the card to you, and you must define the word.
   - If you are correct, keep the card and put the matching pair in front of you. Take another turn.
   - If you are wrong, return the card. Your turn is over.

4. If the player does not have the word, he or she answers, "Pick it." Then you take a card from the draw pile.

5. If the card you draw matches one of your word cards, follow the directions for Step 3 above. If it does not, your turn is over.

6. The game is over when one player has no cards left. The player with the most pairs wins.

Word Box

denominator

eighths

equal parts

equivalent
   fractions

greater than (>)

less than (<)

numerator

unit fractions

© Houghton Mifflin Harcourt Publishing Company • Image Credits: (all) ©Artville/Getty Images

The Write Way

Reflect

Choose one idea. Write about it.

- Juan swam $\frac{3}{5}$ of a mile, and Greg swam $\frac{3}{8}$ of a mile. Explain how you know who swam farther.

- Explain how to compare two fractions.

- Write two examples of equivalent fractions and explain how you know they are equivalent.

Name _____

Problem Solving • Compare Fractions

Essential Question How can you use the strategy *act it out* to solve comparison problems?

Learning Objective You will use the strategy *act it out* to solve comparison problems by modeling and comparing with fraction strips or fraction circles.

🔑 Unlock the Problem

Mary and Vincent climbed up a rock wall at the park. Mary climbed $\frac{3}{4}$ of the way up the wall. Vincent climbed $\frac{3}{8}$ of the way up the wall. Who climbed higher?

You can act out the problem by using manipulatives to help you compare fractions.

Remember
< is less than
> is greater than
= is equal to

Read the Problem

What do I need to find?

_____

What information do I need to use?

Mary climbed _____ of the way.

Vincent climbed _____ of the way.

How will I use the information?

I will use _____

and _____ the lengths of

the models to find who climbed

_____ .

Solve the Problem

Record the steps you used to solve the problem.

1

$\frac{1}{4}$	$\frac{1}{4}$	$\frac{1}{4}$

$\frac{1}{8}$	$\frac{1}{8}$	$\frac{1}{8}$

Compare the lengths.

_____ ◯ _____

The length of the $\frac{3}{4}$ model is _____

than the length of the $\frac{3}{8}$ model.

So, _____ climbed higher on the rock wall.

Math Talk

Math Processes and Practices ④

Use Models When comparing fractions using fraction strips, how do you know which fraction is the lesser fraction?

Chapter 9 **507**

Try Another Problem

Students at day camp are decorating paper circles for placemats. Tracy finished $\frac{3}{6}$ of her placemat. Kim finished $\frac{5}{6}$ of her placemat. Who finished more of her placemat?

Read the Problem	Solve the Problem
What do I need to find?	**Record the steps you used to solve the problem.**
What information do I need to use?	
How will I use the information?	

Math Talk

Math Processes and Practices 2

Use Reasoning How do you know that $\frac{5}{6}$ is greater than $\frac{3}{6}$ without using models?

1. How did your model help you solve the problem? _____

_____

2. Tracy and Kim each had a carton of milk with lunch. Tracy drank $\frac{5}{8}$ of her milk. Kim drank $\frac{7}{8}$ of her milk. Who drank more of her milk? Explain.

_____

_____

Name _____

Unlock the Problem
✓ Circle the question.
✓ Underline important facts.
✓ Act out the problem using manipulatives.

Share and Show MATH BOARD

1. At the park, people can climb a rope ladder to its top. Rosa climbed $\frac{2}{8}$ of the way up the ladder. Justin climbed $\frac{2}{6}$ of the way up the ladder. Who climbed higher on the rope ladder?

   First, what are you asked to find?

   _____

   Then, model and compare the fractions. **Think:** Compare $\frac{2}{8}$ and $\frac{2}{6}$.

   Last, find the greater fraction.

   ____ ⃝ ____

   So, _____ climbed higher on the rope ladder.

2. What if Cara also tried the rope ladder and climbed $\frac{2}{4}$ of the way up? Who climbed highest on the rope ladder: Rosa, Justin, or Cara? Explain how you know.

   _____

   _____

   _____

On Your Own

3. **Math Processes and Practices 5** **Use a Concrete Model** Ted walked $\frac{2}{3}$ mile to his soccer game. Then he walked $\frac{1}{3}$ mile to his friend's house. Which distance is shorter? Explain how you know.

   _____

   _____

Use the table for 4–5.

4. **GO DEEPER** Suri is spreading jam on 8 biscuits for breakfast. The table shows the fraction of biscuits spread with each jam flavor. Which flavor did Suri use on the most biscuits?

   Hint: Use 8 counters to model the biscuits.

   _____

| Suri's Biscuits ||
Jam Flavor	Fraction of Biscuits
Peach	$\frac{3}{8}$
Raspberry	$\frac{4}{8}$
Strawberry	$\frac{1}{8}$

5. **WRITE ▸ Math What's the Question?** The answer is strawberry.

   _____

   _____

WRITE ▸ Math • Show Your Work

6. **THINK SMARTER** Suppose Suri had also used plum jam on the biscuits. She frosted $\frac{1}{2}$ of the biscuits with peach jam, $\frac{1}{4}$ with raspberry jam, $\frac{1}{8}$ with strawberry jam, and $\frac{1}{8}$ with plum jam. Which flavor of jam did Suri use on the most biscuits?

   _____

7. Ms. Gordon has many snack bar recipes. One recipe uses $\frac{1}{3}$ cup oatmeal, $\frac{1}{4}$ cup of milk, and $\frac{1}{2}$ cup flour. Which ingredient will Ms. Gordon use the most of?

   _____

8. **THINK SMARTER** Rick lives $\frac{4}{6}$ mile from school. Noah lives $\frac{3}{6}$ mile from school.

   Use the fractions and symbols to show which distance is longer.

   $\frac{3}{6}$, $\frac{4}{6}$, < and >   ☐ ◯ ☐

Problem Solving • Compare Fractions

Learning Objective You will use the strategy *act it out* to solve comparison problems by modeling and comparing with fraction strips or fraction circles.

Solve.

1. Luis skates $\frac{2}{3}$ mile from his home to school. Isabella skates $\frac{2}{4}$ mile to get to school. Who skates farther?

   Think: Use fraction strips to act it out.

   _____ Luis _____

2. Sandra makes a pizza. She puts mushrooms on $\frac{2}{8}$ of the pizza. She adds green peppers to $\frac{5}{8}$ of the pizza. Which topping covers more of the pizza?

   _____

3. The jars of paint in the art room have different amounts of paint. The green paint jar is $\frac{4}{8}$ full. The purple paint jar is $\frac{4}{6}$ full. Which paint jar is less full?

   _____

4. Jan has a recipe for bread. She uses $\frac{2}{3}$ cup of flour and $\frac{1}{3}$ cup of chopped onion. Which ingredient does she use more of, flour or onion?

   _____

5. **WRITE** ▸*Math* Explain how you can find whether $\frac{5}{6}$ or $\frac{5}{8}$ is greater.

   _____

   _____

Lesson Check

1. Ali and Jonah collect seashells in identical buckets. When they are finished, Ali's bucket is $\frac{2}{6}$ full and Jonah's bucket is $\frac{3}{6}$ full. Compare the fractions using >, < or =.

$\frac{3}{6} \bigcirc \frac{2}{6}$

2. Rosa paints a wall in her bedroom. She puts green paint on $\frac{5}{8}$ of the wall and blue paint on $\frac{3}{8}$ of the wall. Compare the fractions using >, < or =.

$\frac{5}{8} \bigcirc \frac{3}{8}$

Spiral Review

3. Dan divides a pie into eighths. How many equal parts are there?

4. Draw lines to divide the circle into 4 equal parts.

5. Charles places 30 pictures on his bulletin board in 6 equal rows. How many pictures are in each row?

6. Describe a pattern in the table.

Tables	1	2	3	4	5
Chairs	5	10	15	20	25

FOR MORE PRACTICE GO TO THE Personal Math Trainer

Name _____

Compare Fractions with the Same Denominator

Essential Question How can you compare fractions with the same denominator?

Learning Objective You will use visual fraction models and reasoning strategies to compare fractions of a whole and fractions of a group with the same denominator.

Unlock the Problem

Jeremy and Christina are each making a quilt block. Both blocks are the same size and both are made of 4 equal-size squares. $\frac{2}{4}$ of Jeremy's squares are green. $\frac{1}{4}$ of Christina's squares are green. Whose quilt block has more green squares?

- Circle the two fractions you need to compare.
- How are the two fractions alike?

_____

Compare fractions of a whole.

- Shade $\frac{2}{4}$ of Jeremy's quilt block.

- Shade $\frac{1}{4}$ of Christina's quilt block.

- Compare $\frac{2}{4}$ and $\frac{1}{4}$.

The greater fraction will have the larger amount of the whole shaded.

$$\frac{2}{4} \bigcirc \frac{1}{4}$$

Jeremy's Quilt Block   **Christina's Quilt Block**

Math Idea
You can compare two fractions when they refer to the same whole or to groups that are the same size.

So, _____ quilt block has more green squares.

Compare fractions of a group.

Jen and Maggie each have 6 buttons.

- Shade 3 of Jen's buttons to show the number of buttons that are red. Shade 5 of Maggie's buttons to show the number that are red.

- Write a fraction to show the number of red buttons in each group. Compare the fractions.

Jen's Buttons

Maggie's Buttons

There are the same number of buttons in each group, so you can count the number of red buttons to compare the fractions.

$$3 < \underline{\quad}, \text{ so } \frac{}{6} < \frac{}{6}.$$

So, _____ has a greater fraction of red buttons.

🔑 Use fraction strips and a number line.

At the craft store, one piece of ribbon is $\frac{2}{8}$ yard long. Another piece of ribbon is $\frac{7}{8}$ yard long. If Sean wants to buy the longer piece of ribbon, which piece should he buy?

- On a number line, a fraction farther to the right is greater than a fraction to its left.
- On a number line, a fraction farther to the left is _____ a fraction to its right.

Compare $\frac{2}{8}$ and $\frac{7}{8}$.

- Shade the fraction strips to show the locations of $\frac{2}{8}$ and $\frac{7}{8}$.

- Draw and label points on the number line to represent the distances $\frac{2}{8}$ and $\frac{7}{8}$.

- Compare the lengths.

$\frac{1}{8}$	$\frac{1}{8}$	$\frac{1}{8}$	$\frac{1}{8}$	$\frac{1}{8}$	$\frac{1}{8}$	$\frac{1}{8}$	$\frac{1}{8}$
$\frac{1}{8}$	$\frac{1}{8}$	$\frac{1}{8}$	$\frac{1}{8}$	$\frac{1}{8}$	$\frac{1}{8}$	$\frac{1}{8}$	$\frac{1}{8}$

$\frac{0}{8}$　　　　　　　$\frac{8}{8}$

$\frac{2}{8}$ is to the left of $\frac{7}{8}$. It is closer to $\frac{0}{8}$, or _____.

$\frac{7}{8}$ is to the _____ of $\frac{2}{8}$. It is closer to —, or _____.

__ < __ and __ > __

So, Sean should buy the piece of ribbon that is — yard long.

🔑 Use reasoning.

Ana and Omar are decorating same-size bookmarks. Ana covers $\frac{3}{3}$ of her bookmark with glitter. Omar covers $\frac{1}{3}$ of his bookmark with glitter. Whose bookmark is covered with more glitter?

Compare $\frac{3}{3}$ and $\frac{1}{3}$.

- When the denominators are the same, the whole is divided into same-size pieces. You can look at the _____ to compare the number of pieces.

- Both fractions involve third-size pieces. _____ pieces are more than _____ piece. 3 > _____, so — > —.

So, _____ bookmark is covered with more glitter.

Math Talk

Math Processes and Practices ⑥

Explain how you can use reasoning to compare fractions with the same denominator.

514

Name _____

1. Draw points on the number line to show $\frac{1}{6}$ and $\frac{5}{6}$. Then compare the fractions.

Reason Abstractly Why do fractions increase in size as you move right on the number line?

```
←—|——|——|——|——|——|——|—→
   0   1   2   3   4   5   6
   6   6   6   6   6   6   6
```

Think: $\frac{1}{6}$ is to the left of $\frac{5}{6}$ on the number line.

$\frac{1}{6}$ ◯ $\frac{5}{6}$

Compare. Write <, >, or =.

2. $\frac{4}{8}$ ◯ $\frac{3}{8}$ ✓3. $\frac{1}{4}$ ◯ $\frac{4}{4}$ 4. $\frac{1}{2}$ ◯ $\frac{1}{2}$ ✓5. $\frac{3}{6}$ ◯ $\frac{2}{6}$

On Your Own

Compare. Write <, >, or =.

6. $\frac{2}{4}$ ◯ $\frac{3}{4}$ 7. $\frac{2}{3}$ ◯ $\frac{2}{3}$ 8. $\frac{4}{6}$ ◯ $\frac{2}{6}$ 9. $\frac{0}{8}$ ◯ $\frac{2}{8}$

THINK SMARTER Write a fraction less than, greater than, or equal to the given fraction.

10. $\frac{1}{2} < $ ____

11. ____ $< \frac{12}{6}$

12. $\frac{8}{8} = $ ____

13. ____ $> \frac{2}{4}$

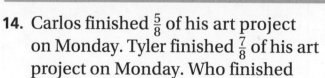

Problem Solving • Applications

14. Carlos finished $\frac{5}{8}$ of his art project on Monday. Tyler finished $\frac{7}{8}$ of his art project on Monday. Who finished more of his art project on Monday?

15. **Use Reasoning** Ms. Endo made two loaves of bread that are the same size. Her family ate $\frac{1}{4}$ of the banana bread and $\frac{3}{4}$ of the cinnamon bread. Which loaf of bread had less left over?

16. **THINK SMARTER**   Todd and Lisa are comparing fraction strips. Which statements are correct? Mark all that apply.

(A) $\frac{1}{4} < \frac{4}{4}$ (B) $\frac{5}{6} < \frac{4}{6}$ (C) $\frac{2}{3} > \frac{1}{3}$ (D) $\frac{5}{8} > \frac{4}{8}$

THINK SMARTER   **What's the Error?**

17. Gary and Vanessa are comparing fractions. Vanessa models $\frac{2}{4}$ and Gary models $\frac{3}{4}$. Vanessa writes $\frac{3}{4} < \frac{2}{4}$. Look at Gary's model and Vanessa's model and describe her error.

Vanessa's Model

Gary's Model

- Describe Vanessa's error.

_____

_____

18. **GO DEEPER**   Explain how to correct Vanessa's error. Then show the correct model.

_____

_____

_____

_____

Compare Fractions with the Same Denominator

Learning Objective You will use visual fraction models and reasoning strategies to compare fractions of a whole and fractions of a group with the same denominator.

Compare. Write <, >, or =.

1. $\frac{3}{4}$ ⟩ $\frac{1}{4}$

2. $\frac{3}{6}$ ◯ $\frac{0}{6}$

3. $\frac{1}{2}$ ◯ $\frac{1}{2}$

4. $\frac{5}{6}$ ◯ $\frac{6}{6}$

5. $\frac{7}{8}$ ◯ $\frac{5}{8}$

6. $\frac{2}{3}$ ◯ $\frac{3}{3}$

7. $\frac{8}{8}$ ◯ $\frac{0}{8}$

8. $\frac{1}{6}$ ◯ $\frac{1}{6}$

9. $\frac{3}{4}$ ◯ $\frac{2}{4}$

10. $\frac{1}{6}$ ◯ $\frac{2}{6}$

11. $\frac{1}{2}$ ◯ $\frac{0}{2}$

12. $\frac{3}{8}$ ◯ $\frac{3}{8}$

13. $\frac{1}{4}$ ◯ $\frac{4}{4}$

14. $\frac{5}{8}$ ◯ $\frac{4}{8}$

15. $\frac{4}{6}$ ◯ $\frac{6}{6}$

 Problem Solving *Real World*

16. Ben mowed $\frac{5}{6}$ of his lawn in one hour. John mowed $\frac{4}{6}$ of his lawn in one hour. Who mowed less of his lawn in one hour?

17. Darcy baked 8 muffins. She put blueberries in $\frac{5}{8}$ of the muffins. She put raspberries in $\frac{3}{8}$ of the muffins. Did more muffins have blueberries or raspberries?

_____   _____

18. **WRITE** ▸*Math* Explain how you can use reasoning to compare two fractions with the same denominator.

_____

_____

Lesson Check

1. Julia paints $\frac{2}{6}$ of a wall in her room white. She paints more of the wall green than white. What fraction could show the part of the wall that is green?

_____

2. Compare. Write <, >, or =.

$$\frac{2}{8} \bigcirc \frac{3}{8}$$

Spiral Review

3. Mr. Edwards buys 2 new knobs for each of his kitchen cabinets. The kitchen has 9 cabinets. How many knobs does he buy?

_____

4. Allie builds a new bookcase with 8 shelves. She can put 30 books on each shelf. How many books can the bookcase hold?

_____

5. The Good Morning Café has 28 customers for breakfast. There are 4 people sitting at each table. How many tables are filled?

_____

6. Ella wants to use the Commutative Property of Multiplication to help find the product 5 × 4. What number sentence can she use?

_____

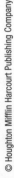

FOR MORE PRACTICE
GO TO THE
Personal Math Trainer

Compare Fractions with the Same Numerator

Essential Question How can you compare fractions with the same numerator?

Learning Objective You will use visual fraction models and reasoning strategies to compare fractions with the same numerator.

Unlock the Problem

Markos is at Athena's Cafe. He can sit at a table with 5 of his friends or at a different table with 7 of his friends. The same-size spinach pie is shared equally among the people at each table. At which table should Markos sit to get more pie?

- Including Markos, how many friends will be sharing pie at each table?

_____

- What will you compare?

_____

_____

Model the problem.

There will be 6 friends sharing Pie A or 8 friends sharing Pie B.

So, Markos will get either $\frac{1}{6}$ or $\frac{1}{8}$ of a pie.

- Shade $\frac{1}{6}$ of Pie A.

- Shade $\frac{1}{8}$ of Pie B.

- Which piece of pie is larger?

- Compare $\frac{1}{6}$ and $\frac{1}{8}$.

$$\frac{1}{6} \bigcirc \frac{1}{8}$$

So, Markos should sit at the table with _____ friends to get more pie.

Pie A   **Pie B**

1. Which pie has more pieces? _____
   The *more* pieces a whole is divided into,

   the _____ the pieces are.

2. Which pie has fewer pieces? _____
   The *fewer* pieces a whole is divided into,

   the _____ the pieces are.

Math Talk

Math Processes and Practices ①

Make Sense of Problems Suppose Markos wants two pieces of one of the pies above. Is $\frac{2}{6}$ or $\frac{2}{8}$ of the pie a greater amount? Explain how you know.

Use fraction strips.

On Saturday, the campers paddled $\frac{2}{8}$ of their planned route down the river. On Sunday, they paddled $\frac{2}{3}$ of their route down the river. On which day did the campers paddle farther?

Compare $\frac{2}{8}$ and $\frac{2}{3}$.

- Place a ✓ next to the fraction strips that show more parts in the whole.

- Shade $\frac{2}{8}$. Then shade $\frac{2}{3}$. Compare the shaded parts.

- $\frac{2}{8}$ ◯ $\frac{2}{3}$

1							
$\frac{1}{8}$	$\frac{1}{8}$	$\frac{1}{8}$	$\frac{1}{8}$	$\frac{1}{8}$	$\frac{1}{8}$	$\frac{1}{8}$	$\frac{1}{8}$

$\frac{1}{3}$	$\frac{1}{3}$	$\frac{1}{3}$

Think: $\frac{1}{8}$ is less than $\frac{1}{3}$, so $\frac{2}{8}$ is less than $\frac{2}{3}$.

So, the campers paddled farther on _____.

Use reasoning.

For her class party, Felicia baked two trays of snacks that were the same size. After the party, she had $\frac{3}{4}$ of the carrot snack and $\frac{3}{6}$ of the apple snack left over. Was more carrot snack or more apple snack left over?

Compare $\frac{3}{4}$ and $\frac{3}{6}$.

- Since the numerators are the same, look at the denominators to compare the size of the pieces. $\frac{3}{4}$ $\frac{3}{6}$

> - The *more* pieces a whole is divided into, the _____ the pieces are.
> - The *fewer* pieces a whole is divided into, the _____ the pieces are.

! **ERROR Alert**

When comparing fractions with the same numerator, be sure the symbol shows that the fraction with fewer pieces in the whole is the greater fraction.

- $\frac{1}{4}$ is _____ than $\frac{1}{6}$ because there are _____ pieces.

- $\frac{3}{4}$ ◯ $\frac{3}{6}$

So, there was more of the _____ snack left over.

520

Name _____

1. Shade the models to show $\frac{1}{6}$ and $\frac{1}{4}$.

   Then compare the fractions.

   $\frac{1}{6}$ ◯ $\frac{1}{4}$

Compare. Write <, >, or =.

☑2. $\frac{1}{8}$ ◯ $\frac{1}{3}$ ☑3. $\frac{3}{4}$ ◯ $\frac{3}{8}$ 4. $\frac{2}{6}$ ◯ $\frac{2}{3}$

5. $\frac{4}{8}$ ◯ $\frac{4}{4}$ 6. $\frac{3}{6}$ ◯ $\frac{3}{6}$ 7. $\frac{8}{4}$ ◯ $\frac{8}{8}$

Math Talk

Math Processes and Practices ①

Evaluate Why is $\frac{1}{2}$ greater than $\frac{1}{4}$?

On Your Own

Compare. Write <, >, or =.

8. $\frac{1}{3}$ ◯ $\frac{1}{4}$ 9. $\frac{2}{3}$ ◯ $\frac{2}{6}$ 10. $\frac{4}{8}$ ◯ $\frac{4}{2}$

11. $\frac{6}{8}$ ◯ $\frac{6}{6}$ 12. $\frac{1}{6}$ ◯ $\frac{1}{2}$ 13. $\frac{7}{8}$ ◯ $\frac{7}{8}$

14. **GO DEEPER** James ate $\frac{3}{4}$ of his quesadilla. David ate $\frac{2}{3}$ of his quesadilla. Both are the same size. Who ate more of his quesadilla?

James said he knows he ate more because he looked at the amounts left. Does his answer make sense? Shade the models. Explain.

James   **David**

_____

_____

Unlock the Problem

15. **Math Processes and Practices ❶** **Make Sense of Problems** Quinton and Hunter are biking on trails in Katy Trail State Park. They biked $\frac{5}{6}$ mile in the morning and $\frac{5}{8}$ mile in the afternoon. Did they bike a greater distance in the morning or in the afternoon?

a. What do you need to know? _____

b. The numerator is 5 in both fractions, so compare $\frac{1}{6}$ and $\frac{1}{8}$. Explain.

   _____

c. How can you solve the problem?

d. Complete the sentences.

   In the morning, the boys biked

   _____ mile. In the afternoon, they biked _____ mile.

   So, the boys biked a greater distance

   in the _____ . $\frac{5}{6} \bigcirc \frac{5}{8}$

16. **THINK SMARTER** Zach has a piece of pie that is $\frac{1}{4}$ of a pie. Max has a piece of pie that is $\frac{1}{2}$ of a pie. Max's piece is smaller than Zach's piece. Explain how this could happen. Draw a picture to show your answer.

_____

_____

Personal Math Trainer

17. **THINK SMARTER +** Before taking a hike, Kate and Dylan each ate part of their same-size granola bars. Kate ate $\frac{1}{3}$ of her bar. Dylan ate $\frac{1}{2}$ of his bar. Who ate more of the granola bar? Explain how you solved the problem.

_____

_____

Compare Fractions with the Same Numerator

Learning Objective You will use visual fraction models and reasoning strategies to compare fractions with the same numerator.

Compare. Write <, >, or =.

1. $\frac{1}{8}$ $<$ $\frac{1}{2}$

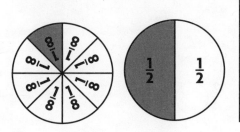

2. $\frac{3}{8}$ ◯ $\frac{3}{6}$

3. $\frac{2}{3}$ ◯ $\frac{2}{4}$

4. $\frac{2}{8}$ ◯ $\frac{2}{3}$

5. $\frac{3}{6}$ ◯ $\frac{3}{4}$

6. $\frac{1}{2}$ ◯ $\frac{1}{6}$

7. $\frac{5}{6}$ ◯ $\frac{5}{8}$

8. $\frac{4}{8}$ ◯ $\frac{4}{8}$

9. $\frac{6}{8}$ ◯ $\frac{6}{6}$

Problem Solving · Real World

10. Javier is buying food in the lunch line. The tray of salad plates is $\frac{3}{8}$ full. The tray of fruit plates is $\frac{3}{4}$ full. Which tray is more full?

_____

11. Rachel bought some buttons. Of the buttons, $\frac{2}{4}$ are yellow and $\frac{2}{8}$ are red. Rachel bought more of which color buttons?

_____

12. **WRITE** ▸ *Math* Explain how the number of pieces in a whole relates to the size of each piece.

_____

_____

Lesson Check

1. What symbol makes the statement true? Write <, >, or =.

$$\frac{3}{4} \bigcirc \frac{3}{8}$$

2. What symbol makes the statement true? Write <, >, or =.

$$\frac{2}{4} \bigcirc \frac{2}{3}$$

Spiral Review

3. Anita divided a circle into 6 equal parts and shaded 1 of the parts. What fraction names the part she shaded?

_____

4. What fraction names the shaded part of the rectangle?

_____

5. Chip worked at the animal shelter for 6 hours each week for several weeks. He worked for a total of 42 hours. How many weeks did Chip work at the animal shelter?

6. Mr. Jackson has 20 quarters. If he gives 4 quarters to each of his children, how many children does Mr. Jackson have?

_____

© Houghton Mifflin Harcourt Publishing Company

FOR MORE PRACTICE GO TO THE Personal Math Trainer

Name _____

Compare Fractions

Essential Question What strategies can you use to compare fractions?

Learning Objective You will use models and strategies involving the sizes of the pieces in the whole to compare fractions of the same whole.

🔑 Unlock the Problem

Luka and Ann are eating the same-size small pizzas. One plate has $\frac{3}{4}$ of Luka's cheese pizza. Another plate has $\frac{5}{6}$ of Ann's mushroom pizza. Whose plate has more pizza?

- Circle the numbers you need to compare.
- How many pieces make up each whole pizza?

_____

🔑 Compare $\frac{3}{4}$ and $\frac{5}{6}$.

Missing Pieces Strategy
- You can compare fractions by comparing pieces missing from a whole.

- Shade $\frac{3}{4}$ of Luka's pizza and $\frac{5}{6}$ of Ann's pizza. Each fraction represents a whole that is missing one piece.

- Since $\frac{1}{6}$ ⃝ $\frac{1}{4}$, a smaller piece is missing from Ann's pizza.

- If a smaller piece is missing from Ann's pizza, she must have more pizza.

So, _____ plate has more pizza.

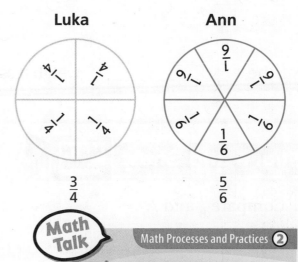

Luka   Ann

$\frac{3}{4}$ $\frac{5}{6}$

Math Talk   Math Processes and Practices ②

Reason Abstractly How does knowing that $\frac{1}{4}$ is less than $\frac{1}{3}$ help you compare $\frac{3}{4}$ and $\frac{2}{3}$?

Morgan ran $\frac{2}{3}$ mile. Alexa ran $\frac{1}{3}$ mile. Who ran farther?

🔑 Compare $\frac{2}{3}$ and $\frac{1}{3}$.

$\frac{}{3} > \frac{}{3}$

Same Denominator Strategy
- When the denominators are the same, you can compare only the number of pieces, or the numerators.

So, _____ ran farther.

Ms. Davis is making a fruit salad with $\frac{3}{4}$ pound of cherries and $\frac{3}{8}$ pound of strawberries. Which weighs less, the cherries or the strawberries?

 Compare $\frac{3}{4}$ and $\frac{3}{8}$.

Same Numerator Strategy

• When the numerators are the same, look at the denominators to compare the size of the pieces.

Think: $\frac{1}{8}$ is smaller than $\frac{1}{4}$ because there are more pieces.

$$\frac{3}{} < \frac{3}{}$$

So, the _____ weigh less.

Share and Show   MATH BOARD

1. Compare $\frac{7}{8}$ and $\frac{5}{6}$.

   Think: What is missing from each whole?

   Write <, >, or =. $\frac{7}{8} \bigcirc \frac{5}{6}$

Compare. Write <, >, or =. Write the strategy you used.

2. $\frac{1}{2} \bigcirc \frac{2}{3}$ _____

✓3. $\frac{3}{4} \bigcirc \frac{2}{4}$ _____

✓4. $\frac{3}{8} \bigcirc \frac{3}{6}$ _____

5. $\frac{3}{4} \bigcirc \frac{7}{8}$ _____

 Math Talk   Math Processes and Practices ①

Make Sense of Problems How do the missing pieces in Exercise 1 help you compare $\frac{7}{8}$ and $\frac{5}{6}$?

Name _____

On Your Own

Compare. Write <, >, or =. Write the strategy you used.

6. $\frac{1}{2} \bigcirc \frac{2}{2}$

_____

7. $\frac{1}{3} \bigcirc \frac{1}{4}$

_____

8. $\frac{2}{3} \bigcirc \frac{5}{6}$

_____

9. $\frac{4}{6} \bigcirc \frac{4}{2}$

_____

Name a fraction that is less than or greater than the given fraction. Draw to justify your answer.

10. less than $\frac{5}{6}$ _____

11. greater than $\frac{3}{8}$ _____

12. **GO DEEPER** Luke, Seth, and Anja have empty glasses. Mr. Gabel pours $\frac{3}{6}$ cup of orange juice in Seth's glass. Then he pours $\frac{1}{6}$ cup of orange juice in Luke's glass and $\frac{2}{6}$ cup of orange juice in Anja's glass. Who gets the most orange juice?

_____

13. **THINK SMARTER** **What's the Error?** Jack says that $\frac{5}{8}$ is greater than $\frac{5}{6}$ because the denominator 8 is greater than the denominator 6. Describe Jack's error. Draw a picture to explain your answer.

_____

_____

_____

_____

Unlock the Problem

14. **Math Processes and Practices ❶ Analyze** Tracy is making blueberry muffins. She is using $\frac{4}{4}$ cup of honey and $\frac{4}{2}$ cups of flour. Does Tracy use more honey or more flour?

a. What do you need to know?

_____

b. What strategy will you use to compare the fractions?

_____

c. Show the steps you used to solve the problem.

d. Complete the comparison.

So, Tracy uses more _____.

15. **THINK SMARTER** Compare the fractions. Circle a symbol that makes the statement true.

$\frac{2}{8}$ $\begin{array}{c} > \\ < \\ = \end{array}$ $\frac{2}{4}$ 　　　　　 $\frac{1}{4}$ $\begin{array}{c} > \\ < \\ = \end{array}$ $\frac{4}{8}$

Name _____

Compare Fractions

Learning Objective You will use models and strategies involving the sizes of the pieces in the whole to compare fractions of the same whole.

Compare. Write <, >, or =. Write the strategy you used.

1. $\frac{3}{8}$ $\boxed{<}$ $\frac{3}{4}$

   Think: The numerators are the same. Compare the denominators. The greater fraction will have the lesser denominator.

   <u>same numerator</u>

2. $\frac{2}{3}$ $\bigcirc$ $\frac{7}{8}$

3. $\frac{3}{4}$ $\bigcirc$ $\frac{1}{4}$

Name a fraction that is less than or greater than the given fraction. Draw to justify your answer.

4. greater than $\frac{1}{3}$ —

5. less than $\frac{3}{4}$ —

Problem Solving · Real World

6. At the third-grade party, two groups each had their own pizza. The blue group ate $\frac{7}{8}$ pizza. The green group ate $\frac{2}{8}$ pizza. Which group ate more of their pizza?

7. Ben and Antonio both take the same bus to school. Ben's ride is $\frac{7}{8}$ mile. Antonio's ride is $\frac{3}{4}$ mile. Who has a longer bus ride?

8. **WRITE** ▶ *Math* Explain how to use the missing pieces strategy to compare two fractions. Include a diagram with your explanation.

Lesson Check

1. Compare $\frac{2}{3}$ and $\frac{7}{8}$. Write <, >, or =.

   $\frac{2}{3}$ $\frac{7}{8}$

2. What symbol makes the statement true? Write <, >, or =.

   $\frac{2}{4}$ $\frac{2}{6}$

Spiral Review

3. Cam, Stella, and Rose each picked 40 apples. They put all their apples in one crate. How many apples are in the crate?

   _____

4. Each shape is 1 whole. What fraction is represented by the shaded part of the model?

   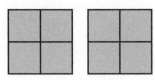

   _____

5. What related multiplication fact can you use to find $16 \div \blacksquare = 2$?

   _____

   _____

   _____

6. What is the unknown factor?

   $9 \times \blacksquare = 36$

   _____

   _____

   _____

FOR MORE PRACTICE GO TO THE
Personal Math Trainer

Name _____

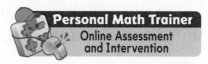

Concepts and Skills

1. When two fractions refer to the same whole, explain why the fraction with a lesser denominator has larger pieces than the fraction with a greater denominator.

_____

_____

_____

2. When two fractions refer to the same whole and have the same denominators, explain why you can compare only the numerators.

_____

_____

_____

Compare. Write $<$, $>$, or $=$.

3. $\dfrac{1}{6}$ ◯ $\dfrac{1}{4}$

4. $\dfrac{1}{8}$ ◯ $\dfrac{1}{8}$

5. $\dfrac{2}{8}$ ◯ $\dfrac{2}{3}$

6. $\dfrac{4}{2}$ ◯ $\dfrac{1}{2}$

7. $\dfrac{7}{8}$ ◯ $\dfrac{3}{8}$

8. $\dfrac{5}{6}$ ◯ $\dfrac{2}{3}$

9. $\dfrac{2}{4}$ ◯ $\dfrac{3}{4}$

10. $\dfrac{6}{6}$ ◯ $\dfrac{6}{8}$

11. $\dfrac{3}{4}$ ◯ $\dfrac{7}{8}$

Name a fraction that is less than or greater than the given fraction. Draw to justify your answer.

12. greater than $\dfrac{2}{6}$ _____

13. less than $\dfrac{2}{3}$ _____

14. Two walls in Tiffany's room are the same size. Tiffany paints $\frac{1}{4}$ of one wall. Roberto paints $\frac{1}{8}$ of the other wall. Who painted a greater amount in Tiffany's room?

_____

15. Matthew ran $\frac{5}{8}$ mile during track practice. Pablo ran $\frac{5}{6}$ mile. Who ran farther?

_____

16. Mallory bought 6 roses for her mother. Two-sixths of the roses are red and $\frac{4}{6}$ are yellow. Did Mallory buy fewer red roses or yellow roses?

_____

17. `GO DEEPER` Lani used $\frac{2}{3}$ cup of raisins, $\frac{3}{8}$ cup of cranberries, and $\frac{3}{4}$ cup of oatmeal to bake cookies. Which ingredient did Lani use the least amount of?

_____

Name _____

Compare and Order Fractions

Essential Question How can you compare and order fractions?

Learning Objective You will use visual fraction models and strategies to compare and order fractions with the same numerator or the same denominator.

🔑 Unlock the Problem

Sierra, Tad, and Dale ride their bikes to school. Sierra rides $\frac{3}{4}$ mile, Tad rides $\frac{3}{8}$ mile, and Dale rides $\frac{3}{6}$ mile. Compare and order the distances from least to greatest.

- Circle the fractions you need to use.
- Underline the sentence that tells you what you need to do.

🔒 Activity 1 Order fractions with the same numerator.

Materials ▪ color pencil

You can order fractions by reasoning about the size of unit fractions.

1

$\frac{1}{4}$	$\frac{1}{4}$	$\frac{1}{4}$	$\frac{1}{4}$

$\frac{1}{8}$	$\frac{1}{8}$	$\frac{1}{8}$	$\frac{1}{8}$	$\frac{1}{8}$	$\frac{1}{8}$	$\frac{1}{8}$	$\frac{1}{8}$

$\frac{1}{6}$	$\frac{1}{6}$	$\frac{1}{6}$	$\frac{1}{6}$	$\frac{1}{6}$	$\frac{1}{6}$

Remember
- The *more* pieces a whole is divided into, the smaller the pieces are.
- The *fewer* pieces a whole is divided into, the larger the pieces are.

STEP 1 Shade one unit fraction for each fraction strip.

_____ is the longest unit fraction.

_____ is the shortest unit fraction.

STEP 2 Shade one more unit fraction for each fraction strip.

Are the shaded fourths still the longest? _____

Are the shaded eighths still the shortest? _____

STEP 3 Continue shading the fraction strips so that three unit fractions are shaded for each strip.

Are the shaded fourths still the longest? _____

Are the shaded eighths still the shortest? _____

$\frac{3}{4}$ mile is the _____ distance. $\frac{3}{8}$ mile is the _____ distance. $\frac{3}{6}$ mile is *between* the other two distances.

So, the distances in order from least to greatest are

_____ mile, _____ mile, _____ mile.

Try This! Order $\frac{2}{6}$, $\frac{2}{3}$, and $\frac{2}{4}$ from greatest to least.

Order the fractions $\frac{2}{6}$, $\frac{2}{3}$, and $\frac{2}{4}$ by thinking about the length of the unit fraction strip. Then label the fractions *shortest*, *between*, or *longest*.

Fraction	Unit Fraction	Length
$\frac{2}{6}$		
$\frac{2}{3}$		
$\frac{2}{4}$		

Math Talk

Math Processes and Practices ⑧

Generalize When ordering three fractions, what do you know about the third fraction when you know which fraction is the shortest and which fraction is the longest? Explain your answer.

• When the numerators are the same, think about the _____ of the pieces to compare and order fractions.

So, the order from greatest to least is _____ , _____ , _____ .

Hands On

🔵 Activity 2 Order fractions with the same denominator.

Materials ■ color pencil

Shade fraction strips to order $\frac{5}{8}$, $\frac{8}{8}$, and $\frac{3}{8}$ from least to greatest.

1

| $\frac{1}{8}$ | $\frac{1}{8}$ | $\frac{1}{8}$ | $\frac{1}{8}$ | $\frac{1}{8}$ | $\frac{1}{8}$ | $\frac{1}{8}$ | $\frac{1}{8}$ | Shade $\frac{5}{8}$. |

| $\frac{1}{8}$ | $\frac{1}{8}$ | $\frac{1}{8}$ | $\frac{1}{8}$ | $\frac{1}{8}$ | $\frac{1}{8}$ | $\frac{1}{8}$ | $\frac{1}{8}$ | Shade $\frac{8}{8}$. |

| $\frac{1}{8}$ | $\frac{1}{8}$ | $\frac{1}{8}$ | $\frac{1}{8}$ | $\frac{1}{8}$ | $\frac{1}{8}$ | $\frac{1}{8}$ | $\frac{1}{8}$ | Shade $\frac{3}{8}$. |

• When the denominators are the same, the size of the pieces is the _____ .

So, think about the _____ of pieces to compare and order fractions.

_____ is the shortest. _____ is the longest.

_____ is between the other two fractions.

So, the order from least to greatest is _____ , _____ , _____ .

534

Name _____

1. Shade the fraction strips to order $\frac{4}{6}$, $\frac{4}{4}$, and $\frac{4}{8}$ from least to greatest.

Math Talk | Math Processes and Practices ⑤

Use a Concrete Model Why does using fraction strips help you order fractions with unlike denominators?

1					
$\frac{1}{6}$	$\frac{1}{6}$	$\frac{1}{6}$	$\frac{1}{6}$	$\frac{1}{6}$	$\frac{1}{6}$

$\frac{1}{4}$	$\frac{1}{4}$	$\frac{1}{4}$	$\frac{1}{4}$

$\frac{1}{8}$	$\frac{1}{8}$	$\frac{1}{8}$	$\frac{1}{8}$	$\frac{1}{8}$	$\frac{1}{8}$	$\frac{1}{8}$	$\frac{1}{8}$

_____ is the shortest. _____ is the longest.

_____ is between the other two lengths. _____, _____, _____

Write the fractions in order from least to greatest.

2. $\frac{1}{2}, \frac{0}{2}, \frac{2}{2}$ _____, _____, _____

3. $\frac{1}{6}, \frac{1}{2}, \frac{1}{3}$ _____, _____, _____

On Your Own

Write the fractions in order from greatest to least.

4. $\frac{6}{6}, \frac{2}{6}, \frac{5}{6}$ _____, _____, _____

5. $\frac{1}{8}, \frac{1}{4}, \frac{1}{2}$ _____, _____, _____

Write the fractions in order from least to greatest.

6. *THINK SMARTER*
   $\frac{6}{3}, \frac{6}{2}, \frac{6}{8}$ _____, _____, _____

7. *THINK SMARTER*
   $\frac{4}{2}, \frac{2}{2}, \frac{8}{2}$ _____, _____, _____

8. Math Processes and Practices ⑥ **Compare** Pam is making biscuits.
   She needs $\frac{2}{6}$ cup of oil, $\frac{2}{3}$ cup of water, and $\frac{2}{4}$ cup of milk.
   Write the ingredients from greatest to least amount.

   _____, _____, _____

Problem Solving • Applications

9. In fifteen minutes, Greg's sailboat went $\frac{3}{6}$ mile, Gina's sailboat went $\frac{6}{6}$ mile, and Stuart's sailboat went $\frac{4}{6}$ mile. Whose sailboat went the longest distance in fifteen minutes?

_____

Whose sailboat went the shortest distance?

_____

10. **GO DEEPER**   Look back at Problem 9. Write a similar problem by changing the fraction of a mile each sailboat traveled, so the answers are different from Problem 9. Then solve the problem.

WRITE ▸ *Math* • **Show Your Work**

_____

_____

_____

_____

_____

11. **THINK SMARTER**   Tom has three pieces of wood. The length of the longest piece is $\frac{3}{4}$ foot. The length of the shortest piece is $\frac{3}{8}$ foot. What might be the length of the third piece of wood?

_____

12. **THINK SMARTER**   Jesse ran $\frac{2}{4}$ mile on Monday, $\frac{2}{3}$ mile on Tuesday, and $\frac{2}{8}$ mile on Wednesday. Order the fractions from least to greatest.

$\boxed{\frac{2}{4}}$, $\boxed{\frac{2}{3}}$ and $\boxed{\frac{2}{8}}$ $\boxed{}$ $\boxed{}$ $\boxed{}$

Name _____

Compare and Order Fractions

Learning Objective You will use visual fraction models and strategies to compare and order fractions with the same numerator or the same denominator.

Write the fractions in order from greatest to least.

1. $\frac{4}{4}, \frac{1}{4}, \frac{3}{4}$ $\frac{4}{4}$, $\frac{3}{4}$, $\frac{1}{4}$

   Think: The denominators are the same, so compare the numerators: $4 > 3 > 1$.

2. $\frac{2}{8}, \frac{5}{8}, \frac{1}{8}$ _____ , _____ , _____

3. $\frac{1}{3}, \frac{1}{6}, \frac{1}{2}$ _____ , _____ , _____

4. $\frac{2}{3}, \frac{2}{6}, \frac{2}{8}$ _____ , _____ , _____

Write the fractions in order from least to greatest.

5. $\frac{2}{4}, \frac{4}{4}, \frac{3}{4}$ _____ , _____ , _____

6. $\frac{4}{6}, \frac{5}{6}, \frac{2}{6}$ _____ , _____ , _____

Problem Solving Real World

7. Mr. Jackson ran $\frac{7}{8}$ mile on Monday. He ran $\frac{3}{8}$ mile on Wednesday and $\frac{5}{8}$ mile on Friday. On which day did Mr. Jackson run the shortest distance?

8. Delia has three pieces of ribbon. Her red ribbon is $\frac{2}{4}$ foot long. Her green ribbon is $\frac{2}{3}$ foot long. Her yellow ribbon is $\frac{2}{6}$ foot long. She wants to use the longest piece for a project. Which color ribbon should Delia use?

_____   _____

9. **WRITE** ▸ *Math* Describe how fraction strips can help you order fractions.

_____

_____

_____

Lesson Check

1. Write the fractions in order from least to greatest.

   $$\frac{1}{8}, \frac{1}{3}, \frac{1}{6}$$

   _____

2. Write the fractions in order from greatest to least.

   $$\frac{3}{6}, \frac{3}{4}, \frac{3}{8}$$

   _____

Spiral Review

3. What fraction of the group of cars is shaded?

   _____

4. Wendy has 6 pieces of fruit. Of these, 2 pieces are bananas. What fraction of Wendy's fruit is bananas?

   _____

5. Toby collects data and makes a bar graph about his classmates' pets. He finds that 9 classmates have dogs, 2 classmates have fish, 6 classmates have cats, and 3 classmates have gerbils. What pet will have the longest bar on the bar graph?

   _____

6. The number sentence is an example of which multiplication property?

   $$6 \times 7 = (6 \times 5) + (6 \times 2)$$

   _____

FOR MORE PRACTICE
GO TO THE
Personal Math Trainer

Model Equivalent Fractions

Essential Question How can you use models to find equivalent fractions?

Learning Objective You will use area models and number lines to recognize and generate equivalent fractions.

Investigate

Hands On

Materials ■ sheet of paper ■ crayon or color pencil

Two or more fractions that name the same amount are called **equivalent fractions**. You can use a sheet of paper to model fractions equivalent to $\frac{1}{2}$.

A. First, fold a sheet of paper into two equal parts. Open the paper and count the parts.

There are _____ equal parts. Each part is _____ of the paper.

Shade one of the halves. Write $\frac{1}{2}$ on each of the halves.

B. Next, fold the paper in half two times. Open the paper.

Now there are _____ equal parts. Each part is

_____ of the paper.

Write $\frac{1}{4}$ on each of the fourths.

Look at the shaded parts. $\frac{1}{2} = \dfrac{}{4}$

C. Last, fold the paper in half three times.

Now there are _____ equal parts. Each part is

_____ of the paper.

Write $\frac{1}{8}$ on each of the eighths.

Find the fractions equivalent to $\frac{1}{2}$ on your paper.

So, $\frac{1}{2}$, ——, and —— are equivalent.

Draw Conclusions

1. Explain how many $\frac{1}{8}$ parts are equivalent to one $\frac{1}{4}$ part on your paper.

_____

_____

2. **THINK SMARTER** What do you notice about how the numerators changed for the shaded part as

you folded the paper? _____

What does this tell you about the change in the

number of parts? _____

How did the denominators change for the shaded

part as you folded? _____

What does this tell you about the change in the

size of the parts? _____

Make Connections

Math Talk Math Processes and Practices ②

Use Reasoning Explain how the number of sixths in a distance on the number line is related to the number of thirds in the same distance.

You can use a number line to find equivalent fractions.

Find a fraction equivalent to $\frac{2}{3}$.

Materials ■ fraction strips

STEP 1 Draw a point on the number line to represent the distance $\frac{2}{3}$.

_____

STEP 2 Use fraction strips to divide the number line into sixths. At the end of each strip, draw a mark on the number line and label the marks to show sixths.

_____

STEP 3 Identify the fraction that names the same point as $\frac{2}{3}$. _____

So, $\frac{2}{3} = \dfrac{\Box}{6}$.

540

Name _____

Shade the model. Then divide the pieces to find the equivalent fraction.

1.

$\frac{1}{4} = \frac{\square}{8}$

2.

$\frac{2}{3} = \frac{\square}{6}$

Use the number line to find the equivalent fraction.

3.

$\frac{1}{2} = \frac{\square}{6}$

4.

$\frac{3}{4} = \frac{\square}{8}$

Problem Solving • Applications (Real World)

5. **Math Processes and Practices 6** **Explain** why $\frac{2}{2} = 1$. Write another fraction that is equal to 1. Draw to justify your answer.

_____

_____

_____

Personal Math Trainer

6. **THINK SMARTER +** For numbers 6a–6d, select True or False to tell whether the fractions are equivalent.

6a. $\frac{6}{6}$ and $\frac{3}{3}$ ○ True   ○ False

6b. $\frac{4}{6}$ and $\frac{1}{3}$ ○ True   ○ False

6c. $\frac{2}{3}$ and $\frac{3}{6}$ ○ True   ○ False

6d. $\frac{1}{3}$ and $\frac{2}{6}$ ○ True   ○ False

Connect to Reading

Summarize

You can *summarize* the information in a problem by underlining it or writing the information needed to answer a question.

Read the problem. Underline the important information.

7. **THINK SMARTER** Mrs. Akers bought three sandwiches that were the same size. She cut the first one into thirds. She cut the second one into fourths and the third one into sixths. Marian ate 2 pieces of the first sandwich. Jason ate 2 pieces of the second sandwich. Marcos ate 3 pieces of the third sandwich. Which children ate the same amount of a sandwich? Explain.

The first sandwich was cut into _____.	The second sandwich was cut into _____.	The third sandwich was cut into _____.
Marian ate _____ pieces of the sandwich. Shade the part Marian ate.	Jason ate _____ pieces of the sandwich. Shade the part Jason ate.	Marcos ate _____ pieces of the sandwich. Shade the part Marcos ate.
Marian ate — of the first sandwich.	Jason ate — of the second sandwich.	Marcos ate — of the third sandwich.

Are all the fractions equivalent? _____

Which fractions are equivalent? — = —

So, _____ and _____ ate the same amount of a sandwich.

542

Model Equivalent Fractions

Learning Objective You will use area models and number lines to recognize and generate equivalent fractions.

Shade the model. Then divide the pieces to find the equivalent fraction.

1.

$$\frac{2}{4} = \frac{4}{8}$$

Use the number line to find the equivalent fraction.

2.
$\frac{0}{8}$ $\frac{1}{8}$ $\frac{2}{8}$ $\frac{3}{8}$ $\frac{4}{8}$ $\frac{5}{8}$ $\frac{6}{8}$ $\frac{7}{8}$ $\frac{8}{8}$

$\frac{0}{4}$ $\frac{1}{4}$ $\frac{2}{4}$ $\frac{3}{4}$ $\frac{4}{4}$

$$\frac{3}{4} = \frac{}{8}$$

Problem Solving · Real World

3. Mike says that $\frac{3}{3}$ of his fraction model is shaded blue. Ryan says that $\frac{6}{6}$ of the same model is shaded blue. Are the two fractions equivalent? If so, what is another equivalent fraction?

4. Brett shaded $\frac{4}{8}$ of a sheet of notebook paper. Aisha says he shaded $\frac{1}{2}$ of the paper. Are the two fractions equivalent? If so, what is another equivalent fraction?

5. **WRITE** ▸*Math* Draw a number line that shows two equivalent fractions. Label your number line and explain how you know the fractions are equivalent.

Lesson Check

1. Name a fraction equivalent to $\frac{2}{3}$.

_____

2. Find the fraction equivalent to $\frac{1}{4}$.

_____

Spiral Review

3. Eric practiced piano and guitar for a total of 8 hours this week. He practiced the piano for $\frac{1}{4}$ of that time. How many hours did Eric practice the piano this week?

_____

4. Kylee bought a pack of 12 cookies. One-third of the cookies are peanut butter. How many of the cookies in the pack are peanut butter?

_____

5. There are 56 students going to the game. The coach puts 7 students in each van. How many vans are needed to take the students to the game?

_____

_____

6. Write a division equation for the picture.

_____

_____

FOR MORE PRACTICE GO TO THE Personal Math Trainer

Name _____

Equivalent Fractions

Essential Question How can you use models to name equivalent fractions?

Learning Objective You will draw circles and shade area models to show equal groups and to find equivalent fractions.

🔑 Unlock the Problem

Cole brought a submarine sandwich to the picnic. He shared the sandwich equally with 3 friends. The sandwich was cut into eighths. What are two ways to describe the part of the sandwich each friend ate?

Cole grouped the smaller pieces into twos. Draw circles to show equal groups of two pieces to show what each friend ate.

> • How many people shared the sandwich?
>
> _____

There are 4 equal groups. Each group is $\frac{1}{4}$ of the whole sandwich. So, each friend ate $\frac{1}{4}$ of the whole sandwich.

How many eighths did each friend eat? _____

$\frac{1}{4}$ and _____ are equivalent fractions since they both name

the _____ amount of the sandwich.

So, $\frac{1}{4}$ and _____ of the sandwich are two ways to describe the part of the sandwich each friend ate.

Try This! Circle equal groups. Write an equivalent fraction for the shaded part of the whole.

$$\frac{4}{8} = \underline{\hspace{1cm}}$$

Apply What is a different way you could have circled the equal groups?

Chapter 9   545

🔑 Example Model the problem.

Heidi ate $\frac{3}{6}$ of her fruit bar. Molly ate $\frac{4}{8}$ of her fruit bar, which is the same size. Which girl ate more of her fruit bar?

Shade $\frac{3}{6}$ of Heidi's fruit bar and $\frac{4}{8}$ of Molly's fruit bar.

- Is $\frac{3}{6}$ greater than, less than, or equal to $\frac{4}{8}$? _____

So, both girls ate the _____ amount.

Heidi

$\frac{1}{6}$	$\frac{1}{6}$	$\frac{1}{6}$
$\frac{1}{6}$	$\frac{1}{6}$	$\frac{1}{6}$

Molly

$\frac{1}{8}$	$\frac{1}{8}$	$\frac{1}{8}$	$\frac{1}{8}$
$\frac{1}{8}$	$\frac{1}{8}$	$\frac{1}{8}$	$\frac{1}{8}$

Try This! Each shape is 1 whole. Write an equivalent fraction for the shaded part of the models.

$$\frac{6}{3} = \frac{}{6}$$

Share and Show MATH BOARD

1. Each shape is 1 whole. Use the model to find the equivalent fraction.

$$\frac{2}{4} = \frac{}{2}$$

Math Talk Math Processes and Practices ②

Use Reasoning Explain why equivalent fractions name the same amount.

Each shape is 1 whole. Shade the model to find the equivalent fraction.

✓ 2.

$$\frac{2}{4} = \frac{}{8}$$

3.

$$\frac{12}{6} = \frac{}{3}$$

4. Andy swam $\frac{8}{8}$ mile in a race. Use the number line to find a fraction that is equivalent to $\frac{8}{8}$.

$$\frac{8}{8} = \frac{}{}$$

Name _____

Circle equal groups to find the equivalent fraction.

5.

$$\frac{3}{6} = \frac{\square}{2}$$

6.

$$\frac{6}{6} = \frac{\square}{3}$$

Each shape is 1 whole. Shade the model to find the equivalent fraction.

7.

$$\frac{1}{2} = \frac{2}{\square} = \frac{\square}{8}$$

8.

$$\frac{8}{\square} = \frac{4}{2}$$

Circle equal groups to find the equivalent fraction.

9.

$$\frac{6}{8} = \frac{\square}{4}$$

10.

$$\frac{2}{6} = \frac{\square}{3}$$

11. Write the fraction that names the shaded part of each circle.

_____   _____   _____   _____   _____

Which pairs of fractions are equivalent? _____

12. **Math Processes and Practices ❸ Apply** Matt cut his small pizza into 6 equal pieces and ate 4 of them. Josh cut his small pizza, which is the same size, into 3 equal pieces and ate 2 of them. Write fractions for the amount they each ate. Are the fractions equivalent? Draw to explain.

_____

Problem Solving • Applications

13. **GO DEEPER** Christy bought 8 muffins. She chose 2 apple, 2 banana, and 4 blueberry. She and her family ate the apple and banana muffins for breakfast. What fraction of the muffins did they eat? Write an equivalent fraction. Draw a picture.

_____

14. **THINK SMARTER** After dinner, $\frac{2}{3}$ of the corn bread is left. Suppose 4 friends want to share it equally. What fraction names how much of the whole pan of corn bread each friend will get? Use the model on the right. Explain your answer.

_____

15. There are 16 people having lunch. Each person wants $\frac{1}{4}$ of a pizza. How many whole pizzas are needed? Draw a picture to show your answer.

_____

16. Lucy has 5 oatmeal bars, each cut in half. What fraction names all of the oatmeal bar halves? $\dfrac{}{2}$

What if Lucy cuts each part of the oatmeal bar into 2 equal pieces to share with friends? What fraction names all of the oatmeal bar pieces now? $\dfrac{}{4}$

$\dfrac{}{2}$ and $\dfrac{}{4}$ are equivalent fractions.

17. **THINK SMARTER** Mr. Peters made a pizza. There is $\frac{4}{8}$ of the pizza left over. Select the fractions that are equivalent to the part of the pizza that is left over. Mark all that apply.

(A) $\frac{5}{8}$ (B) $\frac{3}{4}$ (C) $\frac{2}{4}$ (D) $\frac{1}{2}$

Equivalent Fractions

Learning Objective You will draw circles and shade area models to show equal groups and to find equivalent fractions.

Each shape is 1 whole. Shade the model to find the equivalent fraction.

1.

$$\frac{1}{2} = \frac{3}{6}$$

2.

$$\frac{3}{4} = \frac{6}{\boxed{}}$$

Circle equal groups to find the equivalent fraction.

3.

$$\frac{2}{4} = \frac{\boxed{}}{2}$$

4.

$$\frac{4}{6} = \frac{\boxed{}}{3}$$

Problem Solving *Real World*

5. May painted 4 out of 8 equal parts of a poster board blue. Jared painted 2 out of 4 equal parts of a same-size poster board red. Write fractions to show which part of the poster board each person painted.

_____

6. **WRITE** *Math* Explain how you can find a fraction that is equivalent to $\frac{1}{4}$.

_____

_____

Lesson Check

1. What fraction is equivalent to $\frac{6}{8}$?

_____

2. What fraction is equivalent to $\frac{1}{3}$?

_____

Spiral Review

3. What division number sentence is shown by the array?

_____

_____

4. Cody put 4 plates on the table. He put 1 apple on each plate. What number sentence can be used to find the total number of apples on the table?

_____

_____

5. Write a division number sentence that is a related fact to $7 \times 3 = 21$.

_____

_____

6. Find the quotient.

$$4\overline{)36}$$

_____

_____

FOR MORE PRACTICE
GO TO THE
Personal Math Trainer

Name _____

1. Alexa and Rose read books that have the same number of pages. Alexa's book is divided into 8 equal chapters. Rose's book is divided into 6 equal chapters. Each girl has read 3 chapters of her book.

   Write a fraction to describe what part of the book each girl read. Then tell who read more pages. Explain.

   _____

   _____

   _____

2. David, Maria, and Simone are shading same-sized index cards for a science project. David shaded $\frac{2}{4}$ of his index card. Maria shaded $\frac{2}{8}$ of her index card and Simone shaded $\frac{2}{6}$ of her index card.

   For 2a–2d, choose Yes or No to indicate whether the comparisons are correct.

   2a. $\frac{2}{4} > \frac{2}{8}$ ○ Yes   ○ No

   2b. $\frac{2}{8} > \frac{2}{6}$ ○ Yes   ○ No

   2c. $\frac{2}{6} < \frac{2}{4}$ ○ Yes   ○ No

   2d. $\frac{2}{8} = \frac{2}{4}$ ○ Yes   ○ No

3. Dan and Miguel are working on the same homework assignment. Dan has finished $\frac{1}{4}$ of the assignment. Miguel has finished $\frac{3}{4}$ of the assignment. Which statement is correct? Mark all that apply.

   Ⓐ Miguel has completed the entire assignment.

   Ⓑ Dan has not completed the entire assignment.

   Ⓒ Miguel has finished more of the assignment than Dan.

   Ⓓ Dan and Miguel have completed equal parts of the assignment.

Assessment Options
Chapter Test

4. Bryan cut two peaches that were the same size for lunch. He cut one peach into fourths and the other into sixths. Bryan ate $\frac{3}{4}$ of the first peach. His brother ate $\frac{5}{6}$ of the second peach. Who ate more peach? Explain the strategy you used to solve the problem.

_____

_____

_____

5. A nature center offers 2 guided walks. The morning walk is $\frac{2}{3}$ mile. The evening walk is $\frac{3}{6}$ mile. Which walk is shorter? Explain how you can use the model to find the answer.

_____

_____

6. Chun lives $\frac{3}{8}$ mile from school. Gail lives $\frac{5}{8}$ mile from school.

Use the fractions and symbols to show which distance is longer.

Name _____

7. **THINK SMARTER +** Mrs. Reed baked four pans of lasagna for a family party. Use the rectangles to represent the pans.

☐ ☐ ☐ ☐

Part A

Draw lines to show how Mrs. Reed could cut one pan of lasagna into thirds, one into fourths, one into sixths, and one into eighths.

Part B

At the end of the dinner, equivalent amounts of lasagna in two pans were left. Use the models to show the lasagna that might have been left over. Write two pairs of equivalent fractions to represent the models.

_____

8. Tom rode his horse for $\frac{4}{6}$ mile. Liz rode her horse for an equal distance. What is an equivalent fraction that describes how far Liz rode? Use the models to show your work.

_____

9. Avery prepares 2 equal-size oranges for the bats at the zoo. One dish has $\frac{3}{8}$ of an orange. Another dish has $\frac{2}{8}$ of an orange. Which dish has more orange? Show your work.

_____

10. Jenna painted $\frac{1}{8}$ of one side of a fence. Mark painted $\frac{1}{6}$ of the other side of the same fence. Use >, =, or < to compare the parts that they painted.

_____

11. Bill used $\frac{1}{3}$ cup of raisins and $\frac{2}{3}$ cup of banana chips to make a snack.

    For 11a–11d, select True or False for each comparison.

    11a. $\frac{1}{3} > \frac{2}{3}$ ○ True   ○ False

    11b. $\frac{2}{3} = \frac{1}{3}$ ○ True   ○ False

    11c. $\frac{1}{3} < \frac{2}{3}$ ○ True   ○ False

    11d. $\frac{2}{3} > \frac{1}{3}$ ○ True   ○ False

12. **GO DEEPER**   Jorge, Lynne, and Crosby meet at the playground. Jorge lives $\frac{5}{6}$ mile from the playground. Lynne lives $\frac{4}{6}$ mile from the playground. Crosby lives $\frac{7}{8}$ mile from the playground.

    Part A

    Who lives closer to the playground, Jorge or Lynne? Explain how you know.

    _____

    _____

    _____

    Part B

    Who lives closer to the playground, Jorge or Crosby? Explain how you know.

    _____

    _____

    _____

554

13. Ming needs $\frac{1}{2}$ pint of red paint for an art project. He has 6 jars that have the following amounts of red paint in them. He wants to use only 1 jar of paint. Mark all of the jars of paints that Ming could use.

(A) $\frac{2}{3}$ pint   (D) $\frac{3}{4}$ pint

(B) $\frac{1}{4}$ pint   (E) $\frac{3}{8}$ pint

(C) $\frac{4}{6}$ pint   (F) $\frac{2}{6}$ pint

14. There are 12 people having lunch. Each person wants $\frac{1}{3}$ of a sub sandwich. How many whole sub sandwiches are needed? Use the models to show your answer.

┌─────────────┐   ┌─────────────┐   ┌─────────────┐
│   │   │   │   │   │
└─────────────┘   └─────────────┘   └─────────────┘

┌─────────────┐   ┌─────────────┐   ┌─────────────┐
│   │   │   │   │   │
└─────────────┘   └─────────────┘   └─────────────┘

_____ sub sandwiches

15. Mavis mixed $\frac{2}{4}$ quart of apple juice with $\frac{1}{2}$ quart of cranberry juice. Compare the fractions. Choose the symbol that makes the statement true.

$$\frac{2}{4} \begin{array}{|c|} \hline < \\ = \\ > \\ \hline \end{array} \frac{1}{2}$$

16. Pat has three pieces of fabric that measure $\frac{3}{6}$, $\frac{5}{6}$, and $\frac{2}{6}$ yards long. Write the lengths in order from least to greatest.

_____

17. Cora measures the heights of three plants. Draw a line to match each height on the left to the word on the right that describes its place in the order of heights.

$\frac{4}{6}$ foot •   • least

$\frac{4}{4}$ foot •   • between

$\frac{4}{8}$ foot •   • greatest

18. Danielle drew a model to show equivalent fractions.

Use the model to complete the number sentence.

$\frac{1}{2} =$ _____ $=$ _____

19. Floyd caught a fish that weighed $\frac{2}{3}$ pound. Kira caught a fish that weighed $\frac{7}{8}$ pound. Whose fish weighed more? Explain the strategy you used to solve the problem.

_____

_____

_____

_____

20. Sam went for a ride on a sailboat. The ride lasted $\frac{3}{4}$ hour.

What fraction is equivalent to $\frac{3}{4}$?

_____

Big Idea Measurement

BIG IDEA Develop a conceptual understanding of measurement, including time, linear, and liquid measures. Develop concepts of area and perimeter.

Measurement tools and data are used to design and build a safe and enjoyable playground.

Plan a Playground

Is there a playground at your school, in your neighborhood, or in a nearby park? Playgrounds provide a fun and safe outdoor space for you to climb, swing, slide, and play.

Get Started WRITE Math

Important Facts

Playground Features

- Bench
- Jungle Gym
- Playhouse
- Sandbox
- Seesaw
- Slide
- Swing Set
- Water Fountain

Suppose you want to help plan a playground for a block in your neighborhood.

- Draw a large rectangle on the grid paper to show a fence around your playground. Find the distance around your playground by counting the number of units on each side. Record the distance.

- Use the Important Facts to help you decide on features to have in your playground. Shade parts of your playground to show each feature's location. Then find the number of unit squares the feature covers and record it on your plan.

▲ This drawing shows a plan for a playground.

Completed by _____

Chapter 10 Time, Length, Liquid Volume, and Mass

Show What You Know

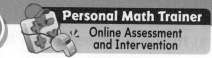

Personal Math Trainer
Online Assessment and Intervention

Check your understanding of important skills.

Name _____

▶ **Time to the Half Hour** Read the clock. Write the time.

1. _____

2. _____

▶ **Skip Count by Fives**

Skip count by fives. Write the missing numbers.

3. 5, 10, 15, ____, 25, ____, 35   4. 55, 60, ____, 70, ____, ____, 85

▶ **Inches** Use a ruler to measure the length to the nearest inch.

5.

6.

about _____ inches   about _____ inch

You can look at the time the sun rises and sets to find the amount of daylight each day. The table shows the time the sun rose and set from January 10 to January 14 in Philadelphia, Pennsylvania. Find which day had the least daylight and which day had the most daylight.

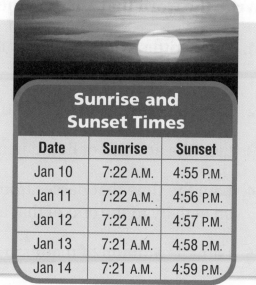

Sunrise and Sunset Times		
Date	Sunrise	Sunset
Jan 10	7:22 A.M.	4:55 P.M.
Jan 11	7:22 A.M.	4:56 P.M.
Jan 12	7:22 A.M.	4:57 P.M.
Jan 13	7:21 A.M.	4:58 P.M.
Jan 14	7:21 A.M.	4:59 P.M.

Vocabulary Builder

▶ **Visualize It** •

Complete the graphic organizer by using the
words with a ✓. Write the words in order from the
greatest to the least length of time.

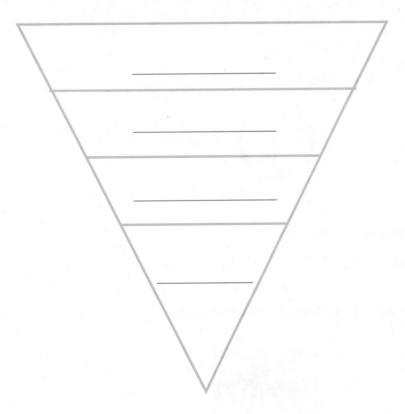

Review Words

analog clock
digital clock
fourth
half
✓ half hour
✓ hour (hr)
inch (in.)
✓ quarter hour

Preview Words

A.M.
elapsed time
gram (g)
kilogram (kg)
liquid volume
liter (L)
mass
midnight
✓ minute (min)
noon
P.M.

▶ **Understand Vocabulary** • • • • • • • • • • • • • • • • • • •

Write the word that answers the riddle.

1. I am written with times after midnight and
   before noon. _____

2. I am the time when it is 12:00 in the daytime. _____

3. I am the amount of liquid in a container. _____

4. I am the time that passes from the start of
   an activity to the end of that activity. _____

5. I am the amount of matter in an object. _____

560

GO DIGITAL
• Interactive Student Edition
• Multimedia eGlossary

Chapter 10 Vocabulary

A.M.

A.M.

1

Elapsed Time

tiempo transcurrido

18

gram (g)

gramo (g)

30

Halves

mitades

32

kilogram (kg)

kilogramo (kg)

39

liquid volume

volumen de un líquido

45

liter (L)

litro (L)

46

mass

masa

47

The time that passes from the start of an activity to the end of that activity

So, the elapsed time is 43 minutes.

The time after midnight and before noon

After Midnight and Before Noon

These are halves

A metric unit used to measure mass
1 kilogram = 1,000 grams

A small paper clip has a mass of about 1 gram.

The amount of liquid in a container

A metric unit used to measure mass
1 kilogram = 1,000 grams

A box of 1,000 paper clips has a mass of about 1 kilogram.

The amount of matter in an object

A metric unit used to measure liquid volume

1 liter

Midnight

medianoche

48

minute

minuto

49

Noon

mediadía

52

P.M.

P.M.

63

A unit used to measure short amounts of time; in one minute, the minute hand on an analog clock moves from one mark to the next minute

12:00 at night

Midnight

The time after noon and before midnight

P.M.

12:00 in the day

Noon

Going to the Playground

Word Box

A.M.
elapsed time
gram (g)
kilogram (kg)
liquid volume
liter (L)
mass
midnight
minute
noon
P.M.

For 2 players

Materials

- 1 red playing piece
- 1 blue playing piece
- 1 number cube

How to Play

1. Each player chooses a playing piece and puts it on START.
2. Toss the number cube to take a turn. Move your playing piece that many spaces.
3. If you land on these spaces, follow the instructions.

    White Space Tell the meaning of the math term, or use it in a sentence. If your answer is correct, jump to the next space with the same term. If your answer is not correct, stay where you are.

    Green Space Follow the directions printed in the space. If there are no directions, stay where you are.

4. The first player to reach FINISH wins.

Game

HOW TO PLAY

1. Each player chooses a playing piece and puts it on START.
2. Toss the number cube to take a turn. Move your playing piece that many spaces.
3. If you land on these spaces, follow the instructions.
   • White Space: Tell the meaning of the math term, or use it in a sentence. If your answer is correct, jump to the next space with the same term. If your answer is not correct, stay where you are.
   • Green Space: Follow the directions printed in the space. If there are no directions, stay where you are.
4. The first player to reach FINISH wins.

MATERIALS

• 1 red playing piece
• 1 blue playing piece
• 1 number cube

FINISH | minute | midnight | mass | liter

kilogram | liquid volume | liter | Go back to | mass

gram | elapsed time | | A.M. | P.M.

midnight | minute | noon | P.M. | A.M.

mass | liter | Go back to | kilogram | gram

START | A.M. | elapsed time | gram | kilogram

Game

Go back to

| liquid volume | kilogram | gram | elapsed time |

| midnight | minute | noon | P.M. | A.M. |

| noon | minute | midnight | mass | Go back to |

| elapsed time | gram | | kilogram | liquid volume |

| elapsed time | A.M. | | noon | minute |

| | liquid volume | liter | mass | midnight |

The Write Way

Reflect

Choose one idea. Write about it.

- Write a paragraph that uses at least **three** of these words or phrases.

  gram   kilogram   liter   mass   liquid volume

- Explain how you solve one kind of measurement problem.

- Write two questions you have about telling time or finding time intervals.

Time to the Minute

Essential Question How can you tell time to the nearest minute?

Learning Objective You will tell and write time to the nearest minute by using analog and digital clocks to write one way you can read the time.

🔑 Unlock the Problem

Groundhog Day is February 2. People say that if a groundhog can see its shadow on that morning, winter will last another 6 weeks. The clock shows the time when the groundhog saw its shadow. What time was it?

- Underline the question.
- Where will you look to find the time?

_____

🔑 Example

Look at the time on this clock face.

- What does the hour hand tell you?

_____

- What does the minute hand tell you?

_____

In 1 **minute**, the minute hand moves from one mark to the next on a clock. It takes 5 minutes for the minute hand to move from one number to the next on a clock.

You can count on by fives to tell time to five minutes. Count zero at the 12.

0, 5, 10, 15, _____, _____, _____, _____

So, the groundhog saw its shadow at _____.

Write: 7:35

Read:

- seven _____

- thirty-five minutes after _____

Math Talk Math Processes and Practices ②

Reason Abstractly How does skip counting by fives help you tell the time when the minute hand points to a number?

- Is 7:35 a reasonable answer? Explain. _____

_____

Time to the Minute

Count by fives and ones to help you.

🔑 One Way   Find minutes after the hour.

Look at the time on this clock face.

- What does the hour hand tell you?

  _____

- What does the minute hand tell you?

  _____

Count on by fives and ones from the 12 on the clock to where the minute hand is pointing. Write the missing counting numbers next to the clock.

When a clock shows 30 or fewer minutes after the hour, you can read the time as a number of minutes *after* the hour.

Write: _____

Read:

- twenty-three minutes after _____

- one _____

🔑 Another Way   Find minutes before the hour.

Look at the time on this clock face.

- What does the hour hand tell you?

  _____

- What does the minute hand tell you?

  _____

Now count by fives and ones from the 12 on the clock back to where the minute hand is pointing. Write the missing counting numbers next to the clock.

When a clock shows 31 or more minutes after the hour, you can read the time as a number of minutes *before* the next hour.

Write: 2:43

Read:

- seventeen _____ before three

- two _____

 ERROR Alert

Remember that time *after* the hour uses the previous hour, and time *before* the hour uses the next hour.

Name _____

Share and Show

1. How would you use counting and the minute hand to find the time shown on this clock? Write the time.

_____

Write the time. Write one way you can read the time.

2.

_____

_____

✓ 3.

_____

_____

✓ 4.

_____

_____

Math Talk

Math Processes and Practices ③

Apply How do you know when to stop counting by fives and start counting by ones when counting minutes after an hour?

On Your Own

Write the time. Write one way you can read the time.

5.

_____

_____

6.

_____

_____

7.

_____

_____

Math Processes and Practices ② **Represent a Problem** **Write the time another way.**

8. 34 minutes after 5

_____

9. 11 minutes before 6

_____

10. 22 minutes after 11

_____

11. 5 minutes before 12

_____

Problem Solving • Applications

Use the clocks for 12–13.

Time of Day the Groundhog Saw Its Shadow

NY   PA

12. How many minutes later in the day did the groundhog in Pennsylvania see its shadow than the groundhog in New York?

_____

13. **GO DEEPER** What if the groundhog in Pennsylvania saw its shadow 5 minutes later? What time would this be?

_____

14. If you look at your watch and the hour hand is between the 8 and the 9 and the minute hand is on the 11, what time is it?

_____

15. **THINK SMARTER** What time is it when the hour hand and the minute hand are both pointing to the same number? Aiden says it is 6:30. Camilla says it is 12:00. Who is correct? Explain.

_____

_____

16. **Math Processes and Practices ❸ Verify the Reasoning of Others** Lucy said the time is 4:46 on her digital watch. Explain where the hands on an analog clock are pointing when it is 4:46.

_____

_____

17. **THINK SMARTER** Write the time that is shown on the clock. Then write the time another way.

_____

Time to the Minute

Learning Objective You will tell and write time to the nearest minute by using analog and digital clocks to write one way you can read the time.

Write the time. Write one way you can read the time.

1.

1:16; sixteen minutes

after one

2.

_____
_____
_____

3.

_____
_____
_____

4.

_____
_____
_____

5.

_____
_____
_____

6.

_____
_____
_____

Write the time another way.

7. 23 minutes after 4

8. 18 minutes before 11

_____

_____

Problem Solving

9. What time is it when the hour hand is a little past the 3 and the minute hand is pointing to the 3?

10. Pete began practicing at twenty-five minutes before eight. What is another way to write this time?

_____

_____

11. **WRITE** ▸*Math* Draw a clock showing a time to the nearest minute. Write the time as many different ways you can.

_____

Lesson Check

1. What is another way to write 13 minutes before 10?

_____

2. What time does the clock show?

_____

Spiral Review

3. Each bird has 2 wings. How many wings do 5 birds have?

_____

4. Find the unknown factor.

$$8 \times \blacksquare = 56$$

_____

5. Mr. Wren has 56 paintbrushes. He places 8 paintbrushes on each of the tables in the art room. How many tables are in the art room?

_____

6. What number completes the equations?

$$4 \times \blacktriangle = 20 \quad 20 \div 4 = \blacktriangle$$

_____

FOR MORE PRACTICE
GO TO THE
Personal Math Trainer

Name _____

A.M. and P.M.

Essential Question How can you tell when to use A.M. and P.M. with time?

Learning Objective You will decide when to use A.M. or P.M. with times by using a number line to show order of events.

Unlock the Problem

Lauren's family is going hiking tomorrow at 7:00. How should Lauren write the time to show that they are going in the morning, not in the evening?

You can use a number line to show the sequence or order of events. It can help you understand the number of hours in a day.

Think: The distance from one mark to the next mark represents one hour.

- Circle the helpful information that tells about the hiking time.
- What do you need to find?

_____

_____

A.M.		P.M.	

12:00 midnight   6:00 A.M.   12:00 noon   6:00 P.M.   12:00 midnight

 Tell time after midnight.

Midnight is 12:00 at night.

The times after midnight and before noon are written with **A.M.**

7:00 in the morning is written as

7:00 _____

So, Lauren should write the hiking time as 7:00 _____

After Midnight and Before Noon

- Find the mark that shows 7:00 A.M. on the number line above. Circle the mark.

 Math Talk

Math Processes and Practices 3

Compare Representations How are the number line on this page and the clock face alike? How are they different?

🔑 **Tell time after noon.**

Callie's family is going for a canoe ride at 3:00 in the afternoon. How should Callie write the time?

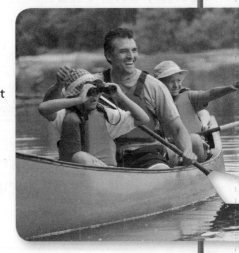

Noon is 12:00 in the daytime.

The times after noon and before midnight are written with **P.M.**

3:00 in the afternoon is written as 3:00 _____

After Noon and Before Midnight

P.M.

So, Callie should write the time as 3:00 _____

Share and Show MATH BOARD

1. Name two things you do in the A.M. hours.
   Name two things you do in the P.M. hours.

_____

_____

Write the time for the activity. Use A.M. or P.M.

2. ride a bicycle

_____

✓ 3. make a sandwich

_____

✓ 4. get ready for bed

_____

5. This morning Sam woke up at the time shown on this clock. Write the time using A.M. or P.M. _____

Math Talk   Math Processes and Practices ❸

Apply How do you decide whether to use A.M. or P.M. when you write the time?

Name _____

Write the time for the activity. Use A.M. or P.M.

6. eat breakfast

_____

7. have science class

_____

8. play softball

_____

Write the time. Use A.M. or P.M.

9. quarter after 9:00 in the morning

_____

10. 6 minutes after 7:00 in the morning

_____

11. Mark is taking a trip on an airplane. His flight leaves at 24 minutes before 9 in the morning. Using A.M. or P.M., at what time does Mark's flight leave?

_____

12. Jennie's class ate lunch at 18 minutes before noon each day. Using A.M. or P.M., write the time that Jennie's class ate lunch.

_____

13. Daylight saving time begins on the second Sunday in March at 2:00 in the morning. Write the time.

Use A.M. or P.M. _____

14. GO DEEPER Jane and her dad are using their new telescope to look at the stars. They start looking at the stars at 23 minutes after 9 and stopped looking at the stars at 10 minutes after 10. Using A.M. or P.M., at what time did they start and stop looking at the stars?

_____

15. THINK SMARTER From midnight to noon each day, how many times does the minute hand on a clock pass 6? Explain how you found your answer.

_____

_____

Unlock the Problem (Real World)

16. Lea and her father arrived at the scenic overlook 15 minutes before noon and left 12 minutes after noon. Using A.M. or P.M., write the time when Lea and her father arrived at the scenic overlook and the time when they left.

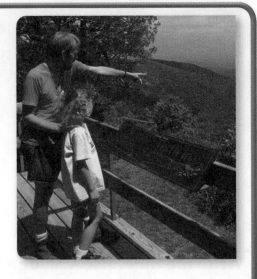

a. What do you need to find? _____

_____

_____

b. What do you need to find first? _____

c. (Math Processes and Practices 6) **Describe a Method** Show the steps you used to solve the problem.

d. They arrived at _____ _____.M.

They left at _____ _____.M.

---

17. (THINK SMARTER) The Davis family spent the day at the lake. Write the letter for each activity next to the time they did it.

A Went swimming soon after lunch.   ☐ 9:50 A.M.

B Ate breakfast at home.   ☐ 7:00 P.M.

C Watched the sunset over the lake.   ☐ 12:15 P.M.

D Got to the lake cabin in the morning.   ☐ 1:30 P.M.

E Had sandwiches for lunch.   ☐ 7:00 A.M.

A.M. and P.M.

Learning Objective You will decide when to use A.M. or P.M. with times by using a number line to show order of events.

Write the time for the activity. Use A.M. or P.M.

1. eat lunch

12:20 P.M.

2. go home after school

_____

3. see the sunrise

_____

4. go for a walk

_____

5. go to school

_____

6. get ready for art class

_____

Write the time. Use A.M. or P.M.

7. one half hour past midnight

_____

8. one-half hour after 4:00 in the morning

_____

9. Jaime is in math class. What time is it? Use A.M. or P.M.

_____

10. Pete began practicing his trumpet at fifteen minutes past three. Write this time using A.M. or P.M.

_____

11. **WRITE** ▸*Math* Write your schedule for today. List each activity with its starting time. Write A.M. or P.M. for each time.

_____

_____

Lesson Check

1. Steven is doing his homework. What time is it? Use A.M. or P.M.

2. After he finished breakfast, Mr. Edwards left for work at fifteen minutes after seven. What time is this? Use A.M. or P.M.

Spiral Review

3. What division equation is related to the multiplication equation

$$4 \times 6 = 24?$$

4. There are 50 toothpicks in each box. Jaime buys 4 boxes for her party platter. How many toothpicks does Jaime buy?

5. A pet store sold 145 bags of beef-flavored dog food and 263 bags of cheese-flavored dog food. How many bags of dog food were sold?

6. Compare. Write <, >, or =.

$$\frac{3}{6} \bigcirc \frac{4}{6}$$

FOR MORE PRACTICE
GO TO THE
Personal Math Trainer

Name _____

Measure Time Intervals

Essential Question How can you measure elapsed time in minutes?

Learning Objective You will measure time intervals in minutes by drawing jumps on a number line or using an analog clock.

🔑 Unlock the Problem

Alicia and her family visited the Kennedy Space Center. They watched a movie that began at 4:10 P.M. and ended at 4:53 P.M. How long did the movie last?

- Circle the times the movie began and ended.
- Underline the question.

To find **elapsed time**, find the amount of time that passes from the start of an activity to the end of the activity.

🔒 One Way Use a number line.

STEP 1 Find the time on the number line that the movie began.

STEP 2 Count on to the ending time, 4:53. Count on by tens for each 10 minutes. Count on by ones for each minute. Write the times below the number line.

STEP 3 Draw the jumps on the number line to show the minutes from 4:10 to 4:53. Record the minutes. Then add them.

10 min + _____ + _____ + _____ + 1 min + _____ + _____

4:10   4:20   _____   _____   4:51   _____

$10 + 10 + 10 + 10 + 1 + 1 + 1 =$ _____

The elapsed time from 4:10 P.M. to

4:53 P.M. is _____ minutes.

So, the movie lasted _____ minutes.

Math Talk Math Processes and Practices ④

Use Models What is another way you can use jumps on the number line to find the elapsed time from 4:10 P.M. to 4:53 P.M?

🔑 Other Ways

Start time: 4:10 P.M. End time: 4:53 P.M.

Ⓐ Use an analog clock.

STEP 1 Find the starting time on the clock.

STEP 2 Count the minutes by counting on by fives and ones to 4:53 P.M. Write the missing counting numbers next to the clock.

So, the elapsed time is _____ minutes.

Ⓑ Use subtraction.

STEP 1 Write the ending time. Then write the starting time so that the hours and minutes line up.

STEP 2 The hours are the same, so subtract the minutes.

$$4 : \boxed{} \quad \leftarrow \text{end time}$$
$$-4 : \boxed{} \quad \leftarrow \text{start time}$$
$$\overline{\boxed{}} \quad \leftarrow \text{elapsed time}$$

Try This! Find the elapsed time in minutes two ways.

Start time: 10:05 A.M. End time: 10:30 A.M.

Ⓐ Use a number line.

STEP 1 Find 10:05 on the number line. Count on from 10:05 to 10:30. Draw marks and record the times on the number line. Then draw and label the jumps.

Think: Count on using longer amounts of time that make sense.

10:05

STEP 2 Add to find the total minutes from 10:05 to 10:30.

From 10:05 A.M. to _____ is _____ minutes.

So, the elapsed time is _____ minutes.

Ⓑ Use subtraction.

Think: The hours are the same, so subtract the minutes.

$$10 : 30$$
$$-10 : 05$$
$$\overline{}$$

Math Talk

Math Processes and Practices ③

Compare Strategies Which method do you prefer to use to find elapsed time?

Name _____

1. Use the number line to find the elapsed time

from 1:15 P.M. to 1:40 P.M. _____

1:15

Find the elapsed time.

✓ **2.** Start: 11:35 A.M.   End: 11:54 A.M.

_____

✓ **3.** Start: 4:20 P.M.   End: 5:00 P.M.

_____

Math Talk   Math Processes and Practices ④

Use a Model How would you use a number line to find the elapsed time from 11:10 A.M. until noon?

On Your Own

Math Processes and Practices ⑤ **Use Appropriate Tools** **Find the elapsed time.**

4. Start: 8:35 P.M.   End: 8:55 P.M.

_____

5. Start: 10:10 A.M.   End: 10:41 A.M.

_____

6. Start: 9:25 A.M.   End: 9:43 A.M.

_____

7. Start: 2:15 P.M.   End: 2:52 P.M.

_____

© Houghton Mifflin Harcourt Publishing Company

Problem Solving • Applications

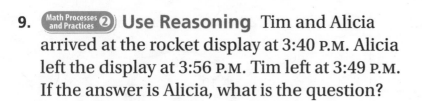

8. John started reading his book about outer space at quarter after nine in the morning. He read until quarter to ten in the morning. How long did John read his book?

_____

9. **Math Processes and Practices ②** **Use Reasoning** Tim and Alicia arrived at the rocket display at 3:40 P.M. Alicia left the display at 3:56 P.M. Tim left at 3:49 P.M. If the answer is Alicia, what is the question?

WRITE *Math* • **Show Your Work**

_____

_____

10. **GO DEEPER** At the space center, Karen bought a model of a shuttle. She started working on the model the next day at 11:13 A.M. She worked until leaving for lunch at 11:51 A.M. After lunch, she worked on the model again from 1:29 P.M. until 1:48 P.M. How long did Karen work on the model?

_____

11. **THINK SMARTER** Aiden arrived at the rocket display at 3:35 P.M. and left at 3:49 P.M. Ava arrived at the rocket display at 3:30 P.M. and left at 3:56 P.M. Ava spent how many more minutes at the rocket display than Aiden?

_____

12. **THINK SMARTER** Kira got on the tour bus at 5:15 P.M. She got off the bus at 5:37 P.M. How long was Kira on the bus?

Select the number to make the sentence true.

Kira was on the bus for _____ minutes.

15
22
37
52

Measure Time Intervals

Learning Objective You will measure time intervals in minutes by drawing jumps on a number line or using an analog clock.

Find the elapsed time.

1. Start: 8:10 A.M.   End: 8:45 A.M.

35 minutes

2. Start: 6:45 P.M.   End: 6:54 P.M.

_____

3. Start: 3:00 P.M.   End: 3:37 P.M.

_____

4. Start: 5:20 A.M.   End: 5:47 A.M.

_____

Problem Solving (Real World)

5. A show at the museum starts at 7:40 P.M. and ends at 7:57 P.M. How long is the show?

_____

6. The first train leaves the station at 6:15 A.M. The second train leaves at 6:55 A.M. How much later does the second train leave the station?

_____

7. **WRITE** ▸*Math* Describe two different methods to find the elapsed time from 2:30 P.M. to 2:58 P.M.

_____

_____

Lesson Check

1. Marcus began playing basketball at 3:30 P.M. and stopped playing at 3:55 P.M. For how many minutes did he play basketball?

2. The school play started at 8:15 P.M. and ended at 8:56 P.M. How long was the school play?

Spiral Review

3. Each car has 4 wheels. How many wheels do 7 cars have?

4. What number completes the equations?

$$3 \times \blacksquare = 27 \quad 27 \div 3 = \blacksquare$$

5. There are 20 napkins in each package. Kelli bought 8 packages for her party. How many napkins did Kelli buy in all?

6. Mr. Martin drove 290 miles last week. This week he drove 125 miles more than last week. How many miles did Mr. Martin drive this week?

FOR MORE PRACTICE
GO TO THE
Personal Math Trainer

Use Time Intervals

Essential Question How can you find a starting time or an ending time when you know the elapsed time?

Learning Objective You will use a number line or a clock to find a starting time or ending time when you know the elapsed time.

Unlock the Problem

Javier begins working on his oceans project at 1:30 P.M. He spends 42 minutes painting a model of Earth and labeling the oceans. At what time does Javier finish working on his project?

• Circle the information you need.
• What time do you need to find?

_____

_____

One Way Use a number line to find the ending time.

STEP 1 Find the time on the number line when Javier started working on the project.

STEP 2 Count forward on the number line to add the elapsed time. Draw and label the jumps to show the minutes.

Think: I can break apart 42 minutes into shorter amounts of time.

STEP 3 Write the times below the number line.

Math Talk Math Processes and Practices ④

Model Mathematics When finding times on the number line, how do you know what size jumps to make?

←————————|————————————————————→
1:30 P.M.

The jumps end at _____

So, Javier finishes working on his project at _____

Another Way Use a clock to find the ending time.

STEP 1 Find the starting time on the clock.

STEP 2 Count on by fives and ones for the elapsed time of 42 minutes. Write the missing counting numbers next to the clock.

So, the ending time is _____

Find Starting Times

Whitney went swimming in the ocean for
25 minutes. She finished swimming at 11:15 A.M.
At what time did Whitney start swimming?

One Way Use a number line to find the starting time.

STEP 1 Find the time on the number line when Whitney finished
swimming in the ocean.

STEP 2 Count back on the number line to subtract the elapsed
time. Draw and label the jumps to show the minutes.

STEP 3 Write the times below the number line.

<——————————————————————|——>
                                         11:15 A.M.

You jumped back to _____

So, Whitney started swimming at _____

Another Way Use a clock to find the starting time.

STEP 1 Find the ending time on the clock.

STEP 2 Count back by fives for the elapsed time of 25 minutes.
Write the missing counting numbers next to the clock.

So, the starting time is _____

Share and Show

Math Talk

Math Processes and Practices ②

Use Reasoning How do
you find the starting
time when you know
the ending time and
the elapsed time?

1. Use the number line to find the starting time if the

   elapsed time is 35 minutes. _____

<——————————————————————|——>
                                         5:10 P.M.

Name _____

Find the ending time.

2. Starting time: 1:40 P.M.
   Elapsed time: 33 minutes

   ←————————————————→

   _____

3. Starting time: 9:55 A.M.
   Elapsed time: 27 minutes

   _____

On Your Own

Find the starting time.

4. Ending time: 3:05 P.M.
   Elapsed time: 40 minutes

   ←————————————————→

   _____

5. Ending time: 8:06 A.M.
   Elapsed time: 16 minutes

   _____

Problem Solving • Applications

6. THINK SMARTER Suzi began fishing at 10:30 A.M.
   and fished until 11:10 A.M. James finished fishing
   at 11:45 A.M. He fished for the same length of time
   as Suzi. At what time did James start fishing? **Explain.**

   _____

   _____

7. GO DEEPER Jessica starts cleaning her room at 5:50 P.M. and
   finishes at 6:44 P.M. Her sister Norah finishes cleaning her
   room at 7:12 P.M. She cleans for the same amount of time as
   Jessica. At what time does Norah start cleaning?

   _____

Personal Math Trainer

8. **THINK SMARTER +** Dante's surfing lesson began at 2:35 P.M. His lesson lasted 45 minutes.

Draw hands on the clock to show the time Dante's surfing lesson ended.

Connect to Science

Tides

If you have ever been to the beach, you have seen the water rise and fall along the shore every day. This change in water level is called the tide. Ocean tides are mostly caused by the pull of the moon and the sun's gravity. High tide is when the water is at its highest level. Low tide is when the water is at its lowest level. In most places on Earth, high tide and low tide each occur about twice a day.

Use the table for 9–10.

9. **GO DEEPER** The first morning, Courtney walked on the beach for 20 minutes. She finished her walk 30 minutes before high tide. At what time did Courtney start her walk?

_____

10. **Math Processes and Practices ②** **Use Reasoning** The third afternoon, Courtney started collecting shells at low tide. She collected shells for 35 minutes. At what time did Courtney finish collecting shells?

Tide Times Atlantic City, NJ		
	Low Tide	High Tide
Day 1	2:12 A.M.	9:00 A.M.
	2:54 P.M.	9:00 P.M.
Day 2	3:06 A.M.	9:36 A.M.
	3:36 P.M.	9:54 P.M.
Day 3	4:00 A.M.	10:12 A.M.
	4:30 P.M.	10:36 P.M.

Use Time Intervals

Learning Objective You will use a number line or a clock to find a starting time or ending time when you know the elapsed time.

Find the starting time.

1. Ending time: 4:29 P.M.
   Elapsed time: 55 minutes

   3:34 P.M.

2. Ending time: 10:08 A.M.
   Elapsed time: 30 minutes

   _____

Find the ending time.

3. Starting time: 2:15 A.M.
   Elapsed time: 45 minutes

   _____

4. Starting time: 6:57 P.M.
   Elapsed time: 47 minutes

   _____

Problem Solving Real World

5. Jenny spent 35 minutes doing research on the Internet. She finished at 7:10 P.M. At what time did Jenny start her research?

   _____

6. Clark left for school at 7:43 A.M. He got to school 36 minutes later. At what time did Clark get to school?

   _____

7. **WRITE** ▸*Math* Describe a situation in your life when you need to know how to find a starting time.

   _____

   _____

Lesson Check

1. Cody and his friends started playing a game at 6:30 P.M. It took them 37 minutes to finish the game. At what time did they finish?

_____

2. Delia worked for 45 minutes on her oil painting. She took a break at 10:35 A.M. At what time did Delia start working on the painting?

_____

Spiral Review

3. Sierra has 30 collector's pins. She wants to put an equal number of pins in each of 5 boxes. How many pins should she put in each box?

30 pins

_____

4. What time is shown on the clock?

_____

5. Ricardo has 32 books to put on 4 shelves. He puts the same number of books on each shelf. How many books does Ricardo put on each shelf?

_____

6. Jon started playing a computer game at 5:35 P.M. He finished the game at 5:52 P.M. How long did Jon play the game?

_____

FOR MORE PRACTICE
GO TO THE
Personal Math Trainer

Name _____

Problem Solving • Time Intervals

Essential Question How can you use the strategy *draw a diagram* to solve problems about time?

Learning Objective You will use the strategy *draw a diagram* to solve problems about time by drawing jumps on number lines to show the elapsed time.

? Unlock the Problem

Zach and his family are going to New York City. Their airplane leaves at 9:15 A.M. They need to arrive at the airport 60 minutes before their flight. It takes 15 minutes to get to the airport. The family needs 30 minutes to get ready to leave. At what time should Zach's family start getting ready?

Read the Problem

What do I need to find?	**What information do I need to use?**	**How will I use the information?**
I need to find what _____ Zach's family should start _____.	the time the _____ leaves; the time the family needs to arrive at the _____; the time it takes to get to the _____; and the time the family needs to _____	I will use a number line to find the answer.

Solve the Problem

• Find 9:15 A.M. on the number line.
  Draw the jumps to show the time.

• Count back _____ minutes to find the time they need to arrive at the airport.

← —————————————————|——→
                                          9:15 A.M.

• Count back _____ minutes to find the time they need to leave for the airport.

• Count back _____ minutes to find the time they need to start getting ready.

So, Zach's family should start getting ready at _____ _____.M.

Math Talk

Math Processes and Practices ①

Analyze How can you check your answer by starting with the time the family starts getting ready?

🔒 Try Another Problem

Bradley gets out of school at 2:45 P.M. It takes him 10 minutes to walk home. Then he spends 10 minutes eating a snack. He spends 8 minutes putting on his soccer uniform. It takes 20 minutes for Bradley's father to drive him to soccer practice. At what time does Bradley arrive at soccer practice?

Read the Problem

What do I need to find?	What information do I need to use?	How will I use the information?

Solve the Problem

Draw a diagram to help you explain your answer.

⟷

1. At what time does Bradley arrive at soccer practice? _____

2. How do you know your answer is reasonable?

_____

_____

_____

Math Talk

Math Processes and Practices ①

Analyze Do you need to draw jumps on the number line in the same order as the times in the problem?

Name _____

Unlock the Problem
√ Circle the question.
√ Underline important facts.
√ Choose a strategy you know.

Share and Show MATH BOARD

1. Patty went to the shopping mall at 11:30 A.M.
   She shopped for 25 minutes. She spent 40 minutes
   eating lunch. Then she met a friend at a movie.
   At what time did Patty meet her friend?

   First, begin with _____ on the number line.

   Then, count forward _____ and _____.

   Think: I can break apart the times into shorter amounts of time
   that make sense.

   11:30 A.M.

   So, Patty met her friend at _____ _____M.

2. What if Patty goes to the mall at 11:30 A.M. and meets a
   friend at a movie at 1:15 P.M.? Patty wants to shop and have
   45 minutes for lunch before meeting her friend. How much
   time can Patty spend shopping?

   _____

3. Avery got on the bus at 1:10 P.M. The trip took 90 minutes.
   Then she walked for 32 minutes to get home. At what time
   did Avery arrive at home?

   _____

On Your Own

4. *GO DEEPER* Kyle and Josh have a total of 64 CDs. Kyle has
   12 more CDs than Josh. How many CDs does each boy
   have?

   _____

5. Jamal spent 60 minutes using the computer. He spent a half hour of the time playing games and the rest of the time researching his report. How many minutes did Jamal spend researching his report?

_____

6. **THINK SMARTER** When Caleb got home from school, he worked on his science project for 20 minutes. Then he studied for a test for 30 minutes. He finished at 4:35 P.M. At what time did Caleb get home from school?

_____

7. **Math Processes and Practices 6** Miguel played video games each day for a week. On Monday, he scored 83 points. His score went up 5 points each day. On what day did Miguel score 103 points? **Explain** how you found your answer.

_____

_____

8. **THINK SMARTER** When Laura arrived at the library, she spent 40 minutes reading a book. Then she spent 15 minutes reading a magazine. She left the library at 4:15 P.M.

Circle the time that makes the sentence true.

Laura arrived at the library at

3:20 P.M.
3:35 P.M.
5:10 P.M.

Problem Solving • Time Intervals

Learning Objective You will use the strategy *draw a diagram* to solve problems about time by drawing jumps on number lines to show the elapsed time.

Solve each problem. Show your work.

1. Hannah wants to meet her friends downtown. Before leaving home, she does chores for 60 minutes and eats lunch for 20 minutes. The walk downtown takes 15 minutes. Hannah starts her chores at 11:45 A.M. At what time does she meet her friends?

_____ 1:20 P.M. _____

2. Katie practiced the flute for 45 minutes. Then she ate a snack for 15 minutes. Next, she watched television for 30 minutes, until 6:00 P.M. At what time did Katie start practicing the flute?

_____

3. Nick gets out of school at 2:25 P.M. He has a 15-minute ride home on the bus. Next, he goes on a 30-minute bike ride. Then he spends 55 minutes doing homework. At what time does Nick finish his homework?

_____

4. **WRITE** ▸*Math* Write a multistep word problem that has at least two amounts of elapsed time. The problem may require finding a starting time or ending time. Include a solution.

_____

_____

Lesson Check

1. Gloria went to the mall and spent 50 minutes shopping. Then she had lunch for 30 minutes. If Gloria arrived at the mall at 11:00 A.M., at what time did she finish lunch?

2. The ball game begins at 2:00 P.M. It takes Ying 30 minutes to get to the ballpark. At what time should Ying leave home to get to the game 30 minutes before it starts?

_____

_____

Spiral Review

3. Write the fractions $\frac{2}{4}$, $\frac{2}{8}$, and $\frac{2}{6}$ in order from least to greatest.

4. Find the unknown factor.

$$6 \times \blacksquare = 36$$

_____

_____

5. There were 405 books on the library shelf. Some books were checked out. Now there are 215 books left on the shelf. How many books were checked out?

6. Savannah has 48 photos. She places 8 photos on each page of her photo album. How many pages in the album does she use?

_____

_____

FOR MORE PRACTICE
GO TO THE
Personal Math Trainer

Name _____

✓ Mid-Chapter Checkpoint

 Personal Math Trainer
Online Assessment
and Intervention

Vocabulary

Choose the best term from the box.

Vocabulary
A.M.
minute
P.M.

1. In one _____ , the minute hand moves from one mark to the next on a clock. (p. 561)

2. The times after noon and before midnight are written

with _____ . (p. 568)

Concepts and Skills

Write the time for the activity. Use A.M. or P.M.

3. play ball

_____

4. eat breakfast

_____

5. do homework

_____

6. sleep

_____

Find the elapsed time.

7. Start: 10:05 A.M.   End: 10:50 A.M.

◄———————————————————►

10:05

_____

8. Start: 5:30 P.M.
   End: 5:49 P.M.

_____

Find the starting time or the ending time.

9. Starting time: _____
   Elapsed time: 50 minutes
   Ending time: 9:05 A.M.

◄——————————————————►
                            9:05 A.M.

10. Starting time: 2:46 P.M.
    Elapsed time: 15 minutes

    Ending time: _____

 © Houghton Mifflin Harcourt Publishing Company

Chapter 10   591

11. Veronica started walking to school at 7:45 A.M. She arrived at school 23 minutes later. At what time did Veronica arrive at school?

_____

12. **GO DEEPER** The clock shows the time the art class ends. At what time does it end? If the class started 37 minutes before the time shown, at what time did the class start?

_____

13. Matt went to his friend's house. He arrived at 5:10 P.M. He left at 5:37 P.M. How long was Matt at his friend's house?

_____

14. Brenda's train leaves at 7:30 A.M. She needs to arrive 10 minutes early to buy her ticket. It takes her 20 minutes to get to the train station. At what time should Brenda leave her house?

_____

15. Write the time you get home from school.

_____

© Houghton Mifflin Harcourt Publishing Company

Measure Length

Essential Question How can you generate measurement data and show the data on a line plot?

Learning Objective You will generate measurement data by measuring lengths to the nearest half or fourth inch and display the measurement data in a line plot.

CONNECT You have learned how to measure length to the nearest inch. Sometimes the length of an object is not a whole unit. For example, a paper clip is more than 1 inch but less than 2 inches.

You can measure length to the nearest half inch or fourth inch. The half-inch markings on a ruler divide each inch into two equal parts. The fourth-inch markings divide each inch into four equal parts.

Math Idea
A ruler is like a number line.

$\frac{0}{4}$ $\frac{1}{4}$ $\frac{2}{4}$ $\frac{3}{4}$ $\frac{4}{4}$

$\frac{0}{2}$ $\frac{1}{2}$ $\frac{2}{2}$

inches

Unlock the Problem · Real World

Example 1 Use a ruler to measure the glue stick to the nearest half inch.

inches

- Line up the left end of the glue stick with the zero mark on the ruler.

- The right end of the glue stick is between the half-inch marks for

  _____ and _____.

- The mark that is closest to the right end of the glue stick is for _____ inches.

So, the length of the glue stick to the

nearest half inch is _____ inches.

Example 2 Use a ruler to measure the paper clip to the nearest fourth inch.

inches

- Line up the left end of the paper clip with the zero mark on the ruler.

- The right end of the paper clip is between the fourth-inch marks for

  _____ and _____.

- The mark that is closest to the right end of the paper clip is for _____ inches.

So, the length of the paper clip to the

nearest fourth inch is _____ inches.

⬤ Activity Make a line plot to show measurement data.

Materials ▪ inch ruler ▪ 10 crayons

Measure the length of 10 crayons to the nearest half inch.
Complete the line plot. Draw an ✗ for each length.

Length of Crayons Measured to the Nearest Half Inch

• Describe any patterns you see in your line plot.

_____

_____

Try This! Measure the length of your fingers to the
nearest fourth inch. Complete the line plot. Draw an
✗ for each length.

Math Processes and Practices ❸

Compare Representations
How do you think your
line plot compares to
line plots your classmates
made?

Length of Fingers Measured to the Nearest Fourth Inch

 Share and Show

☑1. Measure the length to the nearest half inch. Is the
key closest to $1\frac{1}{2}$ inches, 2 inches, or $2\frac{1}{2}$ inches?

_____ inches

Name _____

Measure the length to the nearest fourth inch.

✓2.

_____ inches

On Your Own

Use the lines for 3–4.

3. Measure the length of the lines to the nearest half inch
   and make a line plot.

$$\vdash\!\!+\!\!+\!\!+\!\!+\!\!+\!\!+\!\!+\dashv$$

4. Measure the length of the lines to the nearest fourth inch
   and make a line plot.

$$\vdash\!\!+\!\!+\!\!+\!\!+\!\!+\!\!+\!\!+\!\!+\!\!+\!\!+\!\!+\dashv$$

Problem Solving · Applications

Use the line plot for 5–7.

5. **GO DEEPER** Tara has a magnet collection from places she visited. She measures the length of the magnets to the nearest half inch and records the data in a line plot. Are more magnets longer than $2\frac{1}{2}$ inches or shorter than $2\frac{1}{2}$ inches? Explain.

Length of Magnets

_____

_____

_____

6. **THINK SMARTER** How many magnets measure a whole number of inches? How many magnets have a length between two whole numbers?

_____

_____

7. **Math Processes and Practices ⑥** **Explain** why you think the line plot starts at 1 and stops at 4.

_____

_____

_____

8. **THINK SMARTER** What is the length of the pencil to the nearest half inch?

_____ inches

Explain how you measured the pencil.

_____

_____

Name _____

Measure Length

Learning Objective You will generate measurement data by measuring lengths to the nearest half or fourth inch and display the measurement data in a line plot.

Measure the length to the nearest half inch.

1.

    $1\frac{1}{2}$ _____ inches

2. $\quad$ _____ inches

3. _____ inches

Measure the length to the nearest fourth inch.

4. _____ inches

5. _____ inches

 Problem Solving

Use a separate sheet of paper for 6.

6. Draw 8 lines that are between 1 inch and 3 inches long. Measure each line to the nearest fourth inch, and make a line plot.

7. Alex's dog has a tail that is $5\frac{1}{4}$ inches long. On a ruler, what inch marks are closest to $5\frac{1}{4}$ inches? Name two inch marks.

_____ $\qquad$ _____

8. **WRITE** ▸*Math* Measure the lengths of 10 color pencils to the nearest fourth inch. Then make a line plot of the data.

_____

_____

Lesson Check

1. What is the length of the string to the nearest half inch?

_____

2. What is the length of the leaf to the nearest fourth inch?

_____

Spiral Review

3. Write the equations included in the same set of related facts as $6 \times 8 = 48$.

_____

_____

4. Brooke says there are 49 days until July 4. There are 7 days in a week. In how many weeks will it be July 4?

_____

_____

5. It is 20 minutes before 8:00 in the morning. What time is this? Use A.M. or P.M.

_____

6. Marcy played the piano for 45 minutes. She stopped playing at 4:15 P.M. At what time did she start playing the piano?

_____

FOR MORE PRACTICE
GO TO THE
Personal Math Trainer

Name _____

Estimate and Measure Liquid Volume

Essential Question How can you estimate and measure liquid volume in metric units?

Learning Objective You will estimate and measure liquid volume by writing more than 1 liter, about 1 liter, or less than 1 liter.

🔑 Unlock the Problem

Liquid volume is the amount of liquid in a container. The **liter (L)** is the basic metric unit for measuring liquid volume.

 Activity 1

Materials ■ 1-L beaker ■ 4 containers ■ water ■ tape

STEP 1 Fill a 1-liter beaker with water to the 1-liter mark.

STEP 2 Pour 1 liter of water into a container. Mark the level of the water with a piece of tape. Draw the container below and name the container.

STEP 3 Repeat Steps 1 and 2 with three different-sized containers.

Container 1

_____

Container 2

_____

 Math Talk

Math Processes and Practices ⑧

Draw Conclusions What happens to the liquid volume when you pour the same amount of liquid into different sized containers?

Container 3

_____

Container 4

_____

1. How much water did you pour into each container? _____

2. Which containers are mostly full? Describe them.

_____

3. Which containers are mostly empty? Describe them.

_____

Compare Liquid Volumes

| A full glass holds less than 1 liter. | A water bottle holds about 1 liter. | A fish bowl holds more than 1 liter. |

Activity 2 **Materials** ■ 1-L beaker ■ 5 different containers ■ water

STEP 1   Write the containers in order from the one you think will hold the least water to the one you think will hold the most water.

_____, _____, _____,

_____, _____

STEP 2   Estimate how much each container will hold. Write *more than 1 liter*, *about 1 liter*, or *less than 1 liter* in the table.

STEP 3   Pour 1 liter of water into one of the containers. Repeat until the container is full. Record the number of liters you poured. Repeat for each container.

Container	Estimate	Number of Liters

STEP 4   Write the containers in order from the least to the greatest liquid volume.

_____, _____, _____,

_____, _____

Math Talk

Math Processes and Practices ①

Evaluate Was the order in Step 1 different than the order in Step 4? Explain why they may be different.

© Houghton Mifflin Harcourt Publishing Company • Image Credits: (tr) ©PhotoDisc/Getty Images

Name _____

Share and Show

1. The beaker is filled with water. Is the amount *more than 1 liter*, *about 1 liter*, or *less than 1 liter*?

_____

Estimate how much liquid volume there will be when the container is filled. Write *more than 1 liter*, *about 1 liter*, or *less than 1 liter*.

2. cup of tea	✓ 3. kitchen sink	✓ 4. teapot
_____	_____	_____

On Your Own

Estimate how much liquid volume there will be when the container is filled. Write *more than 1 liter*, *about 1 liter*, or *less than 1 liter*.

Math Talk

Math Processes and Practices 8

Generalize How can you estimate the liquid volume in a container?

5. pitcher	6. juice box	7. punch bowl
_____	_____	_____

Use the pictures for 8–10. Rosario pours juice into four bottles that are the same size.

8. Did Rosario pour the same amount into each bottle? _____

9. Which bottle has the least amount of juice? _____

10. Which bottle has the most juice? _____

W   X   Y   Z

© Houghton Mifflin Harcourt Publishing Company • Image Credits: (tc) ©C Squared Studios/Getty Images; (bc) ©NiKreationS / Alamy; (tcr) ©Stockbyte/Getty Images

Problem Solving · Applications

Use the containers for 11–13. Container _A_ is full when 1 liter of water is poured into it.

11. **GO DEEPER** Estimate how many liters will fill Container _C_ and how many liters will fill Container _E_. Which container will hold more water when filled?

_____

_____

12. **Math Processes and Practices ⑥** Name two containers that will be filled with about the same number of liters of water. **Explain.**

_____

_____

13. **THINK SMARTER** **What's the Error?** Samuel says that you can pour more liters of water into Container _B_ than into Container _D_. Is he correct? Explain.

_____

_____

_____

Personal Math Trainer

14. **THINK SMARTER+** The bottle of tea holds about 1 liter. For numbers 14a–14e, choose Yes or No to tell whether it will hold more than 1 liter.

14a. teacup   ○ Yes   ○ No

14b. kitchen trash can   ○ Yes   ○ No

14c. small pool   ○ Yes   ○ No

14d. fish tank   ○ Yes   ○ No

14e. perfume bottle   ○ Yes   ○ No

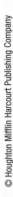

Estimate and Measure
Liquid Volume

Estimate how much liquid volume there will be when the container is filled. Write *more than 1 liter, about 1 liter,* or *less than 1 liter.*

1. large milk container

more than 1 liter

2. small milk container

3. water bottle

4. spoonful of water

5. bathtub

6. eyedropper

Problem Solving Real World

Use the pictures for 7. Alan pours water into four glasses that are the same size.

7. Which glass has the most amount

of water? _____

A   B   C   D

8. **WRITE** ▸Math Name a container that you see at home that when filled has a liquid volume of about 1 liter.

_____

_____

Lesson Check

1. Felicia filled the bathroom sink with water. Is the amount more than 1 liter, about 1 liter, or less than 1 liter?

2. Kyle needed about 1 liter of water to fill a container. Did Kyle most likely fill a small glass, a spoon, or a vase?

Spiral Review

3. Cecil had 6 ice cubes. He put 1 ice cube in each glass. In how many glasses did Cecil put ice cubes?

4. Juan has 12 muffins. He puts $\frac{1}{4}$ of the muffins in a bag. How many muffins does Juan put in the bag?

5. What time is shown on the clock?

6. Julianne drew the line segment below. Use your ruler to measure the segment to the nearest fourth inch.

FOR MORE PRACTICE GO TO THE Personal Math Trainer

Name _____

Estimate and Measure Mass

Essential Question How can you estimate and measure mass in metric units?

Learning Objective You will choose the unit to measure mass as grams or kilograms and compare masses of objects as less than, same as, or more than one to the other.

Unlock the Problem

Pedro has a dollar bill in his pocket. Should Pedro measure the mass of the dollar bill in grams or kilograms?

The **gram (g)** is the basic metric unit for measuring **mass**, or the amount of matter in an object. Mass can also be measured by using the metric unit **kilogram (kg)**.

A small paper clip has a mass of about 1 gram.	A box of 1,000 paper clips has a mass of about 1 kilogram.

Think: The mass of a dollar bill is closer to the mass of a small paper clip than it is to a box of 1,000 paper clips.

So, Pedro should measure the mass of the dollar bill in _____.

Activity 1

Materials ■ pan balance ■ gram and kilogram masses

You can use a pan balance to measure mass.

Do 10 grams have the same mass as 1 kilogram?

- Place 10 gram masses on one side of the balance.

- Place a 1-kilogram mass on the other side of the balance.

Think: If it is balanced, then the objects have the same mass. If it is not balanced, the objects do not have the same mass.

- Complete the picture of the balance above by drawing masses to show your balance.

The pan balance is _____.

So, 10 grams and 1 kilogram _____ the same mass.

Math Talk Math Processes and Practices 4

Use Models How do you tell from the balance which side has greater mass?

© Houghton Mifflin Harcourt Publishing Company

🔑 Activity 2

Materials ■ pan balance ■ gram and kilogram masses ■ classroom objects

STEP 1 Use the objects in the table. Decide if the object should be measured in grams or kilograms.

STEP 2 Estimate the mass of each object. Record your estimates in the table.

STEP 3 Find the mass of each object to the nearest gram or kilogram. Place the object on one side of the balance. Place gram or kilogram masses on the other side until both sides are balanced.

STEP 4 Add the measures of the gram or kilogram masses. This is the mass of the object. Record the mass in the table.

▲ 189 marbles have a mass of 1 kilogram.

Mass		
Object	Estimate	Mass
crayon		
stapler		
eraser		
marker		
small notepad		
scissors		

Math Talk Math Processes and Practices ⑥

Compare How did your estimates compare with the actual measurements?

• Write the objects in order from greatest mass to least mass.

_____ , _____ , _____ ,

_____ , _____ , _____

Share and Show

1. Five bananas have a mass of about _____.

Think: The pan balance is balanced, so the objects on both sides have the same mass.

Name _____

Choose the unit you would use to measure the mass.
Write *gram* or *kilogram*.

2. strawberry

_____

✓3. dog

_____

Math Talk

Math Processes and Practices ②

Use Reasoning How do you decide which unit to use when measuring the mass of different objects?

Compare the masses of the objects. Write
is less than, is the same as, **or** ***is more than.***

4.

The mass of the bowling pin

_____ the mass of the chess piece.

✓5.

The mass of the erasers

_____ the mass of the clips.

On Your Own

Choose the unit you would use to measure the mass.
Write *gram* or *kilogram*.

6. chair

_____

7. sunglasses

_____

8. watermelon

_____

Compare the masses of the objects. Write
is less than, is the same as, **or** ***is more than.***

9.

The mass of the pen _____ the mass of the paper clips.

10.

The mass of the straws _____ the mass of the blocks.

© Houghton Mifflin Harcourt Publishing Company • Image Credits: tc ©GK Hart/Vikki Hart/Getty Images; (b) ©Ryan McVay/Getty Images; (bc) ©comstock/Getty Images; (br) ©artville/Getty Images

Problem Solving • Applications

11. **GO DEEPER** Put the sports balls shown at the right in order from greatest mass to least mass.

_____

_____

Golf ball

Table tennis ball

Bowling ball

12. **Math Processes and Practices ④ Use Diagrams** Choose two objects that have about the same mass. Draw a balance with one of these objects on each side.

13. **Math Processes and Practices ④ Use Diagrams** Choose two objects that have different masses. Draw a balance with one of these objects on each side.

Baseball

Tennis ball

14. **THINK SMARTER** **Pose a Problem** Write a problem about the objects you chose in Exercise 13. Then solve your problem.

_____

_____

15. **THINK SMARTER** **Sense or Nonsense?** Amber is buying produce at the grocery store. She says that a Fuji apple and a green bell pepper would have the same mass because they are the same size. Does her statement make sense? Explain.

_____

_____

_____

16. **THINK SMARTER** Select the objects with a mass greater than 1 kilogram. Mark all that apply.

- Ⓐ skateboard
- Ⓑ laptop computer
- Ⓒ cell phone
- Ⓓ egg
- Ⓔ desk
- Ⓕ pencil

Name _____

Estimate and Measure Mass

Learning Objective You will choose the unit to measure mass as grams or kilograms and compare masses of objects as less than, same as, or more than one to the other.

Choose the unit you would use to measure the mass. Write *gram* or *kilogram*.

1. CD

gram _____

2. boy

_____

3. bag of sugar

_____

Compare the masses of the objects. Write *is less than*, *is the same as*, or *is more than*.

4.

The mass of the candle _____ the mass of the light bulb.

5.

The mass of the watch _____ the mass of the necklace.

Problem Solving

6. A red ball has a mass that is less than 1 kilogram. A blue ball has a mass of 1 kilogram. Is the mass of the blue ball more than or less than the mass of the red ball?

_____

7. Brock's dog is a collie. To find the mass of his dog, should Brock use *grams* or *kilograms*?

_____

8. **WRITE** ▸ *Math* Name an object in your home that has a mass of about 1 kg.

_____

_____

Lesson Check

1. Which unit of measure would you use to measure the mass of a grape? Write *gram* or *kilogram*.

   _____

2. Elsie wants to find the mass of her pony. Which unit should she use? Write *gram* or *kilogram*.

   _____

Spiral Review

3. Marsie blew up 24 balloons. She tied the balloons together in groups of 4. How many groups did Marsie make?

   _____

4. Clark used the order of operations to find the unknown number in $15 - 12 \div 3 = n$. What is the value of the unknown number?

   _____

Use the pictures for 5–6. Ralph pours juice into four bottles that are the same size.

5. Which bottle has the most amount of juice?

   _____

A   B   C   D

6. Which bottle has the least amount of juice?

   _____

FOR MORE PRACTICE
GO TO THE
Personal Math Trainer

Name _____

Solve Problems About Liquid Volume and Mass

Learning Objective You will use bar models then write an equation to solve liquid volume and mass problems.

Essential Question How can you use models to solve liquid volume and mass problems?

Unlock the Problem

A restaurant serves iced tea from a large container that can hold 24 liters. Sadie will fill the container with the pitchers of tea shown below. Will Sadie have tea left over after filling the container?

Example 1 Solve a problem about liquid volume.

_____ L   _____ L   _____ L   _____ L

Since there are _____ equal groups of _____ liters, you can multiply.

_____ ◯ _____ = _____

Circle the correct words to complete the sentences.

_____ liters is *greater than / less than* 24 liters.

So, Sadie *will / will not* have tea left over.

Try This! Use a bar model to solve.

Raul's fish tank contains 32 liters of water. He empties it with a bucket that holds 4 liters of water. How many times will Raul have to fill the bucket?

_____ ◯ _____ = _____

So, Raul will have to fill the bucket _____ times.

_____ times

| 4 L | | 4 L |

32 L

⓵ **Activity** Solve a problem about mass.

Materials ■ pan balance ■ glue stick ■ gram masses

Jeff has a glue stick and a 20-gram mass on one side of a balance and gram masses on the other side. The pan balance is balanced. What is the mass of the glue stick?

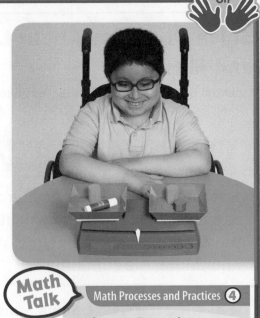

STEP 1 Place a glue stick and a 20-gram mass on one side of the balance.

STEP 2 Place gram masses on the other side until the pans are balanced.

STEP 3 To find the mass of the glue stick, remove 20 grams from each side.

> **Think:** I can remove 20 grams from both sides and the pan balance will still be balanced.

STEP 4 Then add the measures of the gram masses on the balance.

The gram masses have a measure of _____ grams.

So, the glue stick has a mass of _____.

Math Talk

Math Processes and Practices ④

Write an Equation
What equation can you write to find the mass of the glue stick?

Try This! Use a bar model to solve.

A bag of peas has a mass of 432 grams.
A bag of carrots has a mass of 263 grams.
What is the total mass of both bags?

_____ g	_____ g

____ g

_____ ◯ _____ = _____

So, both bags have a total mass of _____ grams.

 Share and Show

1. Ed's Delivery Service delivered three packages to Ms. Wilson. The packages have masses of 9 kilograms, 12 kilograms, and 5 kilograms. What is the total mass of the three packages? Use the bar model to help you solve.

___ kg	___ kg	__ kg

____ kg

_____

Name _____

Write an equation and solve the problem.

2. Ariel's recipe calls for 64 grams of apples and 86 grams of oranges. How many more grams of oranges than apples does the recipe call for?

_____ ◯ _____ = _____

3. Dan's Clams restaurant sold 45 liters of lemonade. If it sold the same amount each hour for 9 hours, how many liters of lemonade did Dan's Clams sell each hour?

_____ ◯ _____ = _____

Math Talk

Math Processes and Practices ④

Use Models How could you use a model to solve Exercise 2?

On Your Own

Math Processes and Practices ④ **Write an Equation** **Write an equation and solve the problem.**

4. Sasha's box holds 4 kilograms of napkins and 29 kilograms of napkin rings. What is the total mass of the napkins and napkin rings?

_____ ◯ _____ = _____

5. Josh has 6 buckets for cleaning a restaurant. He fills each bucket with 4 liters of water. How many liters of water are in the buckets?

_____ ◯ _____ = _____

6. **THINK SMARTER** Ellen will pour water into Pitcher *B* until it has 1 more liter of water than Pitcher *A*. How many liters of water will she pour into Pitcher *B*? Explain how you found your answer.

Pitcher *A*   Pitcher *B*

7. **Practice: Copy and Solve** Use the pictures to write two problems. Then solve your problems.

Grape Juice

Apple Juice

Cereal

Coffee

© Houghton Mifflin Harcourt Publishing Company

Chapter 10 • Lesson 9   613

🔑 Unlock the Problem

8. Ken's Café serves fruit smoothies. Each smoothie has 9 grams of fresh strawberries. How many grams of strawberries are in 8 smoothies?

a. What do you need to find? _____

b. What operation will you use to find the answer? _____

c. **Math Processes and Practices ④ Use Diagrams** Draw a diagram to solve the problem.

d. Complete the sentences.

There are _____ smoothies with _____ grams of strawberries in each.

Since each smoothie is an _____ group, you can _____.

_____ ◯ _____ = _____

So, there are _____ grams of strawberries in 8 smoothies.

9. **GO DEEPER** Arturo has two containers, each filled with 12 liters of water. Daniel has two containers, each filled with 16 liters of water. What is the total liquid volume of the boys' containers?

_____

10. **THINK SMARTER** A deli makes its own salad dressing. A small jar has 3 grams of spices. A large jar has 5 grams of spices. Will 25 grams of spices be enough to make 3 small jars and 3 large jars? Show your work.

Name _____

Solve Problems About Liquid Volume and Mass

Learning Objective You will use bar models then write an equation to solve liquid volume and mass problems.

Write an equation and solve the problem.

1. Luis was served 145 grams of meat and 217 grams of vegetables at a meal. What was the total mass of the meat and the vegetables?

   Think: Add to find how much in all.

   __145__ $\bigoplus$ __217__ = ____   _____

2. The gas tank of a riding mower holds 5 liters of gas. How many 5-liter gas tanks can you fill from a full 20-liter gas can?

   ____ $\bigcirc$ ____ = ____   _____

3. To make a lemon-lime drink, Mac mixed 4 liters of lemonade with 2 liters of limeade. How much lemon-lime drink did Mac make?

   ____ $\bigcirc$ ____ = ____   _____

4. A nickel has a mass of 5 grams. There are 40 nickels in a roll of nickels. What is the mass of a roll of nickels?

   ____ $\bigcirc$ ____ = ____   _____

Problem Solving · Real World

5. Zoe's fish tank holds 27 liters of water. She uses a 3-liter container to fill the tank. How many times does she have to fill the 3-liter container in order to fill her fish tank?

   _____

6. Adrian's backpack has a mass of 15 kilograms. Theresa's backpack has a mass of 8 kilograms. What is the total mass of both backpacks?

   _____

7. **WRITE** ▸*Math* Write a problem that can be solved with a bar model that shows equal groups of liters. Then solve the problem.

   _____

   _____

Lesson Check

1. Mickey's beagle has a mass of 15 kilograms. His dachshund has a mass of 13 kilograms. What is the combined mass of the two dogs?

_____

2. Lois put 8 liters of water in a bucket for her pony. At the end of the day, there were 2 liters of water left. How much water did the pony drink?

_____

Spiral Review

3. Josiah has 3 packs of toy animals. Each pack has the same number of animals. Josiah gives 6 animals to his sister Stephanie. Then Josiah has 9 animals left. How many animals were in each pack?

_____

4. Tom jogged $\frac{3}{10}$ mile, Betsy jogged $\frac{5}{10}$ mile, and Sue jogged $\frac{2}{10}$ mile. Who jogged a distance longer than $\frac{4}{10}$ mile?

_____

5. Bob started mowing at 9:55 A.M. It took him 25 minutes to mow the front yard and 45 minutes to mow the back yard. At what time did Bob finish mowing?

_____

6. Juliana wants to find the mass of a watermelon. What unit should she use?

_____

FOR MORE PRACTICE
GO TO THE
Personal Math Trainer

✓ Chapter 10 Review/Test

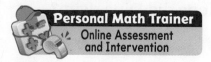

Personal Math Trainer
Online Assessment
and Intervention

1. Yul and Sarah's art class started at 11:25 A.M. The class lasted 30 minutes. Yul left when the class was done. Sarah stayed an extra 5 minutes to talk with the teacher and then left.

   Write the time that each student left. Explain how you found each time.

   _____

   _____

2. Julio measured an object that he found. It was about $\frac{3}{4}$ inch wide.

   For numbers 2a–2d, choose Yes or No to tell whether the object could be the one Julio measured.

   2a.   ○ Yes   ○ No

   2b.   ○ Yes   ○ No

   2c.   ○ Yes   ○ No

   2d.   ○ Yes   ○ No

GO DIGITAL Assessment Options
Chapter Test

3. Dina started swimming at 3:38 P.M. She swam until 4:15 P.M. How long did Dina swim?

_____ minutes

4. Rita's class begins social studies at ten minutes before one in the afternoon. At what time does Rita's class begin social studies? Circle a time that makes the sentence true.

Rita's class begins social studies at

1:10 A.M.
1:10 P.M.
12:50 A.M.
12:50 P.M.

5. Select the objects with a mass greater than 1 kilogram. Mark all that apply.

(A) bicycle   (C) eraser

(B) pen   (D) math book

6. A chicken dish needs to bake in the oven for 35 minutes. The dish needs to cool for at least 8 minutes before serving. Scott puts the chicken dish in the oven at 5:14 P.M.

For numbers 6a–6d, select True or False for each statement.

6a. Scott can serve the dish at 5:51 P.M.   ○ True   ○ False

6b. Scott can serve the dish at 5:58 P.M.   ○ True   ○ False

6c. Scott should take the dish out of the oven at 5:51 A.M.   ○ True   ○ False

6d. Scott should take the dish out of the oven at 5:49 P.M.   ○ True   ○ False

7. Anthony read a book to his little brother. He started reading at the time shown on the clock. He stopped reading at 5:45 P.M.

Part A

How long did Anthony read to his little brother?

_____ minutes

Part B

Explain how you found your answer.

_____

_____

_____

_____

8. Tran checked the time on his watch after he finished his daily run.

Select the time that Tran finished running. Mark all that apply.

Ⓐ   14 minutes before nine   Ⓒ   quarter to nine

Ⓑ   eight forty-six   Ⓓ   nine forty-six

9. Cara uses a balance scale to compare mass.

Circle a symbol that makes the comparison true.

The mass of the blocks | < > = | the mass of the erasers.

10. A large bottle of water holds about 2 liters.

For numbers 10a–10e, choose Yes or No to tell whether the container will hold all of the water.

10a.	kitchen sink	○ Yes	○ No
10b.	water glass	○ Yes	○ No
10c.	ice cube tray	○ Yes	○ No
10d.	large soup pot	○ Yes	○ No
10e.	lunchbox thermos	○ Yes	○ No

11. Select the items that would be best measured in grams. Mark all that apply.

(A) watermelon

(B) lettuce leaf

(C) grape

(D) onion

12. Samir made a list of what he did on Tuesday. Write the letter for each activity next to the time he did it.

(A) Get out of bed.   ☐ 8:05 A.M.

(B) Walk to school.   ☐ 6:25 P.M.

(C) Eat lunch.   ☐ 3:50 P.M.

(D) Go to guitar lesson
after school.   ☐ 11:48 A.M.

(E) Eat dinner at home.   ☐ 6:25 A.M.

Name _____

13. Amy has 30 grams of flour. She puts 4 grams of flour in each pot of chowder that she makes. She puts 5 grams of flour in each pot of potato soup that she makes. She makes 4 pots of chowder. Does Amy have enough flour left over to make 3 pots of potato soup?

14. Use an inch ruler to measure.

Part A

What is the length of the leaf to the nearest fourth inch?

_____

Part B

Explain what happens if you line up the left side of the object with the 1 on the ruler.

_____

_____

15. Mrs. Park takes the 9:38 A.M. train to the city. The trip takes 3 hours and 20 minutes. What time does Mrs. Park arrive in the city?

_____

16. Hector buys two bags of gravel for his driveway. He buys a total of 35 kilograms of gravel. Select the bags he buys.

15 kg	17 kg	18 kg	19 kg
○	○	○	○

17. Ashley measures the shells she collects.
She records the measurements in a chart.

Number of Shells	Length in Inches
1	1
2	$2\frac{1}{2}$
3	$1\frac{1}{2}$
1	2

Part A

Ashley found a razor clam shell this long.
Use an inch ruler to measure. Record the
measurement in the chart.

_____ inches

Part B

Complete the line plot to show the data in the chart. How
many shells are longer than 2 inches? Tell how you know.

Length of Shells Measured to the Nearest Half Inch

_____

_____

18. Lucy fills a bathroom sink with water. Is the amount of
water *more than 1 liter, about 1 liter, or less than 1 liter?*
Explain how you know.

_____

_____

_____

Perimeter and Area

Personal Math Trainer
Online Assessment
and Intervention

✓ Show What You Know

Check your understanding of important skills.

Name _____

▶ **Use Nonstandard Units to Measure Length**
Use paper clips to measure the object.

1.

   about ____

2.

   about ____

▶ **Add 3 Numbers** Write the sum.

3. $2 + 7 + 3 =$ ____   4. $3 + 5 + 2 =$ ____   5. $6 + 1 + 9 =$ ____

▶ **Model with Arrays** Use the array. Complete.

6. 3 rows of 4

   ____ × ____ = ____

7. 4 rows of 2

   ____ × ____ = ____

Math in the Real World

Julia has a picture frame with side lengths of 12 inches
and 24 inches. She wants to cut and glue one color
of ribbon that will fit exactly around the edge. The
green ribbon is 72 inches long. The red ribbon is
48 inches long. Find which ribbon she should use
to glue around the picture frame.

Vocabulary Builder

▶ **Visualize It** ••••••••••••••••••••••••••••••••

Sort the words with a ✔ into the Venn diagram.

Perimeter   Area

Review Words

| addition |
| array |
| centimeter (cm) |
| Distributive Property |
| foot (ft) |
| inch (in.) |
| inverse operations |
| ✔ length |
| meter (m) |
| multiplication |
| pattern |
| rectangle |
| repeated addition |
| ✔ unit |
| ✔ width |

Preview Words

| area |
| perimeter |
| ✔ square unit |
| ✔ unit square |

▶ **Understand Vocabulary** ••••••••••••••••••••••••

Complete the sentences by using the review and preview words.

1. The distance around a figure is the

   _____ .

2. The _____ is the measure of the number of unit squares needed to cover a surface.

3. You can count, use _____, or multiply to find the area of a rectangle.

4. A _____ is a square with a side length of 1 unit and is used to measure area.

5. The _____ shows that you can break apart a rectangle into smaller rectangles and add the area of each smaller rectangle to find the total area.

624

GO DIGITAL
• Interactive Student Edition
• Multimedia eGlossary

Chapter 11 Vocabulary

area

área

3

centimeter (cm)

centímetro (cm)

7

inverse operation

operaciones inversas

37

length

longitud

40

perimeter

perímetro

59

rectangle

rectángulo

69

square unit

unidad cuadrada

75

unit square

caudrado de una unidad

80

A metric unit used to measure length or distance
100 centimeters = 1 meter

centimeters

The measure of the number of unit squares needed to cover a surface

Area = 8 square units

The measurement of the distance between two points

Opposite operations, or operations that undo one another, such as addition and subtraction or multiplication and division

Examples: $16 + 8 = 24$; $24 - 8 = 16$
$4 \times 3 = 12$; $12 \div 4 = 3$

A quadrilateral with two pairs of parallel sides, two pairs of sides of equal length, and four right angles

The distance around a figure

Example: The perimeter of this rectangle is 20 inches.

6 in.

4 in.   4 in.

6 in.

A square with a side length of 1 unit, used to measure area

1 unit

1 unit

A unit used to measure area such as square foot, square meter, and so on

Picture It

Word Box

area

centimeter (cm)

inverse operations

length

perimeter

rectangle

square unit

unit square

For 3 to 4 players

Materials

- timer
- sketch pad

How to Play

1. Take turns to play.
2. To take a turn, choose a word from the Word Box, but do not say the word aloud.
3. Set the timer for 1 minute.
4. Draw pictures and numbers to give clues about the word.
5. The first player to guess the word before time runs out gets 1 point. If that player can use the word in a sentence, he or she gets 1 more point. Then that player gets a turn choosing a word.
6. The first player to score 10 points wins.

Game

The Write Way

Reflect

Choose one idea. Write about it.

- Define perimeter in your own words.
- Write two things you know about area.
- Explain how two rectangles can have the same area, but different perimeter. Give an example.

Name _____

Model Perimeter

Essential Question How can you find perimeter?

Learning Objective You will use dot paper and grid paper to find the perimeter of figures by counting the number of units on each side.

Investigate

Perimeter is the distance around a figure.

Materials ■ geoboard ■ rubber bands

You can find the perimeter of a rectangle on a geoboard or on dot paper by counting the number of units on each side.

A. Make a rectangle on the geoboard that is 3 units on two sides and 2 units on the other two sides.

B. Draw your rectangle on this dot paper.

← 1 Unit

C. Write the length next to each side of your rectangle.

D. Add the number of units on each side.

_____ + _____ + _____ + _____ = _____

E. So, the perimeter of the rectangle

is _____ units.

• How would the perimeter of the rectangle change if the length of two of the sides was 4 units instead of 3 units?

_____

_____

Draw Conclusions

1. Describe how you would find the perimeter of a rectangle that is 5 units wide and 6 units long.

_____

2. **THINK SMARTER** A rectangle has two pairs of sides of equal length. Explain how you can find the unknown length of two sides when the length of one side is 4 units, and the perimeter is 14 units.

_____

_____

3. **Math Processes and Practices ①** **Evaluate** Jill says that finding the perimeter of a figure with all sides of equal length is easier than finding the perimeter of other figures. Do you agree? Explain.

_____

_____

Make Connections

Math Processes and Practices ③

Apply If a rectangle has a perimeter of 12 units, how many units wide and how many units long could it be?

You can also use grid paper to find the perimeter of figures by counting the number of units on each side.

Start at the arrow and trace the perimeter. Begin counting with 1. Continue counting each unit around the figure until you have counted each unit.

Ⓐ

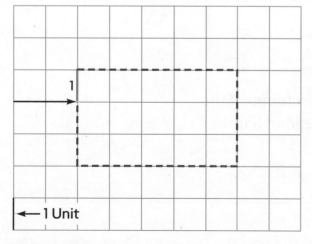

← 1 Unit

Perimeter = _____ units

Ⓑ

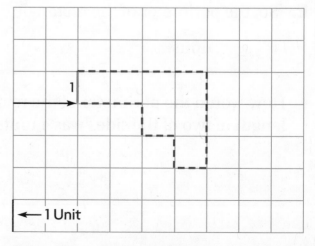

← 1 Unit

Perimeter = _____ units

626

© Houghton Mifflin Harcourt Publishing Company

Name _____

Find the perimeter of the figure. Each unit is 1 centimeter.

1.

_____ centimeters

2.

_____ centimeters

3.

_____ centimeters

4.

_____ centimeters

Find the perimeter.

5. A figure with four sides that measure
4 centimeters, 6 centimeters,
5 centimeters, and 1 centimeter

_____ centimeters

6. A figure with two sides that measure
10 inches, one side that measures
8 inches, and one side that measures
4 inches

_____ inches

 Problem Solving • Applications

7. (Math Processes and Practices ⑥) **Explain** how to find the length of each side of
a triangle with sides of equal length and a perimeter of 27 inches.

_____

_____

8. **THINK SMARTER** Luisa drew a rectangle with a perimeter of 18 centimeters. Select the rectangles that Luisa could have drawn. Mark all that apply. Use the grid to help you.

Ⓐ 9 centimeters long and 2 centimeters wide

Ⓑ 6 centimeters long and 3 centimeters wide

Ⓒ 4 centimeters long and 4 centimeters wide

Ⓓ 5 centimeters long and 4 centimeters wide

Ⓔ 7 centimeters long and 2 centimeters wide

9. **THINK SMARTER** **What's the Error?** Kevin is solving perimeter problems. He counts the units and says that the perimeter of this figure is 18 units.

Look at Kevin's solution.   **Find Kevin's error.**

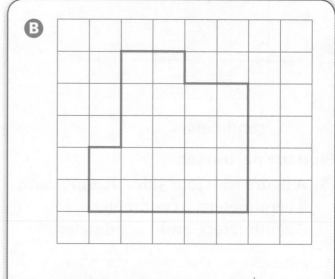

Ⓐ

Perimeter = _____ units

Ⓑ

Perimeter = _____ units

• **GO DEEPER** Describe the error Kevin made. Circle the places in the drawing of Kevin's solution where he made an error.

_____

_____

Name _____

Model Perimeter

Learning Objective You will use dot paper and grid paper to find the perimeter of figures by counting the number of units on each side.

Find the perimeter of the figure. Each unit is 1 centimeter.

1.
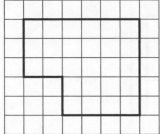

_____ 22 _____ centimeters

2.

_____ centimeters

Problem Solving Real World

Use the drawing for 3–4. Each unit is 1 centimeter.

3. What is the perimeter of Patrick's figure?

    _____

4. How much greater is the perimeter of Jillian's shape than the perimeter of Patrick's figure?

    _____

Patrick's Figure

Jillian's Figure

5. **WRITE** ▸*Math* Draw a rectangle and another figure that is not a rectangle by tracing lines on grid paper. Describe how to find the perimeter of both figures.

    _____

    _____

Lesson Check

1. Find the perimeter of the figure. Each unit is 1 centimeter.

_____

2. Find the perimeter of the figure. Each unit is 1 centimeter.

_____

Spiral Review

3. Order the fractions from least to greatest.

    $$\frac{2}{4}, \frac{2}{3}, \frac{2}{6}$$

_____

4. Kasey's school starts at the time shown on the clock. What time does Kasey's school start?

_____

5. Compare. Write $<$, $>$, or $=$.

    $$\frac{4}{8} \bigcirc \frac{3}{8}$$

6. Aiden wants to find the mass of a bowling ball. Which unit should he use?

_____

FOR MORE PRACTICE
GO TO THE
Personal Math Trainer

Name _____

Find Perimeter

Essential Question How can you measure perimeter?

Learning Objective You will use rulers to estimate and measure the perimeter of figures in inches and centimeters.

You can estimate and measure perimeter in standard units, such as inches and centimeters.

 Unlock the Problem

Find the perimeter of the cover of a notebook.

🔓 **Activity** **Materials** ■ inch ruler

STEP 1 Estimate the perimeter of a notebook in inches. Record your estimate. _____ inches

STEP 2 Use an inch ruler to measure the length of each side of the notebook to the nearest inch.

STEP 3 Record and add the lengths of the sides measured to the nearest inch.

_____ + _____ + _____ + _____ = _____

So, the perimeter of the notebook cover measured to the nearest inch is _____ inches.

Math Talk Math Processes and Practices ①

Evaluate How does your estimate compare with your measurement?

Try This! Find the perimeter.

Use an inch ruler to find the length of each side.	Use a centimeter ruler to find the length of each side.
Add the lengths of the sides:	Add the lengths of the sides:
____ + ____ + ____ + ____ = ____	____ + ____ + ____ + ____ = ____
The perimeter is ____ inches.	The perimeter is ____ centimeters.

Share and Show

1. Find the perimeter of the triangle in inches.

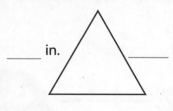

_____ in. _____ in.   **Think:** How long is each side?

_____ in.

_____ inches

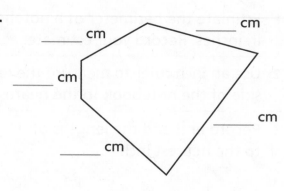

Math Talk

Math Processes and Practices ②

Reason Abstractly How do you use addition to find the perimeter of a figure?

Use a centimeter ruler to find the perimeter.

2.

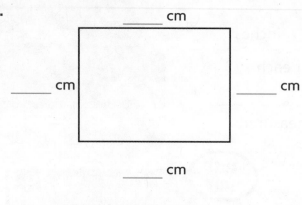

_____ cm

_____ cm   _____ cm

_____ cm

_____ centimeters

✓3.

_____ cm

_____ cm

_____ cm

_____ cm

_____ cm

_____ centimeters

Use an inch ruler to find the perimeter.

4.

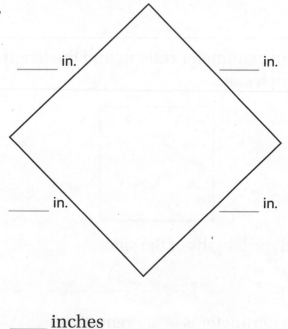

_____ in.   _____ in.

_____ in.   _____ in.

_____ inches

✓5.

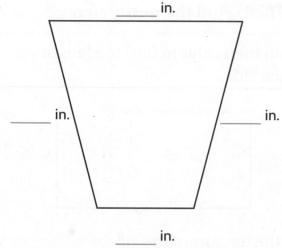

_____ in.

_____ in.   _____ in.

_____ in.

_____ inches

Name _____

Use a ruler to find the perimeter.

6.

_____ in.

_____ in.

_____ in.

_____ in.

_____ inches

7.

_____ cm

_____ cm

_____ cm

_____ cm

_____ cm

_____ cm

_____ centimeters

8. **Math Processes and Practices** ④ **Model Mathematics** Use the grid paper to draw a figure that has a perimeter of 24 centimeters. Label the length of each side.

← 1 cm

Problem Solving • Applications

Use the photos for 9–10.

5 in.

9. Which of the animal photos has a perimeter of 26 inches?

8 in.   8 in.   4 in.   4 in.

_____

5 in.   7 in.

10. **GO DEEPER** How much greater is the perimeter of the bird photo than the perimeter of the cat photo?

WRITE ▸ Math • **Show Your Work**

_____

11. **THINK SMARTER** Erin is putting a fence around her square garden. Each side of her garden is 3 meters long. The fence costs $5 for each meter. How much will the fence cost?

_____

12. **WRITE** ▸Math Gary's garden is shaped like a rectangle with two pairs of sides of equal length, and it has a perimeter of 28 feet. Explain how to find the lengths of the other sides if one side measures 10 feet.

_____

_____

_____

_____

13. **THINK SMARTER** Use an inch ruler to measure this sticker to the nearest inch. Then write an equation you can use to find its perimeter.

_____

Find Perimeter

Learning Objective You will use rulers to estimate and measure the perimeter of figures in inches and centimeters.

Use a ruler to find the perimeter.

1.

_4_ cm

_3_ cm   _3_ cm

_2_ cm

___12___ centimeters

2.

____ cm

____ cm

____ cm

____ cm

____ cm

_____ centimeters

Problem Solving Real World

Draw a picture to solve 3–4.

3. Evan has a square sticker that measures 5 inches on each side. What is the perimeter of the sticker?

_____

4. Sophie draws a shape that has 6 sides. Each side is 3 centimeters. What is the perimeter of the shape?

_____

5. **WRITE** ▸Math Draw two different figures that each have a perimeter of 20 units.

_____

Lesson Check

Use an inch ruler for 1–2.

1. Ty cut a label the size of the shape shown. What is the perimeter, in inches, of Ty's label?

_____

2. Julie drew the shape shown below. What is the perimeter, in inches, of the shape?

_____

Spiral Review

3. What is the perimeter of the shape below?

_____

4. Vince arrives for his trumpet lesson after school at the time shown on the clock. What time does Vince arrive for his trumpet lesson?

_____

5. Matthew's small fish tank holds 12 liters. His large fish tank holds 25 liters. How many more liters does his large fish tank hold?

_____

6. Compare. Write <, >, or =.

$$\frac{1}{6} \bigcirc \frac{1}{4}$$

FOR MORE PRACTICE
GO TO THE
Personal Math Trainer

Algebra • Find Unknown Side Lengths

Essential Question How can you find the unknown length of a side in a plane figure when you know its perimeter?

Learning Objective You will find an unknown side length when you know the perimeter of a figure.

 Unlock the Problem *Real World*

Chen has 27 feet of fencing to put around his garden. He has already used the lengths of fencing shown. How much fencing does he have left for the last side?

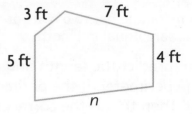

🔑 **Find the unknown side length.**

Write an equation for the perimeter.

$5 + 3 +$ ___ $+$ ___ $+ n = 27$

Think: If I knew the length n, I would add all the side lengths to find the perimeter.

$5 + 3 + 7 + 4 + n = 27$

Add the lengths of the sides you know.

$+ n = 27$

Think: Addition and subtraction are inverse operations.

Write a related equation.

$n = 27 - 19$

So, Chen has _____ feet of fencing left.

_____ $= 27 - 19$

Try This!

The perimeter of the figure is 24 meters. Find the unknown side length, w.

___ $+$ ___ $+$ ___ $+$ ___ $+$ ___ $+ w =$ ___

___ $+ w =$ ___

$w =$ ___ $-$ ___

___ $=$ ___ $-$ ___

So, the unknown side length, w, is ___ meters.

🔑 Example Find unknown side lengths of a rectangle.

Lauren has a rectangular blanket. The perimeter is 28 feet. The width of the blanket is 5 feet. What is the length of the blanket?

Hint: A rectangle has two pairs of opposite sides that are equal in length.

You can predict the length and add to find the perimeter. If the perimeter is 28 feet, then that is the correct length.

5 ft

l   *l*

5 ft

Predict	Check	Does it check?
l = 7 feet	5 + ____ + 5 + ____ = ____	**Think:** Perimeter is not 28 feet, so the length does not check.
l = 8 feet	5 + ____ + 5 + ____ = ____	**Think:** Perimeter is not 28 feet, so the length does not check.
l = 9 feet	5 + ____ + 5 + ____ = ____	**Think:** Perimeter is 28 feet, so the length is correct. ✓

So, the length of the blanket is _____ feet.

Try This! Find unknown side lengths of a square.

The square has a perimeter of 20 inches. What is the length of each side of the square?

Think: A square has four sides that are equal in length.

You can multiply to find the perimeter.

s

s   *s*

s

- Write a multiplication equation for the perimeter. $4 \times s = 20$
- Use a multiplication fact you know to solve. $4 \times \underline{\quad} = 20$

So, the length of each side of the square is _____ inches.

Name _____

Find the unknown side lengths.

1. Perimeter = 25 centimeters

    9 + _____ + _____ + n = 25

    _____ + n = 25

    _____ = _____ − _____

9 cm

n 6 cm

3 cm

n = _____ centimeters

---

2. Perimeter = 34 meters

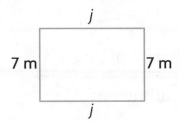

j

7 m   7 m

j

j = _____ meters

3. Perimeter = 12 feet

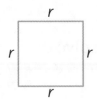

r

r r

r

r = _____ feet

On Your Own

Find the unknown side lengths.

4. Perimeter = 32 centimeters

10 cm

3 cm

6 cm

k

8 cm

k = _____ centimeters

5. THINK SMARTER   Perimeter = 42 feet

g

g g

g g

g

g = _____ feet

---

6. Math Processes and Practices ④ **Use a Diagram** Eleni wants to put up a fence around her square garden. The garden has a perimeter of 28 meters. How long will each side of the fence be? Explain.

a

a a

a

Math Talk   Math Processes and Practices ③

Apply How can you use division to find the length of a side of a square?

_____

_____

Unlock the Problem

7. **GO DEEPER** Latesha wants to make a border with ribbon around a figure she made and sketched at the right. She will use 44 centimeters of ribbon for the border. What is the unknown side length?

3 cm

8 cm

13 cm

6 cm

5 cm

h

a. What do you need to find?

_____

b. How will you use what you know about perimeter to help you solve the problem?

_____

_____

c. Write an equation to solve the problem.

_____

d. So, the length of side *h* is

_____ centimeters.

8. **THINK SMARTER** A rectangle has a perimeter of 34 inches. The left side is 6 inches long. What is the length of the top side?

_____

Personal Math Trainer

9. **THINK SMARTER +** Michael has 40 feet of fencing to make a rectangular dog run for his dog, Buddy. One side of the run will be 5 feet long. For numbers 9a–9d, choose Yes or No to show what the length of another side will be.

9a. 20 feet   ○ Yes   ○ No

9b. 15 feet   ○ Yes   ○ No

9c. 10 feet   ○ Yes   ○ No

9d. 8 feet   ○ Yes   ○ No

Find Unknown Side Lengths

Learning Objective You will find an unknown side length when you know the perimeter of a figure.

Find the unknown side lengths.

1. Perimeter = 33 centimeters

5 cm
x
8 cm
4 cm
7 cm

$5 + 8 + 7 + 4 + x = 33$
$24 + x = 33$
$x = 9$

$x = \underline{\quad 9 \quad}$ centimeters

2. Perimeter = 92 inches

23 in.
7 in.
12 in.
t
12 in.
23 in.

$t = \underline{\qquad}$ inches

Problem Solving (Real World)

3. Steven has a rectangular rug with a perimeter of 16 feet. The width of the rug is 5 feet. What is the length of the rug?

_____

4. Kerstin has a square tile. The perimeter of the tile is 32 inches. What is the length of each side of the tile?

_____

5. WRITE ▸Math Explain how to write and solve an equation to find an unknown side length of a rectangle when given the perimeter.

_____

_____

_____

Lesson Check

1. Jesse is putting a ribbon around a square frame. He uses 24 inches of ribbon. How long is each side of the frame?

2. Davia draws a shape with 5 sides. Two sides are each 5 inches long. Two other sides are each 4 inches long. The perimeter of the shape is 27 inches. What is the length of the fifth side?

Spiral Review

3. What multiplication expression represents $7 + 7 + 7 + 7$?

4. Bob bought 3 packs of model cars. He gave 4 cars to Ann. Bob has 11 cars left. How many model cars were in each pack?

5. Randy read a book in the afternoon. He looked at his watch when he started and finished reading. How long did Randy read?

Start   **End**

6. What fraction and whole number does the model represent?

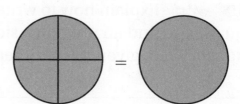

_____ = _____

© Houghton Mifflin Harcourt Publishing Company

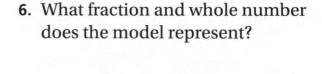

FOR MORE PRACTICE
GO TO THE
Personal Math Trainer

Name _____

Understand Area

Essential Question How is finding the area of a figure different from finding the perimeter of a figure?

Learning Objective You will use dot paper to find the areas of figures by counting the number of unit squares inside a figure and decide when to find area or perimeter for a situation.

🔑 Unlock the Problem

CONNECT You learned that perimeter is the distance around a figure. It is measured in linear units, or units that are used to measure the distance between two points.

Area is the measure of the number of unit squares needed to cover a flat surface. A **unit square** is a square with a side length of 1 unit. It has an area of 1 **square unit**.

Unit Square

Perimeter

1 unit + 1 unit + 1 unit +
1 unit = 4 units

Area

1 square unit

Math Idea
You can count the number of units on each side of a figure to find its perimeter. You can count the number of unit squares inside a figure to find its area in square units.

🔒 Activity **Materials** ■ geoboard ■ rubber bands

A Use your geoboard to form a figure made from 2 unit squares. Record the figure on this dot paper.

· · · · ·
· · · · ·
· · · · ·
· · · · ·
· · · · ·

What is the area of this figure?

Area = _____ square units

B Change the rubber band so that the figure is made from 3 unit squares. Record the figure on this dot paper.

· · · · ·
· · · · ·
· · · · ·
· · · · ·
· · · · ·

What is the area of this figure?

Area = _____ square units

Math Talk

Math Processes and Practices ❸

Compare Representations
For B, did your figure look like your classmate's figure?

Try This! Draw three different figures that are each made from 4 unit squares. Find the area of each figure.

Figure 1 Figure 2 Figure 3

Area = _____ square units | Area = _____ square units | Area = _____ square units

- How are the figures the same? How are the figures different?

Share and Show [MATH BOARD] [Hands On]

1. Shade each unit square in the figure shown. Count the unit squares to find the area.

   Area = _____ square units

Count to find the area of the figure.

2.

3.

✔4.

Area = _____ square units | Area = _____ square units | Area = _____ square units

Write *area* or *perimeter* for the situation.

5. buying a rug for a room

✔6. putting a fence around a garden

_____ | _____

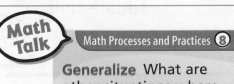

Math Talk — Math Processes and Practices ⑧

Generalize What are other situations where you need to find area?

Name _____

Count to find the area of the figure.

7.

Area = _____ square units

8.

Area = _____ square units

9.

Area = _____ square units

10.

Area = _____ square units

11.

Area = _____ square units

12.

Area = _____ square units

Write *area* or *perimeter* for the situation.

13. painting a wall

_____

14. covering a patio with tiles

_____

15. putting a wallpaper border around a room

_____

16. gluing a ribbon around a picture frame

_____

17. **GO DEEPER** Nicole's mother put tiles on a section of their kitchen floor. The section included 5 rows with 4 tiles in each row. Each tile cost $2. How much money did Nicole's mother spend on the tiles?

_____

Problem Solving · Applications

Juan is building an enclosure for his small dog, Eli. Use the diagram for 18–19.

Eli's Enclosure

18. Juan will put fencing around the outside of the enclosure. How much fencing does he need for the enclosure?

_____

19. **Math Processes and Practices 5** **Use Appropriate Tools** Juan will use grass sod to cover the ground in the enclosure. How much grass sod does Juan need?

_____

20. **THINK SMARTER** Draw two different figures, each with an area of 10 square units.

21. **THINK SMARTER** What is the perimeter and area of this figure? Explain how you found the answer.

Perimeter _____ units

Area _____ square units

_____

_____

_____

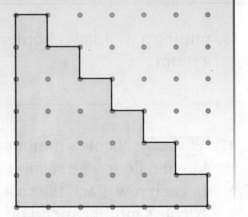

Understand Area

Learning Objective You will use dot paper to find the areas of figures by counting the number of unit squares inside a figure and decide when to find area or perimeter for a situation.

Count to find the area for the shape.

1.

Area = ___6___ square units

2.

Area = _____ square units

3.

Area = _____ square units

Write *area* or *perimeter* for each situation.

4. carpeting a floor

5. fencing a garden

_____

_____

Use the diagram for 6–7.

6. Roberto is building a platform for his model railroad. What is the area of the platform?

_____

7. Roberto will put a border around the edges of the platform. How much border will he need?

_____

8. **WRITE** ▸*Math* Draw a rectangle using dot paper. Find the area, and explain how you found your answer.

_____

Lesson Check

1. Josh used rubber bands to make the shape below on his geoboard. What is the area of the shape?

_____

2. Wilma drew the shape below on dot paper. What is the area of the shape she drew?

_____

Spiral Review

3. Leonardo knows it is 42 days until summer break. How many weeks is it until Leonardo's summer break? (Hint: There are 7 days in a week.)

_____

4. Nan cut a submarine sandwich into 4 equal parts and ate one part. What fraction represents the part of the sandwich Nan ate?

_____

5. Wanda is eating breakfast at fifteen minutes before eight. What time is this? Use A.M. or P.M.

_____

6. Dick has 2 bags of dog food. Each bag contains 5 kilograms of food. How many kilograms of food does Dick have in all?

_____

FOR MORE PRACTICE GO TO THE Personal Math Trainer

Name _____

Measure Area

Essential Question How can you find the area of a plane figure?

Learning Objective You will use square tiles to measure then count unit squares to find the areas of figures.

🔑 Unlock the Problem

Jaime is measuring the area of the rectangles with 1-inch square tiles.

1 square inch

🤚 Activity 1 **Materials** ■ 1-inch grid paper ■ scissors

Cut out eight 1-inch squares. Use the dashed lines as guides to place tiles for *A–C*.

A Place 4 tiles on Rectangle *A*.

- Are there any gaps? _____

- Are there any overlaps? _____

- Jaime says that the area is 4 square inches. Is Jaime's measurement correct? _____

So, when you measure area, there can be no space between the tiles, or no gaps.

Rectangle *A*

B Place 8 tiles on Rectangle *B*.

- Are there any gaps? _____

- Are there any overlaps? _____

- Jaime says that the area is 8 square inches. Is Jaime's measurement correct? _____

So, when you measure the area, the tiles cannot overlap.

Rectangle *B*

C Place 6 tiles on Rectangle C.

- Are there any gaps? _____

- Are there any overlaps? _____

- Jaime says that the area is 6 square inches. Is Jaime's measurement correct? _____

So, the area of the rectangles is

_____ square inches.

Rectangle *C*

Activity 2 Materials ■ green and blue paper ■ scissors

STEP 1 Estimate the number of blue square tiles it will take to cover the gray figure.

_____ blue square tiles

STEP 2 Estimate the number of green tiles it will take to cover the gray figure.

_____ green square tiles

STEP 3 Trace the blue square pattern ten times and cut out the squares.

STEP 4 Trace the green square pattern thirty-six times and cut out the squares.

STEP 5 Cover the gray figure with blue square tiles. Count and write the number of blue square tiles you used. Record the area of the figure.

_____ blue square tiles

Area = _____ blue square units

STEP 6 Cover the gray figure with green square tiles. Count and write the number of green square tiles you used. Record the area of the figure.

_____ green square tiles

Area = _____ green square units

Math Talk

Math Processes and Practices ⑦

Identify Relationships Explain why the number of green square tiles needed to cover the figure is different than the number of blue square tiles needed.

Try This! Count to find the area of the figure.

[ ] is 1 square centimeter.

There are _____ unit squares in the figure.

So, the area is _____ square centimeters.

1				
2				

Name _____

1. Count to find the area of the figure. Each unit square is 1 square centimeter.

Think: Are there any gaps? Are there any overlaps?

There are _____ unit squares in the figure.

So, the area is _____ square centimeters.

Count to find the area of the figure. Each unit square is 1 square centimeter.

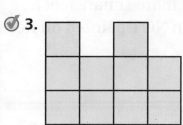

Math Talk

Math Processes and Practices ②

Use Reasoning How can you use square centimeters to find the area of different figures?

2.

Area = _____ square centimeters

3.

Area = _____ square centimeters

On Your Own

Count to find the area of the figure. Each unit square is 1 square inch.

4.

Area = _____ square inches

5.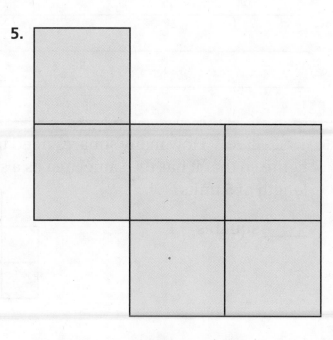

Area = _____ square inches

Problem Solving • Applications

6. **Math Processes and Practices ④** **Use a Diagram** Danny is placing tiles on the floor of an office lobby. Each tile is 1 square meter. The diagram shows the lobby. What is the area of the lobby?

_____

7. **GoDEEPER** Angie is painting a space shuttle mural on a wall. Each section is one square foot. The diagram shows the unfinished mural. How many more square feet has Angie painted than NOT painted on her mural?

_____

Rectangle A

8. **THINK SMARTER** You measure the area of a table top with blue unit squares and green unit squares. Which unit square will give you a greater number of square units for area? **Explain.**

_____

_____

_____

_____

9. **THINK SMARTER** How many squares need to be added to this figure so that it has the same area as a square with a side length of 5 units?

_____ squares

Measure Area

Learning Objective You will use square tiles to measure then count unit squares to find the areas of figures.

Count to find the area of the shape.
Each unit square is 1 square centimeter.

1.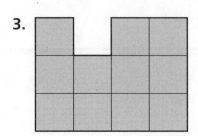

Area = ___14___ square centimeters

2.

Area = _____ square centimeters

3.

Area = _____ square centimeters

4.

Area = _____ square centimeters

Problem Solving

Alan is painting his deck gray. Use the diagram at the right for 5. Each unit square is 1 square meter.

Alan's Deck

5. What is the area of the deck that Alan has already painted gray?

_____

6. **WRITE** ▸*Math* Explain how to find the area of a figure using square tiles.

_____

_____

Lesson Check

Each unit square in the diagram is 1 square foot.

1. How many square feet are shaded?

   _____

2. What is the area that has NOT been shaded?

   _____

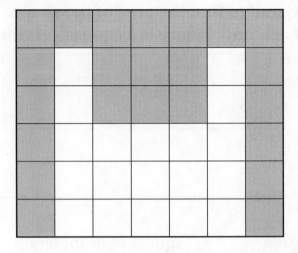

Spiral Review

3. Sonya buys 6 packages of rolls. There are 6 rolls in each package. How many rolls does Sonya buy?

   _____

4. Charlie mixed 6 liters of juice with 2 liters of soda to make fruit punch. How many liters of fruit punch did Charlie make?

   _____

5. What fraction of the circle is shaded?

6. Use the model on the right to name a fraction that is equivalent to $\frac{1}{2}$.

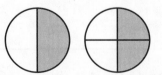

   _____   _____

FOR MORE PRACTICE GO TO THE Personal Math Trainer

Name _____

Use Area Models

Essential Question Why can you multiply to find the area of a rectangle?

Learning Objective You will find the area of a rectangle with whole-number side lengths by modeling with unit squares and by multiplying side lengths.

🔑 Unlock the Problem

Cristina has a garden that is shaped like the rectangle below. Each unit square represents 1 square meter. What is the area of her garden?

• Circle the shape of the garden.

🔑 One Way Count unit squares.

Count the number of unit squares in all.

There are _____ unit squares.

So, the area is _____ square meters.

🔑 Other Ways

A Use repeated addition.

Count the number of rows. Count the number of unit squares in each row.

_____ rows of _____ = ▪

Write an addition equation.

So, the area is _____ square meters.

_____ unit squares

_____ unit squares

_____ unit squares

_____ + _____ + _____ = _____

B Use multiplication.

Count the number of rows. Count the number of unit squares in each row.

_____ rows of _____ = ▪

This rectangle is like an array. How do you find the total number of squares in an array?

_____

Write a multiplication equation.

So, the area is _____ square meters.

_____ unit squares in each row

_____ rows

_____ × _____ = _____

Math Talk

Math Processes and Practices ①

Analyze Can you use all 3 methods mentioned to find the area of all figures?

Try This!

Find the area of the figure.
Each unit square is 1 square foot.

Think: There are 4 rows of 10 unit squares.

_____ × _____ = _____

So, the area is _____ square feet.

Share and Show

1. Look at the figure.

   _____ rows of _____ =

   Add. _____ + _____ + _____ = _____

   Multiply. _____ × _____ = _____

   What is the area of the figure?

   _____ square units

Math Talk

Math Processes and Practices ⑥

Compare Which method do you prefer using?

Find the area of the figure.
Each unit square is 1 square foot.

2.

_____

3.

_____

Find the area of the figure.
Each unit square is 1 square meter.

4.

_____

5.

_____

Name _____

Find the area of the figure.
Each unit square is 1 square foot.

6.

_____

7.

_____

Find the area of the figure.
Each unit square is 1 square meter.

8.

_____

9.

_____

10. (Math Processes and Practices **4**) **Use Diagrams** Draw and shade three rectangles with an area of 24 square units. Then write an addition or multiplication equation for each.

Problem Solving • Applications

11. **GO DEEPER** Compare the areas of the two rugs at the right. Each unit square represents 1 square foot. Which rug has the greater area? Explain.

_____

_____

12. **THINK SMARTER** A tile company tiled a wall using square tiles. A mural is painted in the center. The drawing shows the design. The area of each tile used is 1 square foot.

Write a problem that can be solved by using the drawing. Then solve your problem.

_____

_____

13. **THINK SMARTER** Colleen drew this rectangle. Select the equation that can be used to find the area of the rectangle. Mark all that apply.

Ⓐ $9 \times 6 = n$

Ⓑ $9 + 9 + 9 + 9 + 9 + 9 = n$

Ⓒ $9 + 6 = n$

Ⓓ $6 \times 9 = n$

Ⓔ $6 + 6 + 6 + 6 + 6 + 6 = n$

Lesson Check

1. The entrance to an office has a tiled floor. Each square tile is 1 square meter. What is the area of the floor?

_____

2. Ms. Burns buys a new rug. Each unit square is 1 square foot. What is the area of the rug?

_____

Spiral Review

3. Compare the fractions. Write <, >, or =.

$$\frac{1}{3} \bigcirc \frac{2}{3}$$

4. Claire bought 6 packs of baseball cards. Each pack had the same number of cards. If Claire bought 48 baseball cards in all, how many cards were in each pack?

_____

5. Austin left for school at 7:35 A.M. He arrived at school 15 minutes later. What time did Austin arrive at school?

_____

6. Wyatt's room is a rectangle with a perimeter of 40 feet. The width of the room is 8 feet. What is the length of the room?

_____

FOR MORE PRACTICE
GO TO THE
Personal Math Trainer

Name _____

 Mid-Chapter Checkpoint

Vocabulary

Vocabulary
area
perimeter
square unit

Choose the best term from the box.

1. The distance around a figure is the _____. (p. 625)

2. The measure of the number of unit squares needed to cover a figure with no gaps or overlaps is the _____. (p. 643)

Concepts and Skills

Find the perimeter of the figure. Each unit is 1 centimeter.

3.

_____ centimeters

4.

_____ centimeters

Find the unknown side lengths.

5. Perimeter = 33 centimeters

10 cm
4 cm
6 cm
g
10 cm

g = _____ centimeters

6. Perimeter = 32 feet

12 ft
k   k
12 ft

k = _____ feet

Find the area of the figure. Each unit square is 1 square meter.

7.

_____ square meters

8.

_____ square meters   **Chapter 11 661**

© Houghton Mifflin Harcourt Publishing Company

9. Ramona is making a lid for her rectangular jewelry box. The jewelry box has side lengths of 6 centimeters and 4 centimeters. What is the area of the lid Ramona is making?

6 cm

4 cm

_____

10. Adrienne is decorating a square picture frame. She glued 36 inches of ribbon around the edge of the frame. What is the length of each side of the picture frame?

a

a   *a*

a

_____

11. Margo will sweep a room. A diagram of the floor that she needs to sweep is shown at the right. What is the area of the floor?

_____

12. Jeff is making a poster for a car wash for the Campout Club. What is the perimeter of the poster?

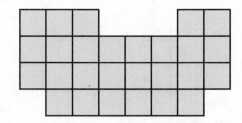

3 ft

1 ft   CAMPOUT CLUB CAR WASH   1 ft

3 ft

_____

13. GO DEEPER   A rectangle has two side lengths of 8 inches and two side lengths of 10 inches. What is the perimeter of the rectangle? What is the area of the rectangle?

_____

Name _____

Problem Solving • Area of Rectangles

Essential Question How can you use the strategy *find a pattern* to solve area problems?

Learning Objective You will use the strategy *find a pattern* to solve area problems by recording measurement data in a table and looking for a pattern of change in the relationships.

🔑 Unlock the Problem

Mr. Koi wants to build storage buildings, so he drew plans for the buildings. He wants to know how the areas of the buildings are related. How does the area change from the area of Building *A* to the area of Building *B*? How does the area change from the area of Building *C* to the area of Building *D*?

Use the graphic organizer to help you solve the problem.

Read the Problem

What do I need to find?	**What information do I need to use?**	**How will I use the information?**
I need to find how the areas will change from *A* to *B* and from _____ to _____.	I need to use the _____ and _____ of each building to find its area.	I will record the areas in a table. Then I will look for a pattern to see how the _____ will change.

Solve the Problem

I will complete the table to find patterns to solve the problem.

	Length	Width	Area		Length	Width	Area
Building *A*	3 ft			Building *C*		4 ft	
Building *B*	3 ft			Building *D*		8 ft	

I see that the lengths will be the same and the widths will be doubled.

The areas will change from _____ to _____ and from _____ to _____.

So, when the lengths are the same and the widths are doubled,

the areas will be _____.

🔒 Try Another Problem

Mr. Koi is building more storage buildings. He wants to know how the areas of the buildings are related. How does the area change from the area of Building *E* to the area of Building *F*? How does the area change from the area of Building *G* to the area of Building *H*?

Use the graphic organizer to help you solve the problem.

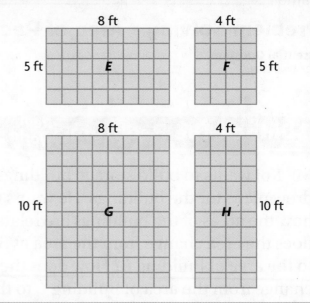

Read the Problem

What do I need to find?	What information do I need to use?	How will I use the information?

Solve the Problem

	Length	Width	Area		Length	Width	Area
Building *E*				Building *G*			
Building *F*				Building *H*			

- How did your table help you find a pattern?

_____

_____

_____

Math Talk

Math Processes and Practices ②

Reason Abstractly
What if the length of both sides is doubled? How would the areas change?

Name _____

Use the table for 1–2.

1. Many pools come in rectangular shapes. How do the areas of the swimming pools change when the widths change?

   First, complete the table by finding the area of each pool.

   Think: I can find the area by multiplying the length and the width.

   Then, find a pattern of how the lengths change and how the widths change.

   The _____ stays the same. The widths

   _____.

   Last, describe a pattern of how the area changes.

   The areas _____ by _____ square feet.

Swimming Pool Sizes			
Pool	Length (in feet)	Width (in feet)	Area (in square feet)
A	8	20	
B	8	30	
C	8	40	
D	8	50	

2. What if the length of each pool was 16 feet? Explain how the areas would change.

   _____

   _____

3. **Math Processes and Practices ⑦** **Look for a Pattern** If the length of each pool in the table is 20 feet, and the widths change from 5, to 6, to 7, and to 8 feet, describe the pattern of the areas.

   _____

   _____

4. **Math Processes and Practices ①** **Analyze Relationships** Jacob has a rectangular garden with an area of 56 square feet. The length of the garden is 8 feet. What is the width of the garden?

_____

5. **GODEEPER** A diagram of Paula's bedroom is at the right. Her bedroom is in the shape of a rectangle. Write the measurements for the other sides. What is the perimeter of the room? (Hint: The two pairs of opposite sides are equal lengths.)

17 ft

12 ft

_____

6. **THINKSMARTER** Elizabeth built a sandbox that is 4 feet long and 4 feet wide. She also built a flower garden that is 4 feet long and 6 feet wide and a vegetable garden that is 4 feet long and 8 feet wide. How do the areas change?

_____

_____

_____

7. **THINKSMARTER** Find the pattern and complete the chart.

Total Area (in square feet)	50	60	70	80	
Length (in feet)	10	10		10	
Width (in feet)	5	6	7		

How can you use the chart to find the length and width of a figure with an area of 100 square feet?

_____

_____

Problem Solving • Area of Rectangles

Learning Objective You will use the strategy *find a pattern* to solve area problems by recording measurement data in a table and looking for a pattern of change in the relationships.

Use the information for 1–3.

An artist makes rectangular murals in different sizes. Below are the available sizes. Each unit square is 1 square meter.

A   B   C   D

1. Complete the table to find the area of each mural.

Mural	Length (in meters)	Width (in meters)	Area (in square meters)
A	2	1	2
B	2	2	4
C	2		
D	2		

2. Find and describe a pattern of how the length changes and how the width changes for murals A through D.

_____

_____

3. How do the areas of the murals change when the width changes?

4. **WRITE** ▸*Math* Write and solve an area problem that illustrates the use of the *find a pattern* strategy.

_____

_____

Lesson Check

1. Lauren drew the designs below. Each unit square is 1 square centimeter. If the pattern continues, what will be the area of the fourth figure?

_____

_____

2. Henry built one garden that is 3 feet wide and 3 feet long. He also built a garden that is 3 feet wide and 6 feet long, and a garden that is 3 feet wide and 9 feet long. How do the areas change?

_____

_____

Spiral Review

3. Joe, Jim, and Jack share 27 football cards equally. How many cards does each boy get?

_____

4. Nita uses $\frac{1}{3}$ of a carton of 12 eggs. How many eggs does she use?

_____

5. Brenda made 8 necklaces. Each necklace has 10 large beads. How many large beads did Brenda use to make the necklaces?

_____

6. Neal is tiling his kitchen floor. Each square tile is 1 square foot. Neal uses 6 rows of tiles with 9 tiles in each row. What is the area of the floor?

_____

© Houghton Mifflin Harcourt Publishing Company

FOR MORE PRACTICE GO TO THE Personal Math Trainer

Area of Combined Rectangles

Essential Question How can you break apart a figure to find the area?

Learning Objective You will use the Distributive Property or a break apart strategy to find the areas of combined rectangles by adding the area of smaller rectangles to find the total area.

 Unlock the Problem

Anna's rug has side lengths of 4 feet and 9 feet. What is the area of Anna's rug?

 Activity **Materials** ■ square tiles

STEP 1 Use square tiles to model 4 × 9.

STEP 2 Draw a rectangle on the grid paper to show your model.

Remember

You can use the Distributive Property to break apart an array.

3 × 3 = 3 × (2 + 1)

STEP 3 Draw a vertical line to break apart the model to make two smaller rectangles.

The side length 9 is broken into _____ plus _____.

STEP 4 Find the area of each of the two smaller rectangles.

Rectangle 1: _____ × _____ = _____

Rectangle 2: _____ × _____ = _____

STEP 5 Add the products to find the total area.

_____ + _____ = _____ square feet

STEP 6 Check your answer by counting the number of square feet.

_____ square feet

So, the area of Anna's rug is _____ square feet.

Math Talk Math Processes and Practices ⑥

Compare Did you draw a line in the same place as your classmates? Explain why you found the same total area.

CONNECT Using the Distributive Property, you found that you could break apart a rectangle into smaller rectangles, and add the area of each smaller rectangle to find the total area.

How can you break apart this figure into rectangles to find its area?

One Way Use a horizontal line.

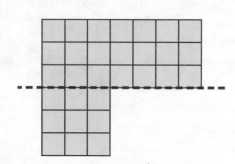

STEP 1 Write a multiplication equation for each rectangle.

Rectangle 1: ___ × ___ = ___

Rectangle 2: ___ × ___ = ___

STEP 2 Add the products to find the total area.

___ + ___ = ___ square units

So, the area is _____ square units.

Another Way Use a vertical line.

STEP 1 Write a multiplication equation for each rectangle.

Rectangle 1: ___ × ___ = ___

Rectangle 2: ___ × ___ = ___

STEP 2 Add the products to find the total area.

___ + ___ = ___ square units

Math Talk Math Processes and Practices ①

Evaluate How can you check your answer?

Share and Show

1. Draw a line to break apart the figure into rectangles. Find the total area of the figure.

Think: I can draw vertical or horizontal lines to break apart the figure to make rectangles.

Rectangle 1: ___ × ___ = ___

Rectangle 2: ___ × ___ = ___

___ + ___ = ___ square units

Name _____

Use the Distributive Property to find the area. Show your multiplication and addition equations.

2.

_____

_____ square units

3.

_____

_____ square units

Use the Distributive Property to find the area. Show your multiplication and addition equations.

4.

_____

_____ square units

5.

_____

_____ square units

Draw a line to break apart the figure into rectangles. Find the area of the figure.

6.

Rectangle 1: ___ × ___ = ___

Rectangle 2: ___ × ___ = ___

___ + ___ = ___ square units

7. **Go DEEPER**

Rectangle 1: ___ × ___ = ___

Rectangle 2: ___ × ___ = ___

Rectangle 3: ___ × ___ = ___

___ + ___ + ___ = ___ square units

Problem Solving • Applications

8. **GO DEEPER** A model of Ms. Lee's classroom is at the right. Each unit square is 1 square foot. Draw a line to break apart the figure into rectangles. What are the areas of the two rectangles? What is the total area of Ms. Lee's classroom?

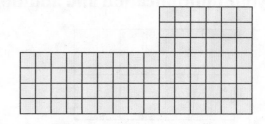

_____

9. David has a rectangular bedroom with a rectangular closet. Each unit square is 1 square foot. Draw a line to break apart the figure into rectangles. What is the total area of David's bedroom?

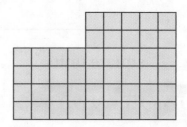

_____

10. **THINK SMARTER** **Explain** how to break apart the figure to find its area.

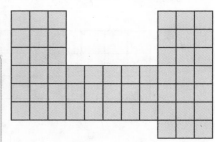

_____

_____

_____

_____

1 unit square = 1 square meter

11. **Math Processes and Practices ④** **Interpret a Result** Use the Distributive Property to find the area of the figure at the right. Write your multiplication and addition equations.

_____

1 unit square = 1 square centimeter

_____

Personal Math Trainer

12. **THINK SMARTER +** Pete drew a diagram of his backyard on grid paper. Each unit square is 1 square meter. The area surrounding the patio is grass.

How much more of the backyard is grass than patio? Show your work.

_____ more square meters

Name _____

Area of Combined Rectangles

Learning Objective You will use the Distributive Property or a break apart strategy to find the areas of combined rectangles by adding the area of smaller rectangles to find the total area.

Use the Distributive Property to find the area. Show your multiplication and addition equations.

1.

    $4 \times 2 = 8; 4 \times 5 = 20$ _____

    $8 + 20 = 28$ _____

    ___28___ square units

2.

    _____

    _____

    _____ square units

Draw a line to break apart the shape into rectangles. Find the area of the shape.

3.

    Rectangle 1: _____ × _____ = _____

    Rectangle 2: _____ × _____ = _____

    _____ + _____ = _____ square units

Problem Solving · Real World

A diagram of Frank's room is at right. Each unit square is 1 square foot.

4. Draw a line to divide the shape of Frank's room into rectangles.

5. What is the total area of Frank's room?

    _____ square feet

6. **WRITE** ▸*Math* Draw a figure that is not a rectangle and find its area. Use grid paper and show each step.

_____

_____

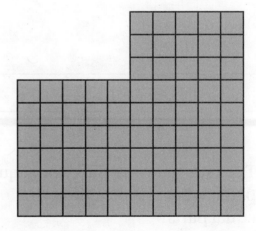

Lesson Check

1. The diagram shows Ben's backyard.
   Each unit square is 1 square yard.
   What is the area of Ben's backyard?

_____

2. The diagram shows a room in an art
   gallery. Each unit square is 1 square
   meter. What is the area of the room?

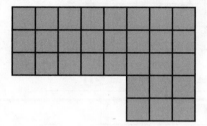

_____

Spiral Review

3. Naomi needs to solve $28 \div 7 = \blacksquare$.
   What related multiplication fact
   can she use to find the unknown
   number?

_____

_____

4. Karen drew a triangle with side
   lengths 3 centimeters, 4 centimeters,
   and 5 centimeters. What is the
   perimeter of the triangle?

_____

_____

5. The rectangle is divided into equal
   parts. What is the name of the
   equal parts?

_____

6. Use an inch ruler. To the nearest half
   inch, how long is this line segment?

├─────────────────┤

_____

Name _____

Same Perimeter, Different Areas

Essential Question How can you use area to compare rectangles with the same perimeter?

Learning Objective You will use square tiles and grid paper to identify and draw rectangles with the same perimeter and tell which rectangle has a greater area.

⚿ Unlock the Problem

Toby has 12 feet of boards to put around a rectangular sandbox. How long should he make each side so that the area of the sandbox is as large as possible?

- What is the greatest perimeter Toby can make for his sandbox?

_____

🔓 Activity

Materials ■ square tiles

Use square tiles to make all the rectangles you can that have a perimeter of 12 units. Draw and label the sandboxes. Then find the area of each.

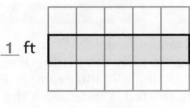

Sandbox 1

<u>1</u> ft

<u>5</u> ft

Sandbox 2

__ ft

__ ft

Sandbox 3

__ ft

__ ft

Find the perimeter and area of each rectangle.

	Perimeter	Area
Sandbox 1	<u>5</u> + <u>1</u> + <u>5</u> + <u>1</u> = <u>12</u> feet	<u>1</u> × <u>5</u> = ___ square feet
Sandbox 2	___ + ___ + ___ + ___ = ___ feet	___ × ___ = ___ square feet
Sandbox 3	___ + ___ + ___ + ___ = ___ feet	___ × ___ = ___ square feet

The area of Sandbox _____ is the greatest.

So, Toby should build a sandbox that is

_____ feet wide and _____ feet long.

Math Talk

Math Processes and Practices ⑥

Compare How are the sandboxes alike? How are the sandboxes different?

🔑 Examples Draw rectangles with the same perimeter and different areas.

Ⓐ Draw a rectangle that has a perimeter of 20 units and an area of 24 square units.

The sides of the rectangle measure

____ units and ____ units.

Ⓑ Draw a rectangle that has a perimeter of 20 units and an area of 25 square units.

The sides of the rectangle measure

____ units and ____ units.

Math Talk   Math Processes and Practices ③

Compare Representations
Explain how the perimeters of Example *A* and Example *B* are related. Explain how the areas are related.

Share and Show   MATH BOARD

1. The perimeter of the rectangle at the right is

____ units. The area is ____ square units.

2. Draw a rectangle that has the same perimeter as the rectangle in Exercise 1 but with a different area.

3. The area of the rectangle in Exercise 2 is

____ square units.

✓ 4. Which rectangle has the greater area?

_____

5. If you were given a rectangle with a certain perimeter, how would you draw it so that it has the greatest area?

_____

Math Talk   Math Processes and Practices ⑥

Explain how you knew what the rectangle for Exercise 5 would look like.

Name _____

**Find the perimeter and the area. Tell which
rectangle has a greater area.**

 6.

A

B

A: Perimeter = _____ ; Area = _____

B: Perimeter = _____ ; Area = _____

Rectangle _____ has a greater area.

On Your Own

**Find the perimeter and the area. Tell which
rectangle has a greater area.**

7.

A

B

8.

B

A

A: Perimeter = _____ ;

   Area = _____

B: Perimeter = _____ ;

   Area = _____

Rectangle ___ has a greater area.

A: Perimeter = _____ ;

   Area = _____

B: Perimeter = _____ ;

   Area = _____

Rectangle ___ has a greater area.

9. **Math Processes and Practices 6** **Use Math Vocabulary** Todd's flower garden
is 4 feet wide and 8 feet long. If the answer is 32 square
feet, what is the question?

_____

Problem Solving • Applications

10. **THINK SMARTER** Draw a rectangle with the same perimeter as Rectangle C, but with a smaller area. What is the area?

Area = _____

C

11. **THINK SMARTER** Which figure has a perimeter of 20 units and an area of 16 square units?

(A)   (B)   (C)   (D)

Connect to Reading

Cause and Effect

Sometimes one action has an effect on another action. The *cause* is the reason something happens. The *effect* is the result.

12. **GO DEEPER** Sam wanted to print a digital photo that is 3 inches wide and 5 inches long. What if Sam accidentally printed a photo that is 4 inches wide and 6 inches long?

Sam can make a table to understand cause and effect.

Cause	Effect
The wrong size photo was printed.	Each side of the photo is a greater length.

Use the information and the strategy to solve the problems.

a. What effect did the mistake have on the perimeter of the photo?

b. What effect did the mistake have on the area of the photo?

Same Perimeter, Different Areas

Learning Objective You will use square tiles and grid paper to identify and draw rectangles with the same perimeter and tell which rectangle has a greater area.

Find the perimeter and the area.
Tell which rectangle has a greater area.

1.

A

B

A: Perimeter = ____**12 units**____ ;

Area = ____**9 square units**____

B: Perimeter = _____ ;

Area = _____

Rectangle _____ has a greater area.

2.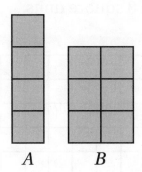

A   B

A: Perimeter = _____ ;

Area = _____

B: Perimeter = _____ ;

Area = _____

Rectangle _____ has a greater area.

Problem Solving · Real World

3. Tara's and Jody's bedrooms are shaped like rectangles. Tara's bedroom is 9 feet long and 8 feet wide. Jody's bedroom is 7 feet long and 10 feet wide. Whose bedroom has the greater area? **Explain**.

_____

_____

4. **WRITE** ▸*Math* Draw three examples of rectangles that have the same perimeter, but different areas. Note which of the areas is greatest and which is the least.

_____

_____

Lesson Check

1. Draw a rectangle that has a perimeter of 12 units and an area of 8 square units.

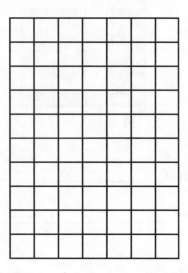

2. Find the perimeter and the area. Tell which rectangle has the greater area.

A

B

A: Perimeter = _____ units

Area = _____ square units

B: Perimeter = _____ units

Area = _____ square units

Rectangle _____ has a greater area.

Spiral Review

3. Kerrie covers a table with 8 rows of square tiles. There are 7 tiles in each row. What is the area that Kerrie covers in square units?

4. Von has a rectangular workroom with a perimeter of 26 feet. The length of the workroom is 6 feet. What is the width of Von's workroom?

FOR MORE PRACTICE GO TO THE Personal Math Trainer

Name _____

Same Area, Different Perimeters

Essential Question How can you use perimeter to compare rectangles with the same area?

Learning Objective You will use square tiles and grid paper to identify and draw rectangles with the same area and tell which rectangle has a greater perimeter.

🔑 Unlock the Problem

Marcy is making a rectangular pen to hold her rabbits. The area of the pen should be 16 square meters with side lengths that are whole numbers. What is the least amount of fencing she needs?

- What does the least amount of fencing represent?

_____

🔓 Activity **Materials** ■ square tiles

Use 16 square tiles to make rectangles. Make as many different rectangles as you can with 16 tiles. Record the rectangles on the grid, write the multiplication equation for the area shown by the rectangle, and find the perimeter of each rectangle.

Math Talk Math Processes and Practices ④

Model Mathematics How did you determine what rectangles to draw?

Area: _____ × _____ = 16 square meters   Perimeter: _____ meters

Area: _____ × _____ = 16 square meters   Perimeter: _____ meters

Area: _____ × _____ = 16 square meters   Perimeter: _____ meters

To use the least amount of fencing, Marcy should make a rectangular

pen with side lengths of _____ meters and _____ meters.

So, _____ meters is the least amount of fencing Marcy needs.

Try This!

Draw three rectangles that have an area of 18 square units on the grid. Find the perimeter of each rectangle. Shade the rectangle that has the greatest perimeter.

Share and Show

1. The area of the rectangle at the right is

   _____ square units. The perimeter is _____ units.

2. Draw a rectangle that has the same area as the rectangle in Exercise 1 but with a different perimeter.

3. The perimeter of the rectangle in Exercise 2 is

   _____ units.

✓ 4. Which rectangle has the greater perimeter?

   _____

5. If you were given a rectangle with a certain area, how would you draw it so that it had the greatest perimeter?

   _____

Math Talk

Math Processes and Practices ③

Compare Representations
Did you and your classmate draw the same rectangle for Exercise 2?

Name _____

Find the perimeter and the area. Tell which rectangle has a greater perimeter.

✓ 6.

A: Area = _____ ; Perimeter = _____

B: Area = _____ ; Perimeter = _____

Rectangle _____ has a greater perimeter.

On Your Own

Find the perimeter and the area. Tell which rectangle has a greater perimeter.

7.
A

B

A: Area = _____ ;

Perimeter = _____

B: Area = _____ ;

Perimeter = _____

Rectangle _____ has a greater perimeter.

8.
A

B

A: Area = _____ ;

Perimeter = _____

B: Area = _____ ;

Perimeter = _____

Rectangle _____ has a greater perimeter.

9. THINK SMARTER **Sense or Nonsense?** Dora says that of all the possible rectangles with the same area, the rectangle with the largest perimeter will have two side lengths that are 1 unit. Does her statement make sense? Explain.

Unlock the Problem (Real World)

10. Roberto has 12 tiles. Each tile is 1 square inch. He will arrange them into a rectangle and glue 1-inch stones around the edge. How can Roberto arrange the tiles so that he uses the least number of stones?

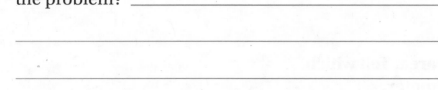

a. **Math Processes and Practices** 6 **Explain a Method** How will you use what you know about area and perimeter to help you solve

the problem? _____

_____

_____

b. **GO DEEPER** Draw possible rectangles to solve the problem, and label them *A*, *B*, and *C*.

_____

_____

c. So, Roberto should arrange

the tiles like Rectangle _____.

11. **THINK SMARTER** Draw 2 different rectangles with an area of 20 square units. What is the perimeter of each rectangle you drew?

Area = 20 square units

Perimeter = _____ units

Perimeter = _____ units

© Houghton Mifflin Harcourt Publishing Company · Image Credits: (tr) ©george doyle/Getty Images; ©Rosemary Calvert/Getty Images

Name _____

Same Area, Different Perimeters

Learning Objective You will use square tiles and grid paper to identify and draw rectangles with the same area and tell which rectangle has a greater perimeter.

Find the perimeter and the area. Tell which rectangle has a greater perimeter.

1.
A

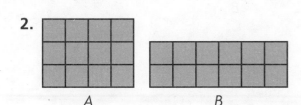
B

A: Area = ___8 square units___ ;

Perimeter = ___18 units___

B: Area = _____ ;

Perimeter = _____

Rectangle _____ has a greater perimeter.

2.

A   B

A: Area = _____ ;

Perimeter = _____

B: Area = _____ ;

Perimeter = _____

Rectangle _____ has a greater perimeter.

Problem Solving Real World

Use the tile designs for 3–4.

3. Compare the areas of Design A and Design B.

_____

_____

Beth's Tile Designs

A

B

4. Compare the perimeters. Which design has the greater perimeter?

_____

5. **WRITE** *Math* Draw two rectangles with different perimeters but the same area.

_____

_____

Lesson Check

1. Jake drew two rectangles. Which rectangle has the greater perimeter?

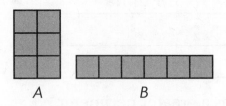

2. Alyssa drew two rectangles. Which rectangle has the greater perimeter?

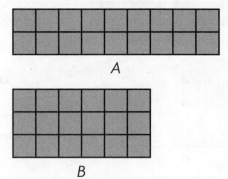

_____

_____

Spiral Review

3. Marsha was asked to find the value of $8 - 3 \times 2$. She wrote a wrong answer. What is the correct answer?

4. What fraction names the point on the number line?

_____

_____

5. Kyle drew three line segments with these lengths: $\frac{2}{4}$ inch, $\frac{2}{3}$ inch, and $\frac{2}{6}$ inch. List the fractions in order from least to greatest.

6. On Monday, $\frac{3}{8}$ inch of snow fell. On Tuesday, $\frac{5}{8}$ inch of snow fell. Write a statement that correctly compares the snow amounts.

_____

_____

Name _____

Personal Math Trainer
Online Assessment
and Intervention

1. Find the perimeter of each figure on the grid. Identify the
    figures that have a perimeter of 14 units. Mark all
    that apply.

Ⓐ   Ⓑ   Ⓒ   Ⓓ

2. Kim wants to put trim around a picture she drew.
    How many centimeters of trim does Kim need for the
    perimeter of the picture?

6 cm
6 cm   6 cm
6 cm

_____ centimeters

3. Sophia drew this rectangle on dot paper. What is the area
    of the rectangle?

_____ square units

© Houghton Mifflin Harcourt Publishing Company

GO
DIGITAL   Assessment Options
           Chapter Test

4. The drawing shows Seth's plan for a fort in his backyard. Each unit square is 1 square foot.

Which equations can Seth use to find the area of the fort? Mark all that apply.

(A) $4 + 4 + 4 + 4 = 16$ (D) $4 \times 4 = 16$

(B) $7 + 4 + 7 + 4 = 22$ (E) $7 \times 7 = 49$

(C) $7 + 7 + 7 + 7 = 28$ (F) $4 \times 7 = 28$

5. Which rectangle has a number of square units for its area equal to the number of units of its perimeter?

(A)

(C)

(B)

(D)

6. Vanessa uses a ruler to draw a square. The perimeter of the square is 12 centimeters. Select a number to complete the sentence.

The square has a side length of
| 3 |
| 4 |
| 5 |
| 6 |
centimeters.

688

Name _____

7. Tomas drew two rectangles on grid paper.

Circle the words that make the sentence true.

A

B

Rectangle *A* has an area that is

less than
the same as
greater than

the area of Rectangle *B*, and a perimeter that is

less than
the same as
greater than

the perimeter of Rectangle *B*.

8. Yuji drew this figure on grid paper. What is the perimeter of the figure?

_____ units

9. What is the area of the figure shown? Each unit square is 1 square meter.

_____ square meters

10. Shawn drew a rectangle that was 2 units wide and 6 units long. Draw a different rectangle that has the same perimeter but a different area.

11. Mrs. Rios put a wallpaper border around the room shown below. She used 72 feet of wallpaper border.

What is the unknown side length? Show your work.

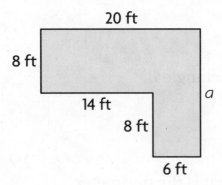

_____ feet

12. Elizabeth has two gardens in her yard. The first garden is 6 feet long and 4 feet wide. The second garden is double the width of the first garden. The area of the second garden is double the area of the first garden. For numbers 12a–12d, select True or False.

12a. The area of the first garden is 24 square feet. ○ True ○ False

12b. The area of the second garden is 48 square feet. ○ True ○ False

12c. The length of the second garden is 12 feet. ○ True ○ False

12d. The length of the second garden is 6 feet. ○ True ○ False

Name _____

13. Marcus bought some postcards. Each postcard had a perimeter of 16 inches. Which could be one of the postcards Marcus bought? Mark all that apply.

(A)   (B)   (C)   (D)

14. **THINK SMARTER +** Anthony wants to make two different rectangular flowerbeds, each with an area of 24 square feet. He will build a wooden frame around each flowerbed. The flowerbeds will have side lengths that are whole numbers.

Part A

Each unit square on the grid below is 1 square foot. Draw two possible flowerbeds. Label each with a letter.

Part B

Which of the flowerbeds will take more wood to frame? Explain how you know.

_____

_____

_____

15. Keisha draws a sketch of her living room on grid paper. Each unit square is 1 square meter. Write and solve a multiplication equation that can be used to find the area of the living room in square meters.

_____

_____ square meters

16. Mr. Wicks designs houses. He uses grid paper to plan a new house design. The kitchen will have an area between 70 square feet and 85 square feet. The pantry will have an area between 4 square feet and 15 square feet. Draw and label a diagram to show what Mr. Wicks could design. Explain how to find the total area.

_____

_____

Big Idea Geometry

BIG IDEA Describe, analyze, and compare two-dimensional shapes. Develop a conceptual understanding of dividing shapes into equal areas and writing the area as a fraction.

Students at Dommerich Elementary helped design and construct a mosaic to show parts of their community and local plants and animals.

Make a Mosaic

Have you ever worked to put puzzle pieces together to make a picture or design? Pieces of paper can be put together to make a colorful work of art called a mosaic.

Get Started | WRITE ▸ Math

Materials ■ construction paper ■ glue ■ ruler ■ scissors

Work with a partner to make a paper mosaic. Use the Important Facts to help you.

- Draw a simple pattern on a piece of paper.

- Cut out shapes, such as rectangles, squares, and triangles of the colors you need from construction paper. The shapes should be about 1 inch on each side.

- Glue the shapes into the pattern. Leave a little space between each shape to make the mosaic effect.

Describe and compare the shapes you used to make your mosaic.

Important Facts

- Mosaics is the art of using small pieces of materials, such as tiles or glass, to make a colorful picture or design.
- Mosaic pieces can be small plane shapes, such as rectangles, squares, and triangles.
- Mosaic designs and patterns can be anything from simple flower shapes to common objects found in your home or patterns in nature.

_____

_____

_____

_____

Completed by _____

✓ **Show What You Know**

Check your understanding of important skills.

Name _____

▶ **Plane Shapes**

1. Color the triangles blue.

2. Color the rectangles red.

▶ **Number of Sides**   Write the number of sides.

3. ___ sides

4. ___ sides

5. Circle the shapes that have 4 or more sides.

Whitney found this drawing that shows 9 small squares. Find larger squares in the drawing. How many squares are there in all? Explain.

Vocabulary Builder

▶ **Visualize It** ••

Complete the tree map by using the words with a ✓.

polygon

▶ **Understand Vocabulary** ••••••••••••••••••••••••••••••••

Draw a line to match the word with its definition.

1. closed shape •

2. line segment •

3. right angle •

4. hexagon •

5. angle •

6. polygon •

• A part of a line that includes two endpoints and all the points between them

• A shape formed by two rays that share an endpoint

• A shape that starts and ends at the same point

• An angle that forms a square corner

• A closed plane shape made up of line segments

• A polygon with 6 sides and 6 angles

Preview Words

angle

closed shape

hexagon

intersecting lines

line

line segment

open shape

parallel lines

perpendicular lines

point

polygon

✓ quadrilateral

ray

✓ rectangle

✓ rhombus

right angle

✓ square

trapezoid

✓ triangle

Venn diagram

vertex

GO DIGITAL
• Interactive Student Edition
• Multimedia eGlossary

angle

ángulo

2

endpoint

extremo

19

intersecting lines

líneas secantes

36

line

línea

42

line segment

segmento

44

octagon

octágono

54

parallel lines

líneas paralelas

56

pentagon

pentágono

58

The point at either end of a line segment

endpoints

A shape formed by two rays that share an endpoint

A straight path extending in both directions with no endpoints

Lines that meet or cross

A polygon with eight sides and eight angles

A part of a line that includes two points, called endpoints, and all of the points between them

A polygon with five sides and five angles

Lines in the same plane that never cross and are always the same distance apart

perpendicular lines

líneas perpendiculares

60

polygon

polígono

64

quadrilateral

cuadrilátero

66

ray

semirrecta

68

rhombus

rombo

71

trapezoid

trapecio

78

Venn diagram

diagrama de Venn

81

vertex

vértice

82

A closed plane shape with straight sides that are line segments

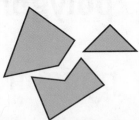

Lines that intersect to form right angles

A part of a line, with one endpoint, that is straight and continues in one direction

A polygon with four sides and four angles

A quadrilateral with at least one pair of parallel sides

A quadrilateral with two pairs of parallel sides and four sides of equal length

The point at which two rays of an angle or two (or more) line segments meet in a plane shape or where three or more edges meet in a solid shape

Examples:

vertex

vertex

A diagram that shows relationships among sets of things

Going to an Art Museum

For 2 players

Materials
- 1 red playing piece
- 1 blue playing piece
- 1 number cube
- Clue Cards

How to Play

1. Choose a playing piece and put it on START.
2. Toss the number cube to take a turn. Move your playing piece that many spaces.
3. If you land on one of these spaces, follow the instructions.

   Blue Space Follow the directions printed in the space.

   Red Space Take a Clue Card from the pile. If you answer the question correctly, keep the Clue Card. If you do not, return the Clue Card to the bottom of the pile.
4. Collect at least 5 Clue Cards. Move around the track as many times as necessary.
5. Only when you have 5 Clue Cards, follow the closest center path to reach FINISH.
6. The first player to reach FINISH wins.

Word Box
- angle
- endpoints
- intersecting lines
- line
- line segment
- octagon
- parallel lines
- pentagon
- perpendicular lines
- polygon
- quadrilateral
- ray
- rhombus
- trapezoid
- Venn diagram
- vertex

TAKE A
CLUE CARD

Your favorite
artist's work is
on display.
Move ahead 1.

FINISH

TAKE A
CLUE CARD

You stand too close
to a painting and
set off the alarms.
Go back 1.

The museum is
closed today.
Go back 1.

TAKE A
CLUE CARD

FINISH

Free tours
today!
Move ahead 1.

TAKE A
CLUE CARD

START ▶

Journal

The Write Way

Reflect

Choose one idea. Write about it.

- In two minutes, draw and label as many examples of polygons that you can. Use a separate piece of paper for your drawing.
- Work with a partner to explain and illustrate parallel, intersecting, and perpendicular lines. Use a separate piece of paper for your drawing.
- A reader of your math advice column writes, "I confuse rhombuses, squares, rectangles, and trapezoids. How can I tell the difference between these quadrilaterals?" Write a letter to your reader offering step-by-step advice.

Name _____

Describe Plane Shapes

Essential Question What are some ways to describe two-dimensional shapes?

Learning Objective You will describe the attributes of two-dimensional shapes and write whether a shape is open or closed.

Unlock the Problem

An architect draws plans for houses, stores, offices, and other buildings. Look at the shapes in the drawing at the right.

A **plane shape** is a shape on a flat surface. It is formed by points that make curved paths, line segments, or both.

point		**line**	
• is an exact position or location	point	• is a straight path • continues in both directions • does not end	
endpoints		**line segment**	
• points that are used to show segments of lines	endpoints	• is straight • is part of a line • has 2 endpoints	

ray

• is straight   • is part of a line   • has 1 endpoint   • continues in one direction

Some plane shapes are made by connecting line segments at their endpoints. One example is a square. Describe a square using math words.

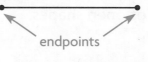

Think: How many line segments and endpoints does a square have?

A square has _____ line segments. The line segments meet only at their _____.

Math Processes and Practices ③

Apply Why can you not measure the length of a line?

Plane shapes have length and width but no thickness, so they are also called **two-dimensional shapes**.

width

length

Try This! Draw plane shapes.

Plane shapes can be open or closed.

A **closed shape** starts and ends at the same point.

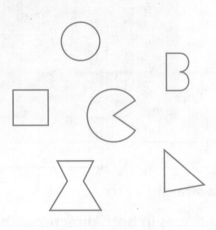

In the space below, draw more examples of closed shapes.

An **open shape** does not start and end at the same point.

In the space below, draw more examples of open shapes.

Math Processes and Practices ⑥

Explain whether a shape with a curved path must be a closed shape, an open shape, or can be either.

- Is the plane shape at the right a closed shape or an open shape? Explain how you know.

_____

_____

Name _____

Share and Show

1. Write how many line segments

   the shape has. _____

Circle all the words that describe the shape.

2.

   ray

   point

3.

   open shape

   closed shape

4.

   open shape

   closed shape

5.

   line

   line segment

Write whether the shape is *open* or *closed*.

6.

_____

7.

_____

8.

_____

9.

_____

> **Math Talk**
>
> Math Processes and Practices ①
>
> **Describe** How do you know whether a shape is open or closed?

On Your Own

Write how many line segments the shape has.

10.

_____ line segments

11.

_____ line segments

12.

_____ line segments

13.

_____ line segments

Write whether the shape is *open* or *closed*.

14.

_____

15.

_____

16.

_____

17.

_____

Problem Solving • Applications

18. **What's the Error?** Brittany says there are two endpoints in the shape shown at the right. Is she correct? Explain.

_____

_____

19. (Math Processes and Practices 6) **Explain** how you can make the shape at the right a closed shape. Change the shape so it is a closed shape.

_____

_____

20. **GO DEEPER** Look at Carly's drawing at the right. What did she draw? How is it like a line? How is it different? Change the drawing so that it is a line.

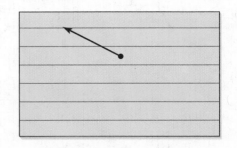

_____

_____

21. **THINK SMARTER** Draw a closed shape in the workspace by connecting 5 line segments at their endpoints.

22. **THINK SMARTER** Draw each shape where it belongs in the table.

Closed Shape	Open Shape

Describe Plane Shapes

Learning Objective You will describe the attributes of two-dimensional shapes and write whether a shape is open or closed.

Write how many line segments the shape has.

1.

___4___ line segments

2.

_____ line segments

Write whether the shape is *open* or *closed*.

3.

_____

4.

_____

5. Carl wants to show a closed shape in his drawing. Show and explain how to make the drawing a closed shape.

_____

_____

6. The shape of a fish pond at a park is shown below. Is the shape open or closed?

_____

7. **WRITE** ▸*Math* Draw an open shape and a closed shape. Label your shapes.

_____

_____

Lesson Check

1. How many line segments does this shape have?

2. What is part of a line, has one endpoint, and continues in one direction?

_____

_____

Spiral Review

3. What multiplication sentence does the array show?

_____

_____

4. What is the unknown factor and quotient?

$9 \times \boxed{} = 27$

$27 \div 9 = \boxed{}$

_____

_____

5. What fraction is equivalent to $\frac{4}{8}$?

6. Mr. MacTavish has 30 students from his class going on a field trip to the zoo. He puts 6 students in each group. How many groups of students will he make?

_____

_____

_____

_____

FOR MORE PRACTICE
GO TO THE
Personal Math Trainer

Describe Angles in Plane Shapes

Essential Question How can you describe angles in plane shapes?

Learning Objective You will describe angles by telling how many of each type of angle a shape has and by measuring to compare an angle measure with the measure of a right angle.

 Unlock the Problem

An **angle** is formed by two rays that share an endpoint. Plane shapes have angles formed by two line segments that share an endpoint. The shared endpoint is called a **vertex**. The plural of *vertex* is *vertices*.

vertex ⟶

Jason drew this shape on dot paper.

- How many angles are in Jason's shape?

_____

Look at the angles in the shape that Jason drew.

How can you describe the angles?

🔑 **Describe angles.**

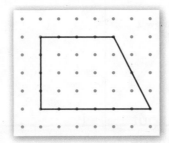

This mark means *right angle*. ⟶

A **right angle** is an angle that forms a square corner.

Some angles are less than a right angle.

Some angles are greater than a right angle.

Look at Jason's shape.

Two angles are _____ angles, _____ angle

is _____ a right angle, and _____ angle

is _____ a right angle.

 Math Talk

Math Processes and Practices ①

Analyze What are some examples of these types of angles that you see in everyday life? Describe where you see them and what types of angles you see.

🔲 Activity Model angles.

Materials ■ bendable straws ■ scissors ■ paper ■ pencil

• Cut a small slit in the shorter section of a bendable straw. Cut off the shorter section of a second straw and the bendable part. Insert the slit end of the first straw into the second straw.

• Make an angle with the straws you put together. Compare the angle you made to a corner of the sheet of paper.

• Open and close the straws to make other types of angles.

In the space below, trace the angles you made with the straws. Label each *right angle, less than a right angle,* or *greater than a right angle.*

Share and Show   MATH BOARD

1. How many angles are in the triangle at the right?

_____

Math Talk   Math Processes and Practices ②

Use Reasoning How do you know an angle is greater than or less than a right angle?

Use the corner of a sheet of paper to tell whether the angle is a *right angle, less than a right angle,* or *greater than a right angle.*

2.

_____

3.

_____

☑4.

_____

Name _____

Write how many of each type of angle the shape has.

5.

_____ right

_____ less than a right

_____ greater than
a right

6.

_____ right

_____ less than a right

_____ greater than
a right

7.

_____ right

_____ less than a right

_____ greater than
a right

On Your Own

Use the corner of a sheet of paper to tell whether the angle is a
right angle, less than a right angle, **or** *greater than a right angle.*

8.

_____

9.

_____

10.

_____

Math Processes and Practices 1 **Analyze Relationships Write how many of each type of angle the shape has.**

11.

_____ right

_____ less than a right

_____ greater than
a right

12.

_____ right

_____ less than a right

_____ greater than
a right

13.

_____ right

_____ less than a right

_____ greater than a right

14. **THINK SMARTER** Describe the types of angles formed when you
divide a circle into 4 equal parts.

_____

Unlock the Problem

15. Holly drew the four shapes below. Which shape does NOT have a right angle?

Q   R   S   T

a. What do you need to know? _____

b. Tell how you might use a sheet of paper to solve the problem.

_____

_____

c. Shape *Q* has _____ right angle(s), _____ angle(s) greater than a right angle, and _____ angle(s) less than a right angle.

Shape *R* has _____ right angle(s), _____ angle(s) greater than a right angle, and _____ angle(s) less than a right angle.

Shape *S* has _____ right angle(s), _____ angle(s) greater than a right angle, and _____ angle(s) less than a right angle.

Shape *T* has _____ right angle(s), _____ angle(s) greater than a right angle, and _____ angle(s) less than a right angle.

So, shape _____ does not have a right angle.

16. THINK SMARTER Circle a number or word from each box to complete the sentence to describe all of the angles in this shape.

There are
| 2 |
| 3 |
| 4 |
right angles and
| 2 |
| 3 |
| 4 |
angles

than a right angle.

Describe Angles in Plane Shapes

Learning Objective You will describe angles by telling how many of each type of angle a shape has and by measuring to compare an angle measure with the measure of a right angle.

Use the corner of a sheet of paper to tell whether the angle is a *right angle, less than a right angle,* or *greater than a right angle.*

1.

   less than a right
   angle
   _____

2.

   _____

3.

   _____

Write how many of each type of angle the shape has.

4.

   _____ right

   _____ less than a right

   _____ greater than
   a right

5.

   _____ right

   _____ less than a right

   _____ greater than
   a right

6.

   _____ right

   _____ less than a right

   _____ greater than
   a right

Problem Solving

7. Jeff has a square piece of art paper. He cuts across it from one corner to the opposite corner to make two pieces. What is the total number of sides and angles in both of the new shapes?

8. **WRITE** *Math* Draw an example of a shape that has at least one right angle, one angle less than a right angle, and one angle greater than a right angle. Label the angles.

_____

_____

_____

_____

Lesson Check

1. What describes this angle?
Write *right angle, less than a right angle,* or *greater than a right angle.*

_____

_____

2. How many right angles does this shape have?

_____

_____

Spiral Review

3. What fraction of the group is shaded?

_____

4. Compare.

$\frac{4}{8}$ ◯ $\frac{3}{8}$

5. What is straight, continues in both directions, and does not end?

_____

6. How many line segments does this shape have?

_____

FOR MORE PRACTICE
GO TO THE
Personal Math Trainer

Name _____

Identify Polygons

Essential Question How can you use line segments and angles to make polygons?

Learning Objective You will use line segments and angles to name and describe polygons by telling the number of sides and the number of angles a shape has.

CONNECT In earlier lessons, you learned about line segments and angles. In this lesson, you will see how line segments and angles make polygons.

A **polygon** is a closed plane shape that is made up of line segments that meet only at their endpoints. Each line segment in a polygon is a **side**.

> **Math Idea**
> All polygons are closed shapes. Not all closed shapes are polygons.

Unlock the Problem

Circle all the words that describe the shape.

A	**B**	**C**	**D**
plane shape	plane shape	plane shape	plane shape
open shape	open shape	open shape	open shape
closed shape	closed shape	closed shape	closed shape
curved paths	curved paths	curved paths	curved paths
line segments	line segments	line segments	line segments
polygon	polygon	polygon	polygon

Try This!

Fill in the blanks with *sometimes*, *always*, or *never*.

Polygons are _____ plane shapes.

Polygons are _____ closed shapes.

Polygons are _____ open shapes.

Plane shapes are _____ polygons.

Math Talk

Math Processes and Practices ②

Reason Abstractly Why are not all closed shapes polygons?

Name Polygons Polygons are named by the number of sides and angles they have.

Some traffic signs are in the shape of polygons. A stop sign is in the shape of which polygon?

angle
side →

🔑 **Count the number of sides and angles.**

triangle	quadrilateral	pentagon
3 sides	4 sides	_____ sides
3 angles	_____ angles	5 angles

hexagon	octagon	decagon
_____ sides	8 sides	_____ sides
6 angles	_____ angles	10 angles

How many sides does the stop sign have? _____

How many angles? _____

So, a stop sign is in the shape of an _____ .

Math Talk

Math Processes and Practices ⑧

Generalize Compare the number of sides and angles. What is a true statement about all polygons?

Share and Show 📝 MATH BOARD

1. The shape at the right is a polygon. Circle all the words that describe the shape.

plane shape   open shape   closed shape   pentagon

curved paths   line segments   hexagon   quadrilateral

710

Name _____

Is the shape a polygon? Write *yes* or *no*.

2.

_____

3.

_____

4.

_____

Math Talk

Math Processes and Practices ③

Apply How can you change the shape in Exercise 4 to make it a polygon?

Write the number of sides and the number of angles. Then name the polygon.

5.

_____ sides

_____ angles

_____

6.

_____ sides

_____ angles

_____

7.

_____ sides

_____ angles

_____

On Your Own

Is the shape a polygon? Write *yes* or *no*.

8.

_____

9.

_____

10.

_____

Write the number of sides and the number of angles. Then name the polygon.

11.

_____ sides

_____ angles

_____

12.

_____ sides

_____ angles

_____

13.

_____ sides

_____ angles

_____

Problem Solving • Applications

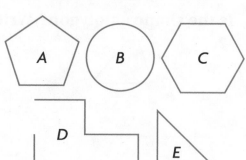

14. **WRITE** ▸*Math* Jake said Shapes *A—E* are all polygons. Does this statement make sense? Explain your answer.

_____

_____

15. **GO DEEPER** I am a closed shape made of 6 line segments. I have 2 angles less than a right angle and no right angles. What shape am I? Draw an example in the workspace.

_____

16. **THINK SMARTER** Is every closed shape a polygon? Use a drawing to help explain your answer.

_____

_____

_____

17. **Math Processes and Practices ③** **Make Arguments** Ivan says that the shape at the right is an octagon. Do you agree or

disagree? Explain. _____

_____

18. **THINK SMARTER** For numbers 18a–18d, select True or False for each description of this shape.

18a. polygon   ○ True   ○ False

18b. open shape   ○ True   ○ False

18c. hexagon   ○ True   ○ False

18d. pentagon   ○ True   ○ False

Identify Polygons

Learning Objective You will use line segments and angles to name and describe polygons by telling the number of sides and the number of angles a shape has.

Is the shape a polygon? Write *yes* or *no*.

1.

   __no__

2.

   _____

Write the number of sides and the number of angles. Then name the polygon.

3.

   _____ sides

   _____ angles

   _____

4.

   _____ sides

   _____ angles

   _____

Problem Solving Real World

5. Mr. Murphy has an old coin that has ten sides. If its shape is a polygon, how many angles does the old coin have?

   _____

6. Lin says that an octagon has six sides. Chris says that it has eight sides. Whose statement is correct?

   _____

7. **WRITE** ▸*Math* Draw a pentagon. Explain how you knew the number of sides and angles to draw.

   _____

   _____

Lesson Check

1. What is a name for this polygon?

_____

2. How many sides does this polygon have?

_____

Spiral Review

3. How many right angles does this shape have?

_____

4. Erica has 8 necklaces. One fourth of the necklaces are blue. How many necklaces are blue?

_____

5. What is straight, is part of a line, and has 2 endpoints?

_____

6. What describes this angle? Write *right angle, less than a right angle,* or *greater than a right angle.*

_____

FOR MORE PRACTICE
GO TO THE
Personal Math Trainer

Name _____

Describe Sides of Polygons

Essential Question How can you describe line segments that are sides of polygons?

Learning Objective You will describe line segments that are sides of polygons and determine whether they appear to be intersecting, perpendicular, or parallel.

Unlock the Problem

Look at the polygon. How many pairs of sides are parallel?

- How do you know the shape is a polygon?

_____

_____

TYPES OF LINES	TYPES OF LINE SEGMENTS
Lines that cross or meet are **intersecting lines**. Intersecting lines form angles.	The orange and blue line segments meet and form an angle. So, they are _____.
Intersecting lines that cross or meet to form right angles are **perpendicular lines**.	The red and blue line segments meet to form a right angle. So, they are _____.
Lines that never cross or meet and are always the same distance apart are **parallel lines**. They do not form any angles.	The green and blue line segments would never cross or meet. They are always the same distance apart. So, they appear to be _____.

So, the polygon above has _____ pair of parallel sides.

 Math Talk

Math Processes and Practices ②

Use Reasoning Why can't parallel lines ever cross?

Try This! Draw a polygon with only 1 pair of parallel sides. Then draw a polygon with 2 pairs of parallel sides. Outline each pair of parallel sides with a different color.

1. Which sides appear to be parallel?

_____

Think: Which pairs of sides appear to be the same distance apart?

Look at the green sides of the polygon. Tell if they appear to be *intersecting*, *perpendicular*, or *parallel*. Write all the words that describe the sides.

2.

_____
_____

☑ 3.

_____
_____

☑ 4.

_____
_____

Math Talk Math Processes and Practices ⑥

Compare How are intersecting and perpendicular lines alike and how are they different?

On Your Own

Look at the green sides of the polygon. Tell if they appear to be *intersecting*, *perpendicular*, or *parallel*. Write all the words that describe the sides.

5.

_____
_____

6.

_____
_____

7.

_____
_____

716

Name _____

Problem Solving • Applications

Use pattern blocks _A–E_ for 8–11.

Chelsea wants to sort pattern blocks by the types of sides.

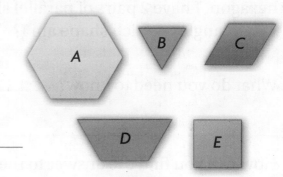

8. Which blocks have intersecting sides?

   _____

9. Which blocks have parallel sides?

   _____

10. Which blocks have perpendicular sides?

    _____

11. Which blocks have neither parallel nor perpendicular sides?

    _____

12. **GO DEEPER** On the box at the right, how many pairs of edges are perpendicular line segments?

    _____

▲ The red line segments show some pairs of perpendicular line segments.

13. **THINK SMARTER** Can the same two lines be parallel, perpendicular, and intersecting? Explain your answer.

    _____

    _____

🔑 Unlock the Problem

14. **Math Processes and Practices ③** **Compare Representations** I am a pattern block that has 2 fewer sides than a hexagon. I have 2 pairs of parallel sides and 4 right angles. Which shape am I?

a. What do you need to know? _____

_____

b. How can you find the answer to the riddle? _____

_____

c. Write *yes* or *no* in the table to solve the riddle.

2 fewer sides than a hexagon						
exactly 2 pairs of parallel sides						
4 right angles						

So, the _____ is the shape.

15. THINK SMARTER Select the shapes that have at least one pair of parallel sides. Mark all that apply.

(A)

(C)

(B)

(D)

Describe Sides of Polygons

Learning Objective You will describe line segments that are sides of polygons and determine whether they appear to be intersecting, perpendicular, or parallel.

Look at the dashed sides of the polygon. Tell if they appear to be *intersecting*, *perpendicular*, or *parallel*. Write all the words that describe the sides.

1.

_____ **parallel**

2.

_____

3.

_____

4.

_____

5.

_____

6.

_____

Problem Solving · Real World

Use shapes *A–D* for 7–8.

7. Which shapes appear to have parallel sides?

_____

8. Which shapes appear to have perpendicular sides?

_____

9. **WRITE** *Math* Give some examples of perpendicular lines inside or outside your classroom.

_____

_____

Lesson Check

1. How many pairs of parallel sides does the quadrilateral appear to have?

_____

2. Which sides appear to be parallel?

_____

Spiral Review

3. Mr. Lance designed a class banner shaped like the polygon shown. What is the name of the polygon?

_____

4. How many angles greater than a right angle does this shape have?

_____

5. How many line segments does this shape have?

6. What fraction names the shaded part?

_____

© Houghton Mifflin Harcourt Publishing Company

FOR MORE PRACTICE
GO TO THE
Personal Math Trainer

Name _____

 Mid-Chapter Checkpoint

Vocabulary

Choose the best term from the box to complete the sentence.

Vocabulary
angle
point
polygon
right angle

1. An _____ is formed by two rays that share an endpoint. (p. 703)

2. A _____ is a closed plane shape made up of line segments. (p. 709)

3. A _____ forms a square corner. (p. 703)

Concepts and Skills

Use the corner of a sheet of paper to tell whether the angle is a *right angle, less than a right angle,* or *greater than a right angle.*

4.

_____

5.

_____

6.

_____

Write the number of sides and the number of angles. Then name the polygon.

7.

____ sides

____ angles

_____

8.

____ sides

____ angles

_____

9.

____ sides

____ angles

_____

© Houghton Mifflin Harcourt Publishing Company

10. Anne drew the shape at the right. Is her shape an open shape or a closed shape?

_____

11. **GO DEEPER** This sign tells drivers there is a steep hill ahead. Write the number of sides and the number of angles in the shape of the sign. Then name the shape.

_____

12. Why is this closed plane shape NOT a polygon?

_____

_____

13. Sean drew a shape with 2 fewer sides than an octagon. Which shape did he draw?

_____

14. John drew a polygon with two line segments that meet to form a right angle. Circle the words that describe the line segments.

intersecting
curved
parallel
perpendicular

Classify Quadrilaterals

Essential Question How can you use sides and angles to help you describe quadrilaterals?

🔑 Unlock the Problem

Quadrilaterals are named by their sides and their angles.

 Describe quadrilaterals.

quadrilateral

_____ sides

_____ angles

> **⚠ ERROR Alert**
>
> Some quadrilaterals cannot be classified as a trapezoid, rectangle, square, or rhombus.

---

trapezoid

at least _____ pair of opposite sides that are parallel
lengths of sides could be the same

---

rectangle

_____ pairs of opposite sides that are parallel

_____ pairs of sides that are of equal length

_____ right angles

square

_____ pairs of opposite sides that are parallel

_____ sides that are of equal length

_____ right angles

rhombus

_____ pairs of opposite sides that are parallel

_____ sides that are of equal length

Math Talk **Math Processes and Practices ⑧**

Generalize Why can a square also be named a rectangle or a rhombus?

Share and Show MATH BOARD

Look at the quadrilateral at the right.

1. Outline each pair of opposite sides that are parallel with a different color. How many pairs of opposite sides appear to be parallel? _____

2. Look at the parallel sides you colored.

   The sides in each pair are of _____ length.

Think: All the angles are right angles.

☑ 3. Name the quadrilateral in as many ways as you can.

   _____

Circle all the words that describe the quadrilateral.

4.

rectangle

rhombus

square

trapezoid

5.

rhombus

quadrilateral

square

rectangle

☑ 6.

rectangle

rhombus

trapezoid

quadrilateral

On Your Own

Math Talk Math Processes and Practices ①

Analyze How can you have a rhombus that is not a square?

Circle all the words that describe the quadrilateral.

7.

rectangle

trapezoid

quadrilateral

rhombus

8.

rectangle

rhombus

trapezoid

square

9.

quadrilateral

square

rectangle

rhombus

Name _____

Problem Solving • Applications

Use the quadrilaterals at the right for 10–12.

10. Which quadrilaterals appear to have 4 right angles?

   _____

11. Which quadrilaterals appear to have 2 pairs of opposite sides that are parallel?

   _____

12. Which quadrilaterals appear to have no right angles?

   _____

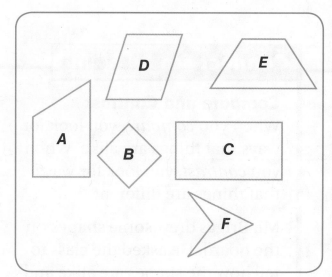

Write *all* or *some* to complete the sentence for 13–18.

13. The opposite sides of _____ rectangles are parallel.

14. _____ sides of a rhombus are the same length.

15. _____ squares are rectangles.

16. _____ rhombuses are squares.

17. _____ quadrilaterals are polygons.

18. _____ polygons are quadrilaterals.

19. **Math Processes and Practices 6** Circle the shape at the right that is not a quadrilateral. **Explain** your choice.

   _____

   _____

   _____

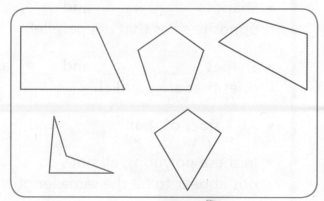

20. **THINK SMARTER** I am a polygon that has 4 sides and 4 angles. At least one of my angles is less than a right angle. Circle all the shapes that I could be.

quadrilateral   rectangle   square   rhombus   trapezoid

21. THINK SMARTER   Identify the quadrilateral that can have two pairs of parallel sides and no right angles.

(A) rhombus   (B) square   (C) rectangle

Connect to Reading

Compare and Contrast

When you *compare*, you look for ways that things are alike. When you *contrast*, you look for ways that things are different.

Mr. Briggs drew some shapes on the board. He asked the class to tell how the shapes are alike and how they are different.

GO DEEPER   **Complete the sentences.**

- Shapes _____, _____, _____, _____, _____, _____, and _____ are polygons.

- Shapes _____, _____, and _____ are not polygons.

- Shapes _____, _____, _____, and _____ are quadrilaterals.

- Shapes _____, _____, and _____ appear to have only 1 pair of opposite sides that are parallel.

- Shapes _____, _____, and _____ appear to have 2 pairs of opposite sides that are parallel.

- All 4 sides of shapes _____ and _____ appear to be the same length.

- In these polygons, all sides do not appear to be the same length. _____

- These shapes can be called rhombuses. _____

- Shapes _____ and _____ are quadrilaterals but cannot be called rhombuses.

- Shape _____ is a rhombus and can be called a square.

Name _____

Classify Quadrilaterals

Learning Objective You will describe, classify, and compare quadrilaterals based on their attributes.

Circle all the words that describe the quadrilateral.

1.

(square)

(rectangle)

(rhombus)

(trapezoid)

2.

square

rectangle

rhombus

trapezoid

3.

square

rectangle

rhombus

trapezoid

Use the quadrilaterals below for 4–6.

A   B   C   D   E

4. Which quadrilaterals appear to have no right angles?

_____

5. Which quadrilaterals appear to have 4 right angles?

_____

6. Which quadrilaterals appear to have 4 sides of equal length?

_____

Problem Solving · Real World

7. A picture on the wall in Jeremy's classroom has 4 right angles, 4 sides of equal length, and 2 pairs of opposite sides that are parallel. What quadrilateral best describes the picture?

_____

_____

8. **WRITE** ▸ Math Explain how a trapezoid and a rectangle are different.

_____

_____

_____

_____

Lesson Check

1. What word describes the quadrilateral?

_____

2. Which quadrilaterals appear to have 2 pairs of opposite sides that are parallel?

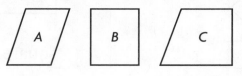

_____

Spiral Review

3. Aiden drew the the polygon shown. What is the name of the polygon he drew?

_____

4. How many pairs of parallel sides does this shape appear to have?

_____

5. What word describes the dashed sides of the shape shown? Write *intersecting*, *perpendicular*, or *parallel*.

_____

6. How many right angles does this shape have?

_____

© Houghton Mifflin Harcourt Publishing Company

FOR MORE PRACTICE
GO TO THE
Personal Math Trainer

Name _____

Draw Quadrilaterals

Essential Question How can you draw quadrilaterals?

Learning Objective You will use grid paper to draw and name quadrilaterals then draw polygons that do not belong in a set of quadrilaterals and explain why.

Unlock the Problem

CONNECT You have learned to classify quadrilaterals by the number of pairs of opposite sides that are parallel, by the number of pairs of sides of equal length, and by the number of right angles.

How can you draw quadrilaterals?

Activity 1 Use grid paper to draw quadrilaterals.

Materials ■ ruler

- Use a ruler to draw line segments from points *A* to *B*, from *B* to *C*, from *C* to *D*, and from *D* to *A*.

- Write the name of your quadrilateral.

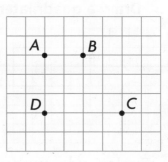

_____

Activity 2 Draw a shape that does not belong.

Materials ■ ruler

A Here are three examples of a quadrilateral. Draw an example of a polygon that is not a quadrilateral.

- Explain why your polygon is not a quadrilateral.

_____

_____

B Here are three examples of a square.
Draw a quadrilateral that is not a square.

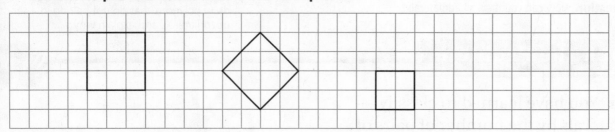

- Explain why your quadrilateral is not a square.

_____

_____

C Here are three examples of a rectangle.
Draw a quadrilateral that is not a rectangle.

- Explain why your quadrilateral is not a rectangle.

_____

_____

D Here are three examples of a rhombus.
Draw a quadrilateral that is not a rhombus.

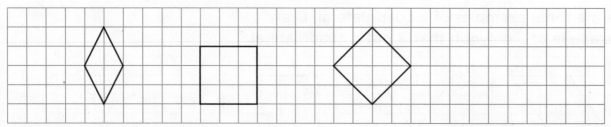

- Explain why your quadrilateral is not a rhombus.

_____

_____

Math Processes and Practices **3**

Compare Representations
Compare your drawings with your classmates. Explain how your drawings are alike and how they are different.

Name _____

Share and Show

1. Choose four endpoints, and connect them to make a rectangle.

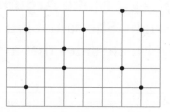

   Think: A rectangle has 2 pairs of opposite sides that are parallel, 2 pairs of sides of equal length, and 4 right angles.

Draw a quadrilateral that is described.
Name the quadrilateral you drew.

2. 2 pairs of sides of equal length

   Name _____

3. 4 sides of equal length

   Name _____

Math Talk

Math Processes and Practices 6

Compare Explain one way the quadrilaterals you drew are alike and one way they are different.

On Your Own

Practice: Copy and Solve Use grid paper to draw a quadrilateral that is described. Name the quadrilateral you drew.

4. exactly 1 pair of opposite sides that are parallel

5. 4 right angles

6. 2 pairs of sides of equal length

Draw a quadrilateral that does not belong. Then explain why.

7.

8.

Problem Solving • Applications (Real World)

9. **Math Processes and Practices ③ Make Arguments** Jacki drew the shape at the right. She said it is a rectangle because it has 2 pairs of opposite sides that are parallel. Describe her error.

_____

_____

10. **GO DEEPER** Adam drew three quadrilaterals. One quadrilateral has no pairs of parallel sides, one quadrilateral has exactly 1 pair of opposite sides that are parallel, and the last quadrilateral has 2 pairs of opposite sides that are parallel. Draw the three quadrilaterals that Adam could have drawn. Name them.

_____   _____   _____

11. **THINK SMARTER** Amy has 4 straws of equal length. Name all the quadrilaterals that can be made using these 4 straws.

_____ Amy cuts one of the straws in half. She uses the two halves and two of the other straws to make a quadrilateral. Name all the quadrilaterals that can be made using these 4 straws.

_____

12. **THINK SMARTER +** Jordan drew one side of a quadrilateral with 2 pairs of opposite sides that are parallel. Draw the other 3 sides to complete Jordan's quadrilateral.

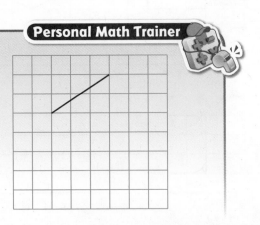

Personal Math Trainer

Draw Quadrilaterals

Learning Objective You will use grid paper to draw and name quadrilaterals then draw polygons that do not belong in a set of quadrilaterals and explain why.

Draw a quadrilateral that is described.
Name the quadrilateral you drew.

1. always has 4 sides of equal length

2. only 1 pair of opposite sides that are parallel

_____ square or rhombus _____

Draw a quadrilateral that does not belong.
Then explain why.

3.

_____

_____

_____

Problem Solving Real World

4. Layla drew a quadrilateral with 4 right angles and 2 pairs of opposite sides that are parallel. What quadrilateral best describes her drawing?

5. **WRITE** *Math* Draw a quadrilateral that is NOT a rectangle. Describe your shape, and explain why it is not a rectangle.

_____

_____

Lesson Check

1. Chloe drew a quadrilateral with 2 pairs of opposite sides that are parallel. Name all the shapes that could be Chloe's quadrilateral.

2. Mike drew a quadrilateral with four right angles. Name all the shapes he could have drawn.

Spiral Review

3. What is the name of the quadrilateral that always has 4 right angles and 4 sides of equal length?

4. Mark drew two lines that form a right angle. What words describe the lines Mark drew?

5. Dennis drew the rectangle on grid paper. What is the perimeter of the rectangle Dennis drew?

6. Jill drew the rectangle on grid paper. What is the area of the rectangle Jill drew?

FOR MORE PRACTICE
GO TO THE
Personal Math Trainer

Name _____

Describe Triangles

Essential Question How can you use sides and angles to help you describe triangles?

Learning Objective You will model, describe, and compare triangles based on the number of sides that have equal length and the types of angles they have.

Unlock the Problem

How can you use straws of different lengths to make triangles?

Activity **Materials** ■ straws ■ scissors ■ MathBoard

STEP 1 Cut straws into different lengths.

STEP 2 Find straw pieces that you can put together to make a triangle. Draw your triangle on the MathBoard.

STEP 3 Find straw pieces that you cannot put together to make a triangle.

1. Compare the lengths of the sides. Describe when you can make a triangle.

_____

_____

Math Talk

Math Processes and Practices ➋

Reason Abstractly What if you have three straws of equal length? Can you make a triangle?

2. (Math Processes and Practices ➊) **Describe** when you cannot make a triangle.

_____

_____

_____

3. Explain how you can change the straw pieces in

Step 3 to make a triangle. _____

_____

Ways to Describe Triangles

What are two ways triangles can be described?

① One Way

Triangles can be described by the number of sides that are of equal length.

Draw a line to match the description of the triangle(s).

No sides are equal in length.

Two sides are equal in length.

Three sides are equal in length.

① Another Way

Triangles can be described by the types of angles they have.

Draw a line to match the description of the triangle(s).

   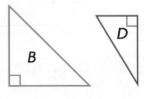

One angle is a right angle.

One angle is greater than a right angle.

Three angles are less than a right angle.

Math Talk

Math Processes and Practices ②

Use Reasoning Can a triangle have two right angles?

Name _____

1. Write the number of sides of equal length the triangle appears to have.

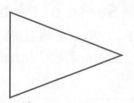

_____

Use the triangles for 2–4. Write _F_, _G_, or _H_.

2. Triangle _____ has 1 right angle.

3. Triangle _____ has 1 angle greater than a right angle.

4. Triangle _____ has 3 angles less than a right angle.

Math Talk

Math Processes and Practices 8

Generalize Explain the ways you can describe a triangle.

On Your Own

Use the triangles for 5–7. Write _K_, _L_, or _M_.
Then complete the sentences.

5. Triangle _____ has 1 right angle and appears to have

_____ sides of equal length.

6. Triangle _____ has 3 angles less than a right angle and

appears to have _____ sides of equal length.

7. Triangle _____ has 1 angle greater than a right angle and

appears to have _____ sides of equal length.

Problem Solving • Applications

8. **Math Processes and Practices ①** **Make Sense of Problems** Martin said a triangle can have two sides that are parallel. Does his statement make sense? Explain.

_____

_____

9. **GO DEEPER** Compare Triangles _R_ and _S_. How are they alike? How are they different?

_____

_____

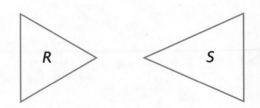

10. **THINK SMARTER** Use a ruler to draw a straight line from one corner of this rectangle to the opposite corner. What shapes did you make? What do you notice about the shapes?

_____

_____

11. **THINK SMARTER** Write the name of each triangle where it belongs in the table. Some triangles might belong in both parts of the table. Some triangles might not belong in either part.

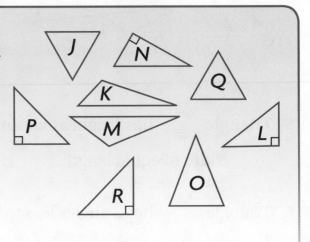

Has 1 Right Angle	Has at Least 2 Sides of Equal Length

Name _____

Describe Triangles

Learning Objective You will model, describe, and compare triangles based on the number of sides that have equal length and the types of angles they have.

Use the triangles for 1–3. Write *A*, *B*, or *C*.
Then complete the sentences.

1. Triangle __*B*__ has 3 angles less than a right angle and

   appears to have __3__ sides of equal length.

2. Triangle _____ has 1 right angle and appears to have

   _____ sides of equal length.

3. Triangle _____ has 1 angle greater than a right angle

   and appears to have _____ sides of equal length.

Problem Solving · Real World

4. Matthew drew the back of his tent. How many sides appear to be of equal length?

_____

5. Sierra made the triangular picture frame shown. How many angles are greater than a right angle?

_____

6. **WRITE** ▸*Math* Draw a triangle that has two sides of equal length and one right angle.

_____

_____

Lesson Check

1. How many angles less than a right angle does this triangle have?

_____

2. How many sides of equal length does this triangle appear to have?

_____

Spiral Review

3. A quadrilateral has 4 right angles, 2 pairs of sides of equal length, and 2 pairs of opposite sides that are parallel. The pairs of opposite sides are not the same length. What quadrilateral could it be?

_____

_____

4. Mason drew a quadrilateral with only one pair of opposite sides that are parallel. What quadrilateral did Mason draw?

_____

_____

5. Draw a rectangle that has an area of 8 square units and a perimeter of 12 units. What are the side lengths of the rectangle?

_____

_____

6. What fraction of the square is shaded?

_____

_____

FOR MORE PRACTICE
GO TO THE
Personal Math Trainer

Name _____

Problem Solving • Classify Plane Shapes

Essential Question How can you use the strategy *draw a diagram* to classify plane shapes?

Learning Objective You will use the strategy *draw a diagram* to classify plane shapes by using a Venn diagram to place shapes that share attributes in each category and determine which shapes fit in the section where the circles overlap.

Unlock the Problem

A **Venn diagram** shows how sets of things are related. In the Venn diagram at the right, one circle has shapes that are rectangles. Shapes that are rhombuses are in the other circle. The shapes in the section where the circles overlap are both rectangles and rhombuses.

What type of quadrilateral is in both circles?

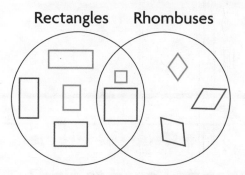

Rectangles   Rhombuses

Read the Problem	Solve the Problem
What do I need to find? _____ _____ _____	What is true about all quadrilaterals? _____ Which quadrilaterals always have 2 pairs of opposite sides that are parallel? _____
What information do I need to use? the circles labeled _____ and _____	Which quadrilaterals always have 4 sides of equal length? _____ Which quadrilaterals always have 4 right angles? _____
How will I use the information? _____ _____ _____	The quadrilaterals in the section where the circles overlap always have _____ pairs of opposite sides that are parallel, _____ sides of equal length, and _____ right angles. So, _____ are in both circles.

Math Talk

Math Processes and Practices ①

Make Sense of Problems Does a △ fit in the Venn diagram? Explain.

🔒 Try Another Problem

The Venn diagram shows the shapes Andrea used to make a picture. Where would the shape shown below be placed in the Venn diagram?

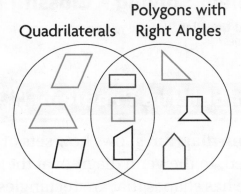

Read the Problem	Solve the Problem
What do I need to find?	**Record the steps you used to solve the problem.**
What information do I need to use?	
How will I use the information?	

1. How many shapes do not have right angles?

_____

2. How many red shapes have right angles but are

not quadrilaterals? _____

3. Math Processes and Practices ② **Reason Abstractly** What is a different way to sort the shapes?

_____

_____

Math Talk

Math Processes and Practices ①

Make Sense of Problems What name can be used to describe all the shapes in the Venn diagram? Explain how you know.

742

Name _____

Share and Show MATH BOARD

Use the Venn diagram for 1–3.

1. Jordan is sorting the shapes at the right in a Venn diagram. Where does a go?

   First, look at the sides and angles of the polygons.

   Next, draw the polygons in the Venn diagram.

   The shape has _____ sides of equal length

   and _____ right angles.

   So, the shape goes in the

   _____ .

2. Where would you place a ⬓?

   _____

3. What if Jordan sorted the shapes by Polygons with Right Angles and Polygons with Angles Less Than a Right Angle? Would the circles still overlap? Explain.

   _____

   _____

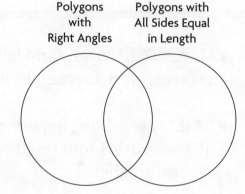

Polygons with Right Angles   Polygons with All Sides Equal in Length

4. **GO DEEPER** Eva drew the Venn diagram below. Write labels she could have used for the diagram.

   _____   _____

   _____   _____

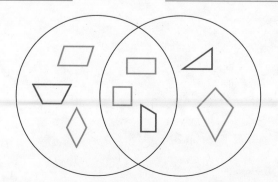

On Your Own

5. Ben and Marta are both reading the same book. Ben has read $\frac{1}{3}$ of the book. Marta has read $\frac{1}{4}$ of the book. Who has read more? _____

6. **Math Processes and Practices ② Represent a Problem** There are 42 students from 6 different classes in the school spelling bee. Each class has the same number of students in the spelling bee. Use the bar model to find how many students are from each class.

42 students

_____ ÷ _____ = _____

7. **THINK SMARTER** Draw and label a Venn diagram to show one way you can sort a rectangle, a square, a trapezoid, and a rhombus.

8. Ashley is making a quilt with squares of fabric. There are 9 rows with 8 squares in each row. How many squares of fabric are there?

_____

Personal Math Trainer

9. **THINK SMARTER +** Sketch where to place these shapes in the Venn diagram. △ □

Polygons with All Sides of Equal Length

Quadrilaterals with Right Angles

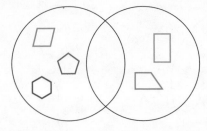

Name _____

Problem Solving • Classify Plane Shapes

Learning Objective You will use the strategy *draw a diagram* to classify plane shapes by using a Venn diagram to place shapes that share attributes in each category and determine which shapes fit in the section where the circles overlap.

Solve each problem.

1. Steve drew the shapes below. Write the letter of each shape where it belongs in the Venn diagram.

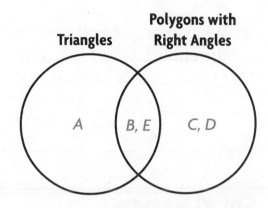

2. Janice drew the shapes below. Write the letter of each shape where it belongs in the Venn diagram.

3. **WRITE** ▸*Math* Draw a Venn diagram with one circle labeled *Quadrilaterals* and the other circle labeled *Polygons with at Least 1 Right Angle*. Draw at least two shapes in each section of the diagram. Explain why you drew the shapes you chose in the overlapping section

Lesson Check

1. What shape could go in the section where the two circles overlap?

   _____

2. What quadrilateral could NOT go in the circle labeled *Polygons with All Sides Equal in Length*?

   _____

Quadrilaterals with 4 Right Angles   Polygons with All Sides Equal in Length

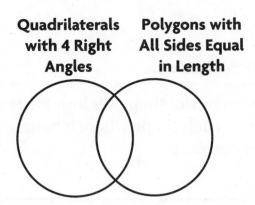

Spiral Review

3. How many angles greater than a right angle does this triangle have?

   _____

4. How many sides of equal length does this triangle appear to have?

   _____

5. Madison drew this shape. How many angles less than a right angle does it have?

6. How many dots are in $\frac{1}{2}$ of this group?

   _____

FOR MORE PRACTICE
GO TO THE
Personal Math Trainer

Relate Shapes, Fractions, and Area

Essential Question How can you divide shapes into parts with equal areas and write the area as a unit fraction of the whole?

Learning Objective You will partition figures into parts with equal areas and express the area of each part as a unit fraction of the whole.

Investigate

Materials ■ pattern blocks ■ color pencils ■ ruler

CONNECT You can use what you know about combining and separating plane shapes to explore the relationship between fractions and area.

A. Trace a hexagon pattern block.

B. Divide your hexagon into two parts with equal area.

C. Write the names of the new shapes. _____

D. Write the fraction that names each part of the whole you divided. ____
Each part is $\frac{1}{2}$ of the whole shape's area.

E. Write the fraction that names the whole area. ____

Math Idea

Equal parts of a whole have equal area.

Draw Conclusions

1. Explain how you know the two shapes have the same area.

_____

_____

2. Predict what would happen if you divide the hexagon into three shapes with equal area. What fraction names the area of each part of the divided hexagon? What fraction names the whole area?

_____

3. **THINK SMARTER** Show how you can divide the hexagon into four shapes with equal area.

   Each part is ____ of the whole shape's area.

Make Connections

The rectangle at the right is divided into four parts with equal area.

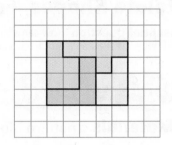

- Write the unit fraction that names each part of the divided whole. _____

- What is the area of each part? _____

- How many $\frac{1}{4}$ parts does it take to make one whole? _____

- Is the shape of each of the $\frac{1}{4}$ parts the same? _____

- Is the area of each of the $\frac{1}{4}$ parts the same? Explain how you know.

_____

_____

Divide the shape into equal parts.

Draw lines to divide the rectangle below into six parts with equal area.

Math Talk

Math Processes and Practices ③

Apply How do you know the areas of all the parts are equal?

- Write the fraction that names each part of the divided whole. _____

- Write the area of each part. _____

- Each part is _____ of the whole shape's area.

Share and Show

1. Divide the trapezoid into 3 parts with equal area. Write the names of the new shapes. Then write the fraction that names the area of each part of the whole.

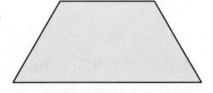

_____

748

Name _____

Draw lines to divide the shape into equal parts that show the fraction given.

2.

$\frac{1}{6}$

3.

$\frac{1}{2}$

4.

$\frac{1}{8}$

Draw lines to divide the shape into parts with equal area. Write the area of each part as a unit fraction.

5.

8 equal parts

_____

6.

6 equal parts

_____

7.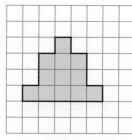

4 equal parts

_____

Problem Solving • Applications Real World

8. **Math Processes and Practices ② Use Reasoning** If the area of three ◇ is equal to the area of one ⬡, the area of how many ◇ equals four ⬡? Explain your answer.

_____

9. **THINK SMARTER** Divide each shape into the number of equal parts shown. Then write the fraction that describes each part of the whole.

2 equal parts   4 equal parts   6 equal parts

_____   _____   _____

10. **THINK SMARTER**   **Sense or Nonsense?**

Divide the hexagon into six equal parts.

Which pattern block represents $\frac{1}{6}$ of the whole area?

_____

Divide the trapezoid into three equal parts.

Which pattern block represents $\frac{1}{3}$ of the whole area?

_____

Alexis said the area of $\frac{1}{3}$ of the trapezoid is greater than the area of $\frac{1}{6}$ of the hexagon because $\frac{1}{3} > \frac{1}{6}$. Does her statement make sense? Explain your answer.

_____

_____

_____

_____

• Write a statement that makes sense.

_____

_____

• **GO DEEPER**   What if you divide the hexagon into 3 equal parts? Write a sentence that compares the area of each equal part of the hexagon to each equal part of the trapezoid.

_____

_____

Name _____

Relate Shapes, Fractions, and Area

Learning Objective You will partition figures into parts with equal areas and express the area of each part as a unit fraction of the whole.

Draw lines to divide the shape into equal parts that show the fraction given.

1.

$\frac{1}{3}$

2.

$\frac{1}{8}$

3.

$\frac{1}{2}$

Draw lines to divide the shape into parts with equal area. Write the area of each part as a unit fraction.

4.

4 equal parts

_____

5.

6 equal parts

_____

6.

3 equal parts

_____

Problem Solving · Real World

7. Robert divided a hexagon into 3 equal parts. Show how he might have divided the hexagon. Write the fraction that names each part of the whole you divided.

8. **WRITE** ▸ *Math* Trace a pattern block. Divide it into two equal parts, and write a unit fraction to describe the area of each part. Explain your work.

_____

Lesson Check

1. What fraction names each part of the divided whole?

_____

2. What fraction names the whole area that was divided?

_____

Spiral Review

3. Lil drew the figure below. Is the shape open or closed?

_____

4. How many line segments does this shape have?

_____

Use the Venn diagram for 5–6.

5. Where would a square be placed in the Venn diagram?

_____

_____

6. Where would a rectangle be placed in the Venn diagram?

_____

_____

Polygons with Right Angles   Polygons with All Sides of Equal Length

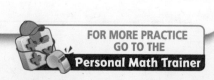

FOR MORE PRACTICE
GO TO THE
Personal Math Trainer

✓ Chapter 12 Review/Test

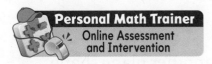

1. Which words describe this shape? Mark all that apply.

   (A) polygon

   (B) open shape

   (C) pentagon

   (D) quadrilateral

2. Umberto drew one side of a quadrilateral with 4 equal sides and no right angles. Draw the other 3 sides to complete Umberto's shape.

3. Mikael saw a painting that included this shape.

   For numbers 3a–3d, select True or False for each statement about the shape.

3a.	The shape has no right angles.	○ True	○ False
3b.	The shape has 2 angles greater than a right angle.	○ True	○ False
3c.	The shape has 2 right angles.	○ True	○ False
3d.	The shape has 1 angle greater than a right angle.	○ True	○ False

Assessment Options
Chapter Test

4. **GO DEEPER** Fran used a Venn Diagram to sort shapes.

Part A

Draw another plane shape that belongs inside the left circle of the diagram but NOT in the section where the circles overlap.

Polygons with Right Angles   Quadrilaterals

Part B

How can you describe the shapes in the section where the circles overlap?

_____

_____

5. Match each object in the left column with its name in the right column.

    • point

    • line

    • ray

    • line segment

6. Describe the angles and sides of this triangle.

_____

Name _____

7. Which words describe this shape. Mark all that apply.

rectangle   rhombus   quadrilateral   square

   Ⓐ   Ⓑ   Ⓒ   Ⓓ

8. Divide each shape into the number of equal parts shown. Then write the fraction that describes each part of the whole.

3 equal parts   **6 equal parts**   **8 equal parts**

_____   _____   _____

9. Han drew a triangle with 1 angle greater than a right angle.

For numbers 9a–9d, choose Yes or No to tell whether the triangle could be the triangle Han drew.

9a.   ○ Yes   ○ No

9b.   ○ Yes   ○ No

9c.   ○ Yes   ○ No

9d.   ○ Yes   ○ No

10. **THINK SMARTER** Look at this group of pattern blocks.

Part A

Sort the pattern blocks by sides. How many groups did you make? Explain how you sorted the shapes.

_____

_____

_____

_____

Part B

Sort the pattern blocks by angles. How many groups did you make? Explain how you sorted the shapes.

_____

_____

_____

_____

11. Teresa drew a quadrilateral that had 4 sides of equal length and no right angles. What quadrilateral did she draw?

_____

Name _____

12. Rhea used a Venn diagram to sort shapes. What label could she use for circle *A*?

13. Colette drew lines to divide a rectangle into equal parts that each represent $\frac{1}{6}$ of the whole area. Her first line is shown. Draw lines to complete Colette's model.

14. Brad drew a quadrilateral. Select the pairs of sides that appear to be parallel. Mark all that apply.

(A) *a* and *b*

(B) *b* and *d*

(C) *c* and *a*

(D) *d* and *c*

15. Give two reasons that this shape is **not** a polygon.

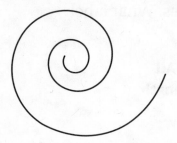

_____

16. The triangle at the right has one angle greater than a right angle. What statements describe the other angles? Mark all that apply.

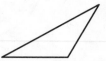

   Ⓐ   At least one is less than a right angle.

   Ⓑ   One is a right angle.

   Ⓒ   Both are less than a right angle.

   Ⓓ   One is greater than a right angle.

17. Ava drew a quadrilateral with 2 pairs of opposite sides that are parallel. The shape has at least 2 right angles. Draw a shape that Ava could have drawn.

18. For 18a–18d, select True or False for each description of a ray.

18a.	straight	○ True	○ False
18b.	has 2 endpoints	○ True	○ False
18c.	part of a line	○ True	○ False
18d.	continues in 1 direction	○ True	○ False

Name _____

In Our Corner of Space

Use with *ScienceFusion* pages 410–413.

Develop Vocabulary

1. Write the definition using your own words.

   solar system: _____

   _____

   _____

   planet: _____

   _____

   _____

Develop Concepts

2. Which characteristics do astronomers use to classify the different bodies found in the solar system?

   _____

   _____

   _____

3. Draw the sun and planets. Make sure that they are in their correct positions in relation to the sun.

Do the Math!

4. Look at the table below that tells each planet's distance from the sun, and use it to answer the questions.

Earth	150 million km	Mars	228 million km
Jupiter	778 million km	Mercury	58 million km

5. How much farther from the sun is Mars than Earth?

_____

_____

6. How much farther from the sun is Jupiter than Mercury?

_____

_____

7. List the planets in the table in order from the closest to the farthest from the sun. Which planet in the table is farthest from the sun?

_____

_____

8. Venus is 50 million km from Mercury. What is Venus's distance from the sun?

_____

_____

Summarize

9. Create a two-column chart and compare the different characteristics of inner and outer planets.

Inner Planets	Outer Planets

Communities of Populations

Use with *ScienceFusion* pages 436–437.

Develop Vocabulary

1. Write the definition using your own words.

   population: _____

   _____

   _____

   community: _____

   _____

   _____

Develop Concepts

2. A park ranger says that there are about 150 grizzly bears in Yellowstone National Park. Is this a population or a community?

   _____

   _____

   _____

3. When bison and wolves interact with each other in the same place, what do they make up?

   _____

   _____

   _____

Do the Math!

4. Use the data in the table on the right to construct a bar graph.

Animal	Population
Gray Wolf	35
Grizzly Bear	25
Bald Eagle	10
Elk	70

5. Which animal has the greatest population in the community? Which has the smallest?

_____

_____

_____

6. In the Yellowstone community, there are 45 Bull Snakes. How many more Bull Snakes than Gray Wolves are there?

_____

_____

_____

Summarize

7. What are some ways that animals and plants interact in a community?

_____

_____

_____

Reflection and Refraction

Use with *ScienceFusion*
pages 184–185.

Develop Vocabulary

1. Write the definition using your own words.

reflection: _____

_____

_____

refraction: _____

_____

_____

Develop Concepts

2. Give an example of an object that refracts light. How does it do this?

_____

_____

_____

3. Do binoculars reflect or refract light? What is the result of this reflection or refraction?

_____

_____

_____

Do the Math!

4. The table below lists how tall each of the objects appeared to be when Tom viewed them with and without binoculars. Complete the table by calculating the magnification of each item.

Object	Height without binoculars	Height with binoculars	Magnification
Robin	3 inches	9 inches	
American flag	5 inches	25 inches	
Cat	2 inches	6 inches	

5. Which object appeared to be the largest?

_____

_____

_____

6. Susie appeared to be 6 inches tall when Tom saw her without binoculars, but 18 inches tall with binoculars. How many times as tall as Susie looks without binoculars does she look with binoculars?

_____

_____

_____

Summarize

7. Name 4 different devices that depend on refracting lenses to work.

_____

_____

_____

Name _____

Big Changes: Fire, Water, Mud

Use with *ScienceFusion* pages 288-289.

Develop Vocabulary

1. Write the definition using your own words. Write the first definition as a noun and the second as a verb.

flood (n): _____

_____

_____

flood (v): _____

_____

_____

Develop Concepts

2. What is a small change in water going to cause? What about a big change in water?

_____

_____

_____

3. When can fire cause a small change? When can fire cause a big change?

_____

_____

_____

Do the Math!

4. Skip count by fives to find the time it would take for a river to overflow if rain fell at 5 centimeters per hour and the river needed 55 centimeters of water to overflow.

_____

_____

_____

5. Write an equation for the problem above.

_____

_____

_____

6. Rain is falling at 5 centimeters each hour. Write an equation for each body of water given the rainfall needed for the water to overflow. Use this equation to determine the time until the water overflows.

	Rainfall needed to overflow	Equation	Time (in hours) until the water overflows
River	30 centimeters		
Stream	25 centimeters		
Lake	40 centimeters		

Summarize

7. Describe some conditions that can lead to flooding and mudslides.

_____

_____

_____

© Houghton Mifflin Harcourt Publishing Company

Stargazing

Use with *ScienceFusion* pages 404–405.

Develop Vocabulary

1. Write the definition using your own words.

   telescope: _____

   _____

   _____

Develop Concepts

2. How do you think telescopes help scientists study space?

   _____

   _____

   _____

3. What does *tele-* in *telescope* mean in Greek? What are some other words that use that word part *tele-* in them?

   _____

   _____

   _____

4. How are a hand lens and a telescope alike? How are they different?

   _____

   _____

   _____

Do the Math!

5. Max sees 8 stars each time he looks into the night sky behind his house. When he uses his telescope, he sees 7 times as many stars. Write an equation for how many stars Max sees through the telescope.

_____

_____

6. How many stars would Max see if he saw only 4 times as many stars?

_____

_____

7. Which part of the sentence in problem 5 tells you which operation to use?

_____

_____

8. Max's friend sees 6 stars without the telescope and 5 times as many stars with the telescope. How many stars does he see when he looks through the telescope?

_____

_____

Summarize

9. Compare how stars look with your eyes and through a telescope.

_____

_____

_____

Name _____

Cool! It's Freezing!

Use with *ScienceFusion* pages 118–119.

Develop Vocabulary

1. Write the definition using your own words.

freezing: _____

_____

_____

_____

change of state: _____

_____

_____

_____

Develop Concepts

2. How can water in the liquid state change to water in the solid state?

_____

_____

_____

_____

3. At what temperature does water change from liquid to solid?

_____

_____

_____

_____

Do the Math!

4. The temperature of a puddle of water is 20°C. Draw a thermometer below and shade up to 20°C.

5. The temperature of the water in the puddle cools by 2 degrees every hour. At what temperature does water start to freeze?

_____

6. Predict how long it will take for the water in the puddle to start to freeze. Use division to help you find the answer.

_____

7. Predict how cooling will change the state of the water if the puddle doesn't reach 0°C.

_____

_____

8. How long will it take for the water in the puddle to start to freeze if the temperature is 10°C.

_____

Summarize

9. Refer back to the pictures on the last page of this activity. Identify the causes and effects in each picture.

_____

_____

Chemical Changes

Use with *ScienceFusion* pages 134–137

Develop Vocabulary

1. Write the definition using your own words.

   physical change: _____

   _____

   _____

   chemical change: _____

   _____

   _____

Develop Concepts

2. What type of change is folding paper? Explain why.

   _____

   _____

   _____

3. Name a physical and a chemical change that can occur when you eat an apple.

   _____

   _____

   _____

4. In the activity, look at the picture of the rusted mailbox. How do you know that rusting is a chemical change?

   _____

   _____

   _____

Do the Math!

5. Max placed three types of food on a plate and recorded how much mold he saw on each after 3 days. Complete the bar graph below by labeling the title and each axis.

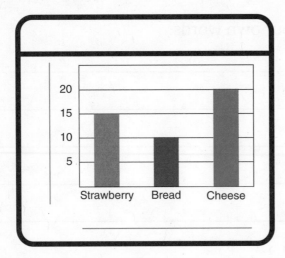

6. Which type of food had the most mold on it after 3 days? Is this a physical or a chemical change?

_____

_____

7. For a campfire, scouts want to burn 20 pieces of wood. If 1 match can light 4 pieces of wood on fire, how many pieces of wood can the scouts burn if they have only 5 matches? Do they need more matches?

_____

_____

8. Is burning wood an example of a physical or a chemical change?

_____

_____

Summarize

9. Compare a physical and a chemical change.

_____

_____

Water Moves All Around

Use with *ScienceFusion*
pages 344–345.

Develop Vocabulary

1. Write the definition using your own words.

salt water: _____

_____

_____

_____

fresh water: _____

_____

_____

_____

Develop Concepts

2. Is fresh water a natural resource? What do people use fresh water for?

_____

_____

_____

3. What are some places on Earth that contain fresh water?

_____

_____

_____

Do the Math!

4. Complete the table below. Write the fraction in the right-hand column.

Only 3 out of every 100 liters of water on Earth is fresh water. What fraction of Earth's water is fresh water?	
If Earth is divided into 10 equal parts, 7 of those would be covered by water. What fraction of Earth's surface is land?	

5. Draw a circle. Divide the circle into 10 equal parts. Color blue the number of parts of the circle that is equal to the number of parts of Earth covered by water. Color green the number of parts that are land.

6. If Earth's surface is $\frac{3}{10}$ land, what does this fraction help us understand?

_____

_____

_____

Summarize

7. Is Earth's surface mostly land or mostly water? Is most of Earth's water fresh water or salt water?

_____

_____

_____

Using a Wheel-and-Axle

Use with *ScienceFusion*
pages 214–215.

Develop Vocabulary

1. Write the definition using your own words.

wheel-and-axle: _____

_____

_____

_____

fulcrum: _____

_____

_____

_____

Develop Concepts

2. What part of the wheel-and-axle is like the fulcrum of the lever?

_____

_____

_____

3. What is a real-world example of an object that uses a wheel-and-axle?

_____

_____

_____

Do the Math!

4. A wheel turns on an axle. The arrow of each circle shows the direction in which the wheel turns. The shaded part shows how far the wheel turns. Write a fraction below each circle to indicate how far the wheel turned.

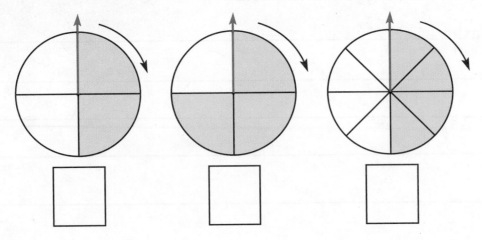

5. Compare the fractions you found for the circle on the left to the fraction you found for the circle on the right.

_____

_____

_____

6. Does the middle circle show the same whole as the last circle? Why?

_____

_____

_____

Summarize

7. How does a wheel-and-axle do work? Provide an example.

_____

_____

_____

Measure It!

Use with *ScienceFusion* pages 20–21.

Develop Vocabulary

1. Write the definition using your own words.

gram: _____

_____

_____

_____

graduated cylinder: _____

_____

_____

_____

Develop Concepts

2. When you look at a recipe, how do you know how much of each ingredient to add?

_____

_____

_____

3. What is a good tool to use if you want to measure the length of your desk at school? What are some units of measurement that this tool uses?

_____

_____

_____

Do the Math!

4. Complete the table by thinking about what you are measuring on the left column and filling in what would be a good tool used to measure it and a possible unit of measurement you could use.

Measure	Tool used to measure it	Unit of measurement
Time		
Length		
Liquid		
Weight		

5. How many millimeters are in one centimeter? How many centimeters are in one meter?

_____

_____

_____

6. What are some uses of a graduated cylinder?

_____

_____

_____

Summarize

7. Name a tool to measure each of the following: length, liquid volume, mass.

_____

_____

_____

What's the Volume?

Use with *ScienceFusion*
pages 98–99.

Develop Vocabulary

1. Define the following terms in your own words.

volume: _____

_____

_____

cubic centimeter: _____

_____

_____

_____

Develop Concepts

2. How would you find the volume of a book?

_____

_____

_____

3. A book has a length of 13 cm, a width of 12 cm, and a height of 16 cm. What is the volume of the book?

_____

_____

_____

Do the Math!

4. A shell is added to a graduated cylinder with a specific volume of water. Complete the table by finding the volume of the shell.

	Volume of water	Volume of water + shell	Volume of the shell
Shell A	53 milliliters	64 milliliters	
Shell B	32 milliliters	35 milliliters	
Shell C	45 milliliters	70 milliliters	

5. What is the process called when a solid object is added to a liquid and the volume of the liquid is increased?

_____

_____

_____

6. A box is 4 cm long, 5 cm wide, and 8 cm high. What is the volume of that box?

_____

_____

_____

Summarize

7. What are some ways in which volume is measured?

_____

_____

_____

Planning and Building

Develop Vocabulary

Use with *ScienceFusion*
pages 60–61.

1. Write the definition using your own words.

   prototype: _____

   _____

   _____

   _____

Develop Concepts

2. If a team of engineers is planning on building a new bridge, what will help them know what kind of bridge to build?

   _____

   _____

   _____

   _____

3. What are some objects around your house that might use a prototype when they are being designed and created?

   _____

   _____

   _____

4. Read the process for designing a bridge. What is the last step in the design process? What is the purpose of this step?

   _____

   _____

   _____

   _____

Do the Math!

5. Look at the bridge in the picture. What geometric shapes do you see?

_____

_____

_____

6. Are the angles at the top of the bridge greater than or less than a right angle? Are there any right angles on the bridge?

_____

_____

_____

7. In the space below, use geometric shapes such as triangles and rectangles to draw a bridge. Label the shapes and angles in your design.

Summarize

8. What is the main idea of the S.T.E.M. activity on pages 60 – 61?

_____

_____

_____

© Houghton Mifflin Harcourt Publishing Company

Glossary

Pronunciation Key

a	add, map	f	fit, half	n	nice, tin	p	pit, stop	û(r)	burn, term
ā	ace, rate	g	go, log	ng	ring, song	r	run, poor	yo͞o	fuse, few
â(r)	care, air	h	hope, hate	o	odd, hot	s	see, pass	v	vain, eve
ä	palm, father	i	it, give	ō	open, so	sh	sure, rush	w	win, away
b	bat, rub	ī	ice, write	ô	order, jaw	t	talk, sit	y	yet, yearn
ch	check, catch	j	joy, ledge	oi	oil, boy	th	thin, both	z	zest, muse
d	dog, rod	k	cool, take	ou	pout, now	th	this, bathe	zh	vision, pleasure
e	end, pet	l	look, rule	o͞o	took, full	u	up, done		
ē	equal, tree	m	move, seem	o͞o	pool, food	u̇	pull, book		

ə the schwa, an unstressed vowel representing the sound spelled *a* in *above*, *e* in *sicken*, *i* in *possible*, *o* in *melon*, *u* in *circus*

Other symbols:
- • separates words into syllables
- ′ indicates stress on a syllable

A

addend [a′dend] **sumando** Any of the numbers that are added in addition
Examples: 2 + 3 = 5
      ↑ ↑
  addend addend

addition [ə•dish′ən] **suma** The process of finding the total number of items when two or more groups of items are joined; the opposite operation of subtraction

A.M. [ā•em] **a.m.** The time after midnight and before noon

analog clock [an′ə•log kläk] **reloj analógico** A tool for measuring time, in which hands move around a circle to show hours and minutes
Example:

angle [ang′gəl] **ángulo** A shape formed by two rays that share an endpoint
Example:

Word History

When the letter *g* is replaced with the letter *k* in the word *angle*, the word becomes *ankle*. Both words come from the same Latin root, *angulus*, which means "a sharp bend."

area [âr′ē•ə] **área** The measure of the number of unit squares needed to cover a surface
Example:

Area = 6 square units

array [ə•rā′] **matriz** A set of objects arranged in rows and columns
Example:

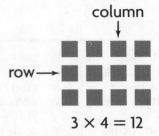

column

row→

$3 \times 4 = 12$

Associative Property of Addition [ə•sō′shē•āt•iv präp′ər•tē əv ə•dish′ən] **propiedad asociativa de la suma** The property that states that you can group addends in different ways and still get the same sum
Example:
$4 + (2 + 5) = 11$
$(4 + 2) + 5 = 11$

Associative Property of Multiplication
[ə•sō′shē•āt•iv präp′ər•tē əv mul•tə•pli•kā′shən]
propiedad asociativa de la multiplicación The property that states that when the grouping of factors is changed, the product remains the same
Example:
$(3 \times 2) \times 4 = 24$
$3 \times (2 \times 4) = 24$

bar graph [bär graf] **gráfica de barras** A graph that uses bars to show data
Example:

Favorite Food

capacity [kə•pas′i•tē] **capacidad** The amount a container can hold
Example:
1 liter = 1,000 milliliters

cent sign (¢) [sent sīn] **símbolo de centavo** A symbol that stands for *cent* or *cents*
Example: 53¢

centimeter (cm) [sen′tə•mēt•ər] **centímetro (cm)** A metric unit that is used to measure length or distance
Example:

1 cm

circle [sûr′kəl] **círculo** A round closed plane shape
Example:

closed shape [klōzd shāp] **figura cerrada** A shape that begins and ends at the same point
Examples:

Commutative Property of Addition
[kə•myoōt′ə•tiv präp′ər•tē əv ə•dish′ən]
propiedad conmutativa de la suma
The property that states that you can add two or more numbers in any order and get the same sum
Example: $6 + 7 = 13$
$7 + 6 = 13$

Commutative Property of Multiplication
[kə•myoōt′ə•tiv präp′ər•tē əv mul•tə•pli•kā′shən]
propiedad conmutativa de la multiplicación The property that states that you can multiply two factors in any order and get the same product
Example: $2 \times 4 = 8$
$4 \times 2 = 8$

compare [kəm•pâr′] **comparar** To describe whether numbers are equal to, less than, or greater than each other

compatible numbers [kəm•pat′ə•bəl num′bərz] **números compatibles** Numbers that are easy to compute with mentally

cone [kōn] **cono** A three-dimensional, pointed shape that has a flat, round base
Example:

base

counting number [kount'ing num'bər] **número natural** A whole number that can be used to count a set of objects (1, 2, 3, 4 . . .)

cube [kyōōb] **cubo** A three-dimensional shape with six square faces of the same size
Example:

cylinder [sil'ən•dər] **cilindro** A three-dimensional object that is shaped like a can
Example:

data [dāt'ə] **datos** Information collected about people or things

decagon [dek'ə•gän] **decágono** A polygon with ten sides and ten angles
Example:

decimal point [des'ə•məl point] **punto decimal** A symbol used to separate dollars from cents in money
Example: $4.52
⌐ decimal point

denominator [dē•näm'ə•nāt•ər] **denominador** The part of a fraction below the line, which tells how many equal parts there are in the whole or in the group
Example: $\frac{3}{4}$ ← denominator

difference [dif'ər•əns] **diferencia** The answer to a subtraction problem
Example: 6 − 4 = 2
⌐difference

digital clock [dij'i•təl kläk] **reloj digital** A clock that shows time to the minute, using digits
Example:

digits [dij'its] **dígitos** The symbols 0, 1, 2, 3, 4, 5, 6, 7, 8, and 9

dime [dīm] **moneda de 10¢** A coin worth 10 cents and with a value equal to that of 10 pennies; 10¢
Example:

Distributive Property [di•strib'yōō•tiv präp'ər•tē] **propiedad distributiva** The property that states that multiplying a sum by a number is the same as multiplying each addend by the number and then adding the products
Example:
5 × 8 = 5 × (4 + 4)
5 × 8 = (5 × 4) + (5 × 4)
5 × 8 = 20 + 20
5 × 8 = 40

divide [də•vīd'] **dividir** To separate into equal groups; the opposite operation of multiplication

dividend [div'ə•dend] **dividendo** The number that is to be divided in a division problem
Example: 35 ÷ 5 = 7
⌐dividend

division [də•vizh′ən] **división** The process of sharing a number of items to find how many groups can be made or how many items will be in a group; the opposite operation of multiplication

divisor [de•vī′zər] **divisor** The number that divides the dividend
Example: $35 \div 5 = 7$

divisor

dollar [däl′ər] **dólar** Paper money worth 100 cents and equal to 100 pennies; $1.00
Example:

edge [ej] **arista** A line segment formed where two faces meet

edge

eighths [ātths] **octavos**

These are eighths

elapsed time [ē•lapst′ tīm] **tiempo transcurrido** The time that passes from the start of an activity to the end of that activity

endpoint [end′point] **extremo** The point at either end of a line segment

equal groups [ē′kwəl groopz] **grupos iguales** Groups that have the same number of objects

equal parts [ē′kwəl pärts] **partes iguales** Parts that are exactly the same size

equal sign (=) [ē′kwəl sīn] **signo de igualdad** A symbol used to show that two numbers have the same value
Example: $384 = 384$

equal to (=) [ē′kwəl too] **igual a** Having the same value
Example: $4 + 4$ is equal to $3 + 5$.

equation [ē•kwā′zhən] **ecuación** A number sentence that uses the equal sign to show that two amounts are equal
Examples:
$$3 + 7 = 10$$
$$4 - 1 = 3$$
$$6 \times 7 = 42$$
$$8 \div 2 = 4$$

equivalent [ē•kwiv′ə•lənt] **equivalente** Two or more sets that name the same amount

equivalent fractions [ē•kwiv′ə•lənt frak′shənz] **fracciones equivalentes** Two or more fractions that name the same amount
Example:

$$\frac{3}{4} = \frac{6}{8}$$

estimate [es′tə•māt] *verb* **estimar** To find about how many or how much

estimate [es′tə•mit] *noun* **estimación** A number close to an exact amount

even [ē′vən] **par** A whole number that has a 0, 2, 4, 6, or 8 in the ones place

expanded form [ek•span′did fôrm] **forma desarrollada** A way to write numbers by showing the value of each digit
Example: $721 = 700 + 20 + 1$

experiment [ek•sper′ə•mənt] **experimento** A test that is done in order to find out something

F

face [fās] **cara** A polygon that is a flat surface of a solid shape

factor [fak'tər] **factor** A number that is multiplied by another number to find a product
Examples: 3 × 8 = 24
↑   ↑
factor   factor

foot (ft) [fŏŏt] **pie** A customary unit used to measure length or distance;
1 foot = 12 inches

fourths [fôrths] **cuartos**

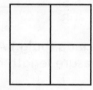

These are fourths

fraction [frak'shən] **fracción** A number that names part of a whole or part of a group
Examples:

$\frac{1}{3}$

Word History

Often, a *fraction* is a part of a whole that is broken into pieces. *Fraction* comes from the Latin word *frangere*, which means "to break."

fraction greater than 1 [frak'shən grāt'ər than wun] **fracción mayor que 1** A number which has a numerator that is greater than its denominator
Examples:

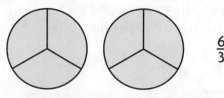

$\frac{6}{3}$ $\frac{2}{1}$

frequency table [frē'kwən•sē tā'bəl] **tabla de frecuencia** A table that uses numbers to record data
Example:

Favorite Color	
Color	**Number**
Blue	10
Green	8
Red	7
Yellow	4

G

gram (g) [gram] **gramo (g)** A metric unit that is used to measure mass;
1 kilogram = 1,000 grams

greater than (>) [grāt'ər than] **mayor que** A symbol used to compare two numbers when the greater number is given first
Example:
Read 6 > 4 as "six is greater than four."

Grouping Property of Addition [grōōp'ing präp'ər•tē əv ə•dish'ən] **propiedad de agrupación de la suma** *See* Associative Property of Addition.

Grouping Property of Multiplication [grōōp'ing präp'ər•tē əv mul•tə•pli•kā'shən] **propiedad de agrupación de la multiplicación** *See* Associative Property of Multiplication.

H

half dollar [haf dol'ər] **moneda de 50¢**
A coin worth 50 cents and with a value
equal to that of 50 pennies; 50¢
Example:

half hour [haf our] **media hora** 30 minutes
Example: Between 4:00 and 4:30 is one
half hour.

halves [havz] **mitades**

These are halves

hexagon [hek'sə•gän] **hexágono** A polygon
with six sides and six angles
Examples:

horizontal bar graph [hôr•i•zänt'l bär graf]
gráfica de barras horizontales A bar graph
in which the bars go from left to right
Examples:

hour (hr) [our] **hora (h)** A unit used to measure
time; in one hour, the hour hand on an analog
clock moves from one number to the next;
1 hour = 60 minutes

hour hand [our hand] **horario** The short hand on
an analog clock

I

Identity Property of Addition [ī•den'tə•tē
präp'ər•tē əv ə•dish'ən] **propiedad de
identidad de la suma** The property that
states that when you add zero to a number,
the result is that number
Example: 24 + 0 = 24

Identity Property of Multiplication [ī•den'tə•tē
präp'ər•tē əv mul•tə•pli•kā'shən] **propiedad de
identidad de la multiplicación** The property
that states that the product of any number
and 1 is that number
Examples: 5 × 1 = 5
1 × 8 = 8

inch (in.) [inch] **pulgada (pulg.)** A customary
unit used to measure length or distance
Example:

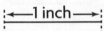

intersecting lines [in•tər•sekt'ing līnz] **líneas
secantes** Lines that meet or cross
Example:

inverse operations [in'vûrs äp•ə•rā'shənz]
operaciones inversas Opposite operations,
or operations that undo one another, such
as addition and subtraction or multiplication
and division

K

key [kē] **clave** The part of a map or graph
that explains the symbols

kilogram (kg) [kil'ō•gram] **kilogramo (kg)**
A metric unit used to measure mass;
1 kilogram = 1,000 grams

length [lengkth] **longitud** The measurement of the distance between two points

less than (<) [les _than_] **menor que** A symbol used to compare two numbers when the lesser number is given first
Example:
Read 3 < 7 as "three is less than seven."

line [līn] **línea** A straight path extending in both directions with no endpoints
Example:

⟵————————⟶

> ### Word History
>
> The word *line* comes from *linen*, a thread spun from the fibers of the flax plant. In early times, thread was held tight to mark a straight line between two points.

line plot [līn plät] **diagrama de puntos** A graph that records each piece of data on a number line
Example:

**Height of Bean Seedlings
to the Nearest Centimeter**

line segment [līn seg′mənt] **segmento** A part of a line that includes two points, called endpoints, and all of the points between them
Example:

●————————●

liquid volume [lik′wid väl′yo͞om] **volumen de un líquido** The amount of liquid in a container

liter (L) [lēt′ər] **litro (L)** A metric unit used to measure capacity and liquid volume; 1 liter = 1,000 milliliters

mass [mas] **masa** The amount of matter in an object

meter (m) [mēt′ər] **metro (m)** A metric unit used to measure length or distance; 1 meter = 100 centimeters

midnight [mid′nīt] **medianoche** 12:00 at night

milliliter (mL) [mil′i•lēt•ər] **mililitro (mL)** A metric unit used to measure capacity and liquid volume

minute (min) [min′it] **minuto (min)** A unit used to measure short amounts of time; in one minute, the minute hand on an analog clock moves from one mark to the next

minute hand [min′it hand] **minutero** The long hand on an analog clock

multiple [mul′tə•pəl] **múltiplo** A number that is the product of two counting numbers
Examples:

6	6	6	6	counting
× 1	× 2	× 3	× 4	← numbers
6	12	18	24	← multiples of 6

multiplication [mul•tə•pli•kā′shən] **multiplicación** The process of finding the total number of items in two or more equal groups; the opposite operation of division

multiply [mul′tə•plī] **multiplicar** To combine equal groups to find how many in all; the opposite operation of division

nickel [nik′əl] **moneda de 5¢** A coin worth 5 cents and with a value equal to that of 5 pennies; 5¢
Example:

noon [no͞on] **mediodía** 12:00 in the day

number line [num′bər līn] **recta numérica**
A line on which numbers can be located
Example:

number sentence [num′bər sent′ns] **enunciado numérico** A sentence that includes numbers, operation symbols, and a greater than symbol, a less than symbol, or an equal sign
Example: 5 + 3 = 8

numerator [noo′mər•āt•ər] **numerador** The part of a fraction above the line, which tells how many parts are being counted
Example: $\frac{3}{4}$ ← numerator

octagon [äk′tə•gän] **octágono** A polygon with eight sides and eight angles
Examples:

odd [od] **impar** A whole number that has a 1, 3, 5, 7, or 9 in the ones place

open shape [ō′pən shāp] **figura abierta** A shape that does not begin and end at the same point
Examples:

order [ôr′dər] **orden** A particular arrangement or placement of numbers or things, one after another

order of operations [ôr′dər əv äp•ə•rā′shənz] **orden de las operaciones** A special set of rules that gives the order in which calculations are done

Order Property of Addition [ôr′dər präp′ər•tē əv ə•dish′ən] **propiedad de orden de la suma** *See* Commutative Property of Addition.

Order Property of Multiplication [ôr′dər präp′ər•tē əv mul•tə•pli•kā′shən] **propiedad de orden de la multiplicación** *See* Commutative Property of Multiplication.

parallel lines [pâr′ə•lel līnz] **líneas paralelas** Lines in the same plane that never cross and are always the same distance apart
Example:

pattern [pat′ərn] **patrón** An ordered set of numbers or objects in which the order helps you predict what will come next
Examples:
2, 4, 6, 8, 10

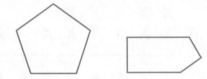

pentagon [pen′tə•gän] **pentágono** A polygon with five sides and five angles
Examples:

perimeter [pə•rim′ə•tər] **perímetro** The distance around a figure
Example:

perpendicular lines [pər•pən•dik′yoo•lər līnz] **líneas perpendiculares** Lines that intersect to form right angles
Example:

picture graph [pik′chər graf] **gráfica con dibujos** A graph that uses pictures to show and compare information
Example:

How We Get to School	
Walk	
Ride a Bike	
Ride a Bus	
Ride in a Car	
Key: Each ✳ = 10 students.	

place value [plās val′yoo] **valor posicional** The value of each digit in a number, based on the location of the digit

plane [plān] **plano** A flat surface that extends without end in all directions
Example:

plane shape [plān shāp] **figura plana** A shape in a plane that is formed by curves, line segments, or both
Example:

P.M. [pē·em] **p.m.** The time after noon and before midnight

point [point] **punto** An exact position or location

polygon [päl′i·gän] **polígono** A closed plane shape with straight sides that are line segments
Examples:

polygons   not polygons

© Houghton Mifflin Harcourt Publishing Company

Word History

Did you ever think that a *polygon* looks like a bunch of knees that are bent? This is how the term got its name. *Poly-* is from the Greek word *polys*, which means "many." The ending *-gon* is from the Greek word *gony*, which means "knee."

product [präd′əkt] **producto** The answer in a multiplication problem
Example: 3 × 8 = 24
              ↑ product

 Q

quadrilateral [kwäd·ri·lat′ər·əl] **cuadrilátero** A polygon with four sides and four angles
Example:

quarter [kwôrt′ər] **moneda de 25¢** A coin worth 25 cents and with a value equal to that of 25 pennies; 25¢
Example:

quarter hour [kwôrt′ər our] **cuarto de hora** 15 minutes
Example: Between 4:00 and 4:15 is one quarter hour.

quotient [kwō′shənt] **cociente** The number, not including the remainder, that results from division
Example: 8 ÷ 4 = 2
              ↑ quotient

R

ray [rā] **semirrecta** A part of a line, with one endpoint, that is straight and continues in one direction
Example:

rectangle [rek'tang•gəl] **rectángulo** A quadrilateral with two pairs of parallel sides, two pairs of sides of equal length, and four right angles
Example:

rectangular prism [rek•tang'gyə•lər priz'əm] **prisma rectangular** A three-dimensional shape with six faces that are all rectangles
Example:

regroup [rē•grōōp'] **reagrupar** To exchange amounts of equal value to rename a number
Example: 5 + 8 = 13 ones or 1 ten 3 ones

related facts [ri•lāt'id fakts] **operaciones relacionadas** A set of related addition and subtraction, or multiplication and division, number sentences
Examples: 4 × 7 = 28   28 ÷ 4 = 7
7 × 4 = 28   28 ÷ 7 = 4

remainder [ri•mān'dər] **residuo** The amount left over when a number cannot be divided evenly

results [ri•zults'] **resultados** The answers from a survey

rhombus [räm'bəs] **rombo** A quadrilateral with two pairs of parallel sides and four sides of equal length
Example:

right angle [rīt ang'gəl] **ángulo recto** An angle that forms a square corner
Example:

round [round] **redondear** To replace a number with another number that tells about how many or how much

S

scale [skāl] **escala** The numbers placed at fixed distances on a graph to help label the graph

side [sīd] **lado** A straight line segment in a polygon

sixths [siksths] **sextos**

These are sixths

skip count [skip kount] **contar salteado** A pattern of counting forward or backward
Example: 5, 10, 15, 20, 25, 30, . . .

solid shape [sä'lid shāp] **cuerpo geométrico** *See* three-dimensional shape.

sphere [sfir] **esfera** A three-dimensional shape that has the shape of a round ball
Example:

square [skwâr] **cuadrado** A quadrilateral with two pairs of parallel sides, four sides of equal length, and four right angles
Example:

square unit [skwâr yōō'nit] **unidad cuadrada**
A unit used to measure area such as square
foot, square meter, and so on

standard form [stan'dərd fôrm] **forma normal**
A way to write numbers by using the digits
0–9, with each digit having a place value
Example: 345 ← standard form

subtraction [səb•trak'shən] **resta** The process of
finding how many are left when a number of
items are taken away from a group of items;
the process of finding the difference when two
groups are compared; the opposite operation
of addition

sum [sum] **suma o total** The answer to an
addition problem
Example: 6 + 4 = 10
⎿—sum

survey [sûr'vā] **encuesta** A method of gathering
information

tally table [tal'ē tā'bəl] **tabla de conteo** A table
that uses tally marks to record data
Example:

Favorite Sport	
Sport	**Tally**
Soccer	卌 |||
Baseball	|||
Football	卌
Basketball	卌	

thirds [thûrdz] **tercios**

These are thirds

three-dimensional shape [thrē də•men'shə•nəl shāp]
figura tridimensional A shape that has length,
width, and height
Example:

time line [tīm līn] **línea cronológica**
A drawing that shows when and in what
order events took place

trapezoid [trap'i•zoid] **trapecio**
A quadrilateral with at least one pair of
parallel sides
Example:

triangle [trī'ang•gəl] **triángulo** A polygon with
three sides and three angles
Examples:

two-dimensional shape [tōō də•men'shə•nəl shāp]
figura bidimensional A shape that has only
length and width
Example:

unit fraction [yōō'nit frak'shən] **fracción
unitaria** A fraction that has 1 as its top
number, or numerator
Examples: $\frac{1}{2}$ $\frac{1}{3}$ $\frac{1}{4}$

unit square [yōō'nit skwâr] **cuadrado de una unidad**
A square with a side length of 1 unit, used to
measure area

Venn diagram [ven dī'ə•gram] **diagrama de Venn**
A diagram that shows relationships among
sets of things
Example:

vertex [vûr'teks] **vértice** The point at which
two rays of an angle or two (or more) line
segments meet in a plane shape or where
three or more edges meet in a solid shape
Examples:

vertical bar graph [vûr'ti•kəl bär graf] **gráfica
de barras verticales** A bar graph in which the
bars go up from bottom to top

whole [hōl] **entero** All of the parts of a shape
or group
Example:

$$\frac{2}{2} = 1$$

This is one whole.

whole number [hōl num'bər] **número entero**
One of the numbers 0, 1, 2, 3, 4, . . .
The set of whole numbers goes on
without end

word form [wûrd fôrm] **en palabras** A way
to write numbers by using words
Example: The word form of 212 is
two hundred twelve.

Zero Property of Multiplication [zē'rō
präp'ər•tē əv mul•tə•pli•kā'shən] **propiedad
del cero de la multiplicación** The property
that states that the product of zero and
any number is zero
Example: $0 \times 6 = 0$

H12 Glossary

Index

© Houghton Mifflin Harcourt Publishing Company

© Houghton Mifflin Harcourt Publishing Company

Math in the Real World, 3, 85, 137, 189, 259, 299, 363, 441, 505, 559, 623, 695

Math on the Spot Videos, In every Student Edition lesson. Some examples are: 26, 102, 200, 263, 380, 470, 542, 666, 712

Math Talk, In every lesson. Some examples are: 5, 43, 377, 409, 715, 747

Measurement
    area
        defined, 643
        finding, 643–646, 649–652, 655–658, 669–672
        patterns and, 663–666
        perimeter related to, 643, 675–678, 681–684
        solving problems, 663–666
        unknown lengths and, 675–678, 681–684
    customary units,
        for length
            feet, 151, 634, 638, 664
            inches, 126, 593–596, 631–633
        for liquid volume and capacity, cups, 217
        for weight, ounces, 148
    distinguish between linear and area, 675–678, 681–684
    length
        customary units for
            feet, 151
            inches, 126, 593–596, 631–633
        measure in centimeters, 631–634
        measure to nearest half inch, 593–596
        measure to nearest fourth inch, 593–596
        measure to nearest inch, 126
        metric units for
            centimeters, 89, 627, 631–634
    liquid volume
        defined, 599
        measuring, 599–602
        liters, 599–602
        solving problems, 599–602, 611–614
    mass
        defined, 605
        grams, 605–608
        kilograms, 605–608
        measuring, 605–608
        solving problems, 605–608, 611–614

    metric units
        for length
            centimeters, 89, 627, 631–634
        for liquid volume and capacity, liters, 599–602
        for mass
            grams, 605–608
            kilograms, 605–608
    perimeter
        area related to, 643, 675–678, 681–684
        defined, 625
        estimate and measure, 631–634
        modeling, 625–628
        unknown side lengths and, 637–640
    Table of Measures, H39
    weight
        ounces, 148

Metric units
    for length
        centimeters, 89, 627, 631–634
    for liquid volume and capacity, liters, 599–602
    for mass
        grams, 605–608
        kilograms, 605–608

Mid-Chapter Checkpoint, 47–48, 105–106, 157–158, 221–222, 273–274, 331–332, 401–402, 473–474, 531–532, 591–592, 661–662, 721–722

Midnight, 567

Minute hand, 561–564

Minutes, 561–564
    add and subtract, 573–576, 579–582
    after the hour, 562
    before the hour, 562
    defined, 561
    elapsed time in, 573–576, 579–582, 585–588
    time intervals in, 573–576, 579–582, 585–588

Modeling
    analog clock, 561–564, 567–570, 574–575, 580–581
    angles, 704
    area, 643–646, 655–658
    area models, 333–336, 643–646, 655–658
    bar models, 73–75, 119–122, 159–161, 198–200, 319–322, 339–342, 611–614
    with base-ten blocks, 281, 287

with counters, 191–194, 301–304, 307–310, 313–316, 319–322, 365–368, 383–386, 395–396, 415–416, 481–484, 487–490, 493–496

division with arrays, 333–336, 340–342, 389–391, 403–406

equivalent fractions, 539–542, 545–548

fractions

with fraction circles, 508, 519–522, 525–528

with fraction strips, 467–470, 507, 513–516, 520–522, 533–536, 540

fractions greater than 1, 475–478, 482–483

multiplication, 159–162

multiplication with arrays, 165–168, 209–212, 340–342

multiplication with base-ten blocks, 281, 287

with number lines. *See* Number lines

part of a group, 481–484, 487–490

perimeter, 625–628

with square tiles, 165–168, 171–174, 267–268, 333–336, 345–348, 386, 403, 649, 669

triangles, 735–738

Money, 90, 142, 198, 226, 250, 262, 270, 278, 283, 342, 377, 392, 421, 428, 430

Multiples

defined, 197

of ten, 275–278, 281–284, 287–290

Multiplication

area models, 275–278, 655–658, 663–666

as inverse operation, 339–342

bar models, 159–161, 197–200, 339–342

describe a number pattern, 229–232

doubles, 191–194, 204, 235

draw a diagram, 159–162, 275–278

factors, 146

eight, 235–238

five, 197–200, 204

four, *179*, 191–194

nine, 241–244

one, 177–180

seven, 215–218

six, 203–206

ten, 197–200

three, *179*, 203–206

two, 191–194

unknown factors, 173, 205, 225, 267–270, 396–397, 415–418

zero, 177–180

of equal groups, 139–142, 145–148, 151–154, 301–304, 307–310

of liquid volume, 611–614

of mass, 611–614

place value strategy, 281–284

products, 146

properties of

Associative Property of Multiplication, 223–226, 236

Commutative Property of Multiplication, 171–174, 215, 224

Distributive Property, 209–212, 215, 241, 275–278, 669–672

Grouping Property of Multiplication, 223–226

Identity Property of Multiplication, 177–180

Zero Property of Multiplication, 177–180

regrouping, 287–290

related facts, 345–348

related to addition, 145–148

related to area, 655–658, 663–666, 669–672

related to division, 339–342

related to perimeter, 638

strategies, 281–284

with arrays, 165–168, 209–212, 223, 267–268, 339–342

with measurement quantities, 611–614

with multiples of ten, 275–278, 281–284, 287–290

with multiplication table, 204

with number lines, 151–154, 197–198, 235, 281–283

Multiplication tables, 204

find unknown divisor, 410

find unknown factor, 267–270

make a table, 247–250

patterns on the, 229–232

Multiply, 146

N

Nickels, 377

Noon, 568

Number lines

add and subtract minutes, 573, 580

adding with, 23–26, 573–576, 579

comparing fractions on, 514–515

counting back on, 55, 326–328, 371–374, 377–380, 384

counting up on, 55, 378–379

dividing with, 325–328, 371, 377–380, 384

elapsed time. *See* Time

fractions greater than 1, 495–501

fractions on, 467–470

multiplying with, 151–154, 197–200, 235, 281–284

number line for hours in a day, 567

round numbers and, 11–14

skip counting, 151–154

    by eights, 235

    by fives, 197–198

    by sixes, 151

    by tens, 197–198

    time intervals. *See* Time

    by twos, 192

subtracting with, 55–58

take away tens and ones, 55–58

use to represent

    distances, 467–470

    elapsed time, 573–575, 579–582, 585–588

whole numbers on, 467–470, 475–478

Number patterns, 5–8, 229–232, 242, 261–264

Numbers

compatible, 17–20, 24–25, 49–52

counting, 281, 562, 438, 625

even, 5–8, 229–232, 235–236

expanded form of, 24, 35–38, 42, 56

fractions, 443–446, 449–452, 437–440, 455–458, 467–470, 475–478, 481–484, 487–490, 493–496, 507–510, 513–516, 519–522, 525–528, 533–536, 539–542, 545–548

hundreds, 11–14, 18–20, 35–38, 41–44, 50–52, 56–57, 61–64, 67–70, 281–284, 287–290

odd, 5–8, 229–232, 235–238

ones, 23–26, 29–32, 35–38, 41–44, 50–52, 55–58, 61–64, 67–70, 177–180, 351–354

ordering, 533–536

rounding, 11–14, 17–20

standard form of, 36

tens, 11–14, 23–26, 29–32, 35–38, 41–44, 55–58, 61–64, 67–70, 197–200, 287–290

unknown, 63, 193, 199, 225, 267–270, 367, 390–391, 396–397, 404–405, 410–411, 417, 429

zero, 177–180, 351–354

Numerators, 461

comparing fractions with same, 519–522, 525–528

defined, 461

fractions greater than 1, 476–478

ordering fractions with same, 533–536

O

Octagons

angles of, 709–712

sides of, 709–712

Odd numbers, 5–8, 229–232, 235–236

Ones, 12–14, 23–26, 29–32, 35–38, 41–44, 50–52, 55–58, 61–64, 67–70, 177–180, 287–290

On Your Own, In most lessons. Some examples are: 7, 43, 379, 411, 731, 744

Open shapes, 698–700

Ordering

fractions, 533–536

fraction strips, 533–536

liquid volume, 600

mass, 606

Order of operations, 427–430

Organize data, 87–90

P

Parallel lines, 715–718

Partitioning

fractions, 443–446, 449–452

shapes, 747–750

Patterns

addition, 5–8, 261–264

on the addition table, 5–8

arithmetic, 5–8, 229–232, 261–264

defined, 5

describing, 261–264

explaining using properties, 5–8, 229–232, 236

finding, 663–666

multiplication, 229–232, 242, 261–264

on the multiplication table, 229–232

with nine, 241–244

number, 5–8, 229–232

in a table, 261–264

© Houghton Mifflin Harcourt Publishing Company

Table of Measures

METRIC | CUSTOMARY

Length

1 centimeter (cm) = 10 millimeters (mm)

1 decimeter (dm) = 10 centimeters (cm)   1 foot (ft) = 12 inches (in.)

1 meter (m) = 100 centimeters   1 yard (yd) = 3 feet, or 36 inches

1 meter (m) = 10 decimeters   1 mile (mi) = 1,760 yards, or 5,280 feet

1 kilometer (km) = 1,000 meters

Capacity and Liquid Volume

1 liter (L) = 1,000 milliliters (mL)   1 pint (pt) = 2 cups (c)

1 quart (qt) = 2 pints

1 gallon (gal) = 4 quarts

Mass/Weight

1 kilogram (kg) = 1,000 grams (g)   1 pound (lb) = 16 ounces (oz)

TIME

1 minute (min) = 60 seconds (sec)   1 year (yr) = 12 months (mo), or

1 hour (hr) = 60 minutes   about 52 weeks

1 day = 24 hours   1 year = 365 days

1 week (wk) = 7 days   1 leap year = 366 days

1 decade = 10 years

1 century = 100 years

MONEY

1 penny = 1 cent (¢)

1 nickel = 5 cents

1 dime = 10 cents

1 quarter = 25 cents

1 half dollar = 50 cents

1 dollar ($) = 100 cents

SYMBOLS

< is less than

> is greater than

= is equal to